PRACTICING
PRESENCE

Practicing Presence

Simple Self-Care Strategies for Teachers

Lisa J. Lucas

STENHOUSE PUBLISHERS
PORTSMOUTH, NEW HAMPSHIRE

Stenhouse Publishers
www.stenhouse.com

Library of Congress Cataloging-in-Publication Data

Names: Lucas, Lisa J., 1964- author.
Title: Practicing presence : tools for the overwhelmed teacher / Lisa J. Lucas.
Description: Portland, Maine : Stenhouse Publishers, 2017. | Includes
    bibliographical references.
Identifiers: LCCN 2017023608 (print) | LCCN 2017041861 (ebook) |
    ISBN 9781625311924 (ebook) | ISBN 9781625311917 (pbk. : alk. paper)
Subjects: LCSH: Classroom management. | Mindfulness (Psychology)
Classification: LCC LB3013 (ebook) | LCC LB3013 .L83 2017 (print) |
    DDC 371.102/4--dc23
LC record available at https://lccn.loc.gov/2017023608

Book design by Blue Design, Portland, Maine (www.bluedes.com)

Printed in the United States of America

This book is printed on paper certified by third-party standards for sustainably
manged forestry.

23 22 21   4371   3 2 1

This book is dedicated to children everywhere.
My wish is that present teachers who ignite the presence in
each and every one of you guide you on your journey.

TABLE OF CONTENTS

Preface: Overwhelmed to Optimistic ix

Acknowledgments xiii

Introduction: The Practice of Presence: Paths to Mindful Teaching 1

Chapter 1: **P**racticing Presence 9

Pause, Plan, and Prioritize 9

Becoming More Present 15

Personal Practices to Support Mindful Teaching 26

Classroom Connections 31

Chapter 2: **R**esponding Rather than Reacting 35

Recognize Mindlessness and Restore Gratitude 38

Recognize a Reframe Is Possible 38

Personal Practices to Support Mindful Teaching 50

Classroom Connections 55

Chapter 3: **E**pigenetics: Ever Heard of It? 56

Enjoying Experiencing Life: Making Epigenetics Work for YOU 56

Personal Practices to Support Mindful Teaching 68

Chapter 4: **S**imple Self-Care 70

Time Analysis 70

Personal Practices to Support Mindful Teaching 84

Classroom Connections 92

Chapter 5: **E**ver-Lasting Focus 94

Eliminate Extraneous Distractions. 94

Personal Practices to Support Mindful Teaching Aligned with the Ten Productivity Tips 109

Classroom Connections. 120

A Look Ahead to Chapter 6: Noticing the Negativity Bias 122

Chapter 6: **N**oticing the Negativity Bias 123

Nuts and Bolts of Neuroscience 123

Personal Practices to Support Mindful Teaching 142

Classroom Connections. 145

Chapter 7: **C**an't We Just Get Along? 149

Collaboration Versus Conflict. 149

Personal Practices to Support Mindful Teaching 160

Classroom Connections. 169

Chapter 8: **E**nvisioning Endless Possibilities for Education. 171

Envision and Establish Mind-Set 171

Personal Practices to Support Mindful Teaching 178

Resources 187

References 198

Index 205

Overwhelmed to Optimistic

2008—It was March. Outside, I was greeted by dreary, gray skies and a constant drizzle. It was the kind of rain that makes you feel chilled to the bone. Inside, I felt equally dreary. I was the director of organizational and professional development at a suburban school district. It was the month of mandated state testing, so teachers were unsettled, administrators were on edge, and students looked resigned to another day of bubbling circles on the state test as they trudged to their classrooms. It was also the month for report cards and parent conferences, which created another layer of work and stress for everyone. As I stood in my office, greeting my administrative assistant and admiring the mahogany furniture and private bathroom, I realized that I felt cold inside. As I gazed out the window, I realized I wasn't just cold. I was numb.

Something wasn't right. I picked up the phone and made an appointment with a doctor. I sat for what felt like hours in the waiting room only to be seen and discharged in just minutes by the doctor. After asking me a few cursory questions about my health, the doctor pulled out a pad and wrote me a prescription for an antidepressant. She didn't ask any questions about my current life situation. If she had, she would have learned that my mother was recently diagnosed with Alzheimer's disease, my father was in the end stage of pulmonary fibrosis, my son was struggling in middle school, my oldest daughter was starting to look at colleges—which meant she would be soon leaving home—and I was in a new administrative position at a workplace with zero collegiality. There was too much change happening at one time.

I went home, filled the prescription, and hid it in a shoebox in my closet so no one at home would know I was taking any medication. This was uncharacteristic of the Lisa they knew. I was known for being able to handle it all. I had been raised to be strong, resilient, and independent. My friends would have described me as easygoing and always ready to have fun. I took the prescription for about three weeks. During that time, my father died. I found it difficult to cry. Normally, I cry easily. Enough, I thought. I stopped taking the prescription. This is not something I advise anyone doing, and I know that taking antidepressants can be necessary and lifesaving to many people. But for me, in my situation, I decided to sit down on my outside deck and create my own prescription. I listed all the things that made me feel good. My list looked like this:

- Spending time with my family
- Genuine and faithful friends
- My pets
- Exercise
- Walks outside and sunshine
- Yoga and meditation
- A good night's sleep
- Healthy food
- Cooking and baking
- Reading and journaling
- Venturing anyplace new and different
- Teaching and coaching
- Feeling like I make a difference
- Having healthy relationships at work

Next, I drove to the bookstore and stared at the offerings in the self-help section. They all seemed to offer quick fixes, such as ten simple steps to happiness. I ended up buying Finding Your Own North Star, a book by Martha Beck (2001), an author I had never heard of. Looking back now, I find it fitting that I was reading a book by a coach, a role that I now embrace myself. That book nudged me to take stock of my life. I realized I was getting through my life rather than enjoying it.

I began noticing that many teachers were also in survival mode. They complained of having more to do than was feasible; it was as if the joy of teaching had evaporated. The feeling of being overwhelmed that seemed prevalent in schools was contagious, and spreading fast.

The next day, I began to intentionally do things that were on my custom-made prescription list. I bought a sign that said, "Do one thing every day that makes you happy." When I slowed down long enough to notice and pause, I realized I had opportunities for happiness all around me. Often we don't notice what's right in front of us because we're in a hurry to get to the next thing. We lack presence.

I also realized that my work no longer made me happy. I was rarely in schools, with children, or among colleagues I cared about. I was in an office, surrounded by administrators, many of whom were more concerned with climbing the ladder than doing what was best for students. Often I felt like I was putting into place mandates that I didn't agree with. My primary mentor and friend at the district had left, and I was being bullied by a coworker to endorse a program I didn't support. So much for making a difference in education. I was miserable.

To make a long story short, I was offered a job at a university that was known as the best teaching college in the state. Accepting the position meant that I had to take a significant pay cut and that I would enter the world of academia in a tenure-track position, which meant tenuous job stability. It made no sense, but I kept getting signs that it was the right thing to do. So I listened to the still, small, wise voice inside and resigned from my administrative position. It wouldn't be the last time I listened to that voice. I worked through the summer, finished the strategic plan, made sure the induction program was ready for the fall, and walked out the door. It's true what they say: as one door closes, another opens. Although in my case it felt more like a window that was slightly cracked and that I crawled through.

Slowly but steadily, my life improved. I achieved tenure at the university. I began to give presentations at conferences on topics I was passionate about. I was teaching again, and I began to teach courses that I found meaningful. I supervised student teachers and taught a preschool field-based practicum course, so I was active in the field—I was back in schools with colleagues I respected and students who made me remember why I went into education. I began training teachers in a writing program I completely believed in, and I opened my own coaching business. My coaching business thrived and I noticed that by helping others I felt more purposeful.

However, when I'm in schools, I still see "signs of March." Teachers look weary, administrators seem tense, and I don't see nearly enough joy in students' faces. So many of my clients experience the same issues I had encountered.

I've wrestled with the question of why educators aren't happier. I think we can all agree there is no silver bullet, but we can also agree that the best place to start is with ourselves, and it's important that we do something. I began researching mindfulness and stress reduction.

At the time, the terms *mindfulness* and *presence* were rarely seen in the mainstream. I never imagined that practices like meditation, yoga, visualization, setting intentions, and repeating affirmations would be accepted in education journals or publishing houses. Recently, the mindfulness strategies I had practiced for years have started appearing in print, and I realized I wanted to share what has worked for me. It seems that everywhere, teachers are feeling overwhelmed. I wanted to share my "prescription" for bringing a sense of presence and peace to daily life.

I don't think anyone needs to walk out the door like I did; it's not what made the real difference. What made all the difference for me were the lifestyle choices I adopted and the conscious effort I made to become more present. Researchers have found that we find the greatest meaning in life when we value the roles we play, the goals we pursue, and the integrative story we tell about it all. I'm on a quest to live every moment in the present, and I want to share with others how to join me on this quest. *Presence* can make us better teachers and, as a result, improve the classroom environment and foster students who are more engaged and are poised to learn and thrive. Students learn from teachers who project enthusiasm and optimism and clearly enjoy what they do. They are *present* for their students. You can't fake presence, but you can learn to cultivate it.

The subsequent chapters will provide methods to achieve a state of presence that I've collected from recent science, brain-based research, ancient wisdom traditions, and the happiest people I know. This book doesn't describe a path of continuous success, but rather small steps forward, and unfortunately, often a few steps backward on my journey toward presence. However, many of the incidents that at the time I thought were failures became stepping-stones on my path to presence. My missteps were always followed by growth spurts. So, this journey begins by looking back at the times when I first began noticing I lacked presence. After all, we're teachers, and we know that we often learn the most by examining our mistakes.

Acknowledgments

I often think of life like a curriculum: each of us have individual goals and objectives, daily experiences comprise the content, and to achieve our goals we are all provided specific resources. The overarching essential question is, how can we each do the best we can, using what we have, to support one another? This book is intended to be a resource to support others, but I couldn't have written it without receiving a tremendous amount of support from my own resources. I would like to acknowledge and express gratitude to them all. My husband, Andy, and children, Chelsea and Craig, are at the top of that list, but there have been countless others, far too many to name. My primary resource has been the presence within. We are all in this journey together, and if this book helps even one person, it will have been worth the time and energy it took to create.

The Practice of Presence: Paths to Mindful Teaching

Some teachers, when you watch them teach, radiate an inner light, and you can feel that they are completely present for their students. These teachers rarely have classroom management issues, they bring happiness to the classroom, and it's clear they love what they do. Why aren't all teachers like that? How did they get like that? How can you become a teacher like that? Weren't we all like that once? This book is about kindling or rekindling that state.

For more than two decades, I've studied presence. I've read hundreds of books and articles by academic researchers, writers in the field of psychology, ancient scholars, and current neurologists. I've attended and presented multiple workshops on the topic of presence in school districts, child care settings, and educational conferences. Most importantly, I'm still on the journey to live in the present moment myself. The old adage is true: you teach what you need to learn. I've learned that cultivating presence is clearly an inside job. It begins with bringing attention to your own thoughts and feelings. You have to notice things, be curious, and be willing to question your beliefs. It is from a place of presence that a peaceful perception of the world arises.

This book is an invitation to learn to fully inhabit the present moment.

What you have in your hands is a resource for *you*. It's the glue that holds all the swirling components of being an exceptional teacher together; it will help hold *you* together. It will help counterbalance the more difficult demands of teaching, which encompass the ever-changing standards, the eternally revised curriculum, report cards, and assessments. The strategies in this book can help you put the classroom management dilemmas, the endless committee work, and the student, colleague, and parent challenges into perspective so that you can be a quiet presence of contentment, no matter what chaos comes your way. By coupling what's in this book with your own considerable inner resources, you can revamp your daily routines and become more present.

This book provides pathways to presence. Similar to routes on a map, there are multiple pathways to get to a specific destination. Each chapter of this book will explore different topics and offer distinctive strategies, and as a reader, you'll choose which path you might want to explore.

Think of presence as a cousin of mindfulness meditation, which had its origins over 2,500 years ago. Prince Siddhartha, who became the Buddha, dedicated his life to finding the cause of suffering and recommended mindfulness as a way of overcoming grief, sorrow, pain, and anxiety. In 1979, mindfulness was used therapeutically by Dr. Jon Kabat-Zinn and colleagues at the Stress Reduction Clinic at the University of Massachusetts Hospital. In addition, mindfulness is currently being taught in Fortune 500 companies, in the military, in hospitals, and even in the world of politics.

Mindful seems to be the word of the moment, and mindfulness in education has exploded. This text is unique in that it takes mindfulness a step further and heads down a slightly different path. Mindfulness is being aware of your thoughts and being content with whatever is. When your thoughts run rampant, you redirect your attention and bring your mind back to the present moment. However, I've found that sometimes my thoughts about the present moment aren't so blissful. This is where some of my practices take a slight detour from traditional mindfulness. I have found that reframing *some* of those thoughts are helpful. The moment that you are aware of a negative thought, it sometimes helps to reach for a more positive one. I once heard someone say, "My mind is like a bad neighborhood. I don't like to go there alone." When I find myself in "my bad neighborhood," I head down another path.

For this reason, I use the word *presence* instead of *mindfulness*. *Presence*, as used in this text, is a secular, informal term, intended to be applicable to daily life.

Practicing presence has elements of cognitive behavior therapy. Once I'm present, I can shine a light on inaccurate or negative thinking to view a challenging situation more clearly and respond rather than react. I believe that a combination of strategies allows individuals to choose the approach that works best for them at any given moment. Just as we differentiate instruction for students, mindfulness tools should be differentiated for educators. Learning how to assess your situation and select an appropriate tool for change to rekindle that present, calm state takes practice.

Practicing presence gives us the ability to anchor ourselves so we aren't carried away by the ever-changing challenges of being an educator. A lot of those challenges have to do with our rampant thoughts. Our thoughts become our words, our words reflect our beliefs, and our beliefs drive our actions.

If you picked up this book because you are tired, wired, and running in circles, you need to know you are not alone.

Approximately 50 percent of new teachers leave the education field before they hit the five-year mark. Moreover, the attrition rates of first-year teachers have increased by about one-third in the past two decades. So, not only are more beginners entering the teaching force, but these beginners are also less likely to stay in teaching. If you are a veteran teacher, congratulate yourself for remaining in this profession; thankfully, you are one of many dedicated, caring teachers who make a difference. Students need you. However, you need to take as good care of yourself as you do your students—actually better. Making your own self-care a priority is the opposite of selfish; it allows you to be more present and supportive of others, and more content in your work.

The National Commission on Teaching and America's Future estimated that the cost of turnover among public school teachers in the United States is more than $7.3 billion a year. That's not taking into account the money recent graduates invested in their college educations to become teachers and the loans they have incurred. That $7.3 billion number also does not include the amount of *time* it takes administrators to interview and train new teachers.

A recent survey conducted by the National Center for Educational Statistics suggests that an exceedingly high percentage of teachers who abandoned their careers may have entered the teaching profession underprepared, overwhelmed, and undersupported—resulting in frustrated teachers who became discouraged after only a few years. What does every student need to be well adjusted and happy? Not discouraged, frustrated teachers. Students need well-adjusted, happy teachers. The greatest gift you can give to your students is your authentic presence. Classrooms should be places where teachers and students can learn, dream, create, and be themselves.

No matter how many times the pendulum swings in education, we know that focusing on the whole child makes sense. Focusing on the whole teacher makes sense as well. This book explores multiple aspects of a teacher's life, including topics that are rarely addressed in teacher preparation, induction, or professional development programs.

Numerous books and programs address the training of teachers, but most focus primarily on pedagogy and curriculum. This book focuses not on *doing*, but rather on *being—being* present. The reality is that programs and curriculum don't teach; teachers teach. The teacher is the determining factor in student achievement. It's time we began to focus on the variable that matters most: the teacher.

How to Navigate This Book

This book is a compilation of simple strategies and resources for educators to manage being overwhelmed, written in an informal, conversational tone. My goal is to keep it simple. Knowledge is power, but the real change is in the implementation of knowledge and information. Each chapter contains research and reflections, but the essence of the book is in the section on personal practices to support mindful teaching. The action is where we implement the strategies, which is where the change happens.

The acronym PRESENCE is used to divide the text into eight chapters.

Here is a sneak peak at the chapters ahead:

P Chapter 1, "Practicing Presence," opens with an overview of the concept of presence and an explanation of what being present can do for us as teachers and the impact our presence can have on students. A prioritizing tool precedes an overview of the benefit of purposeful planning and prioritizing. We dabble with a minimeditation (a four-minute presence pause), and then the chapter concludes with classroom connections, an opportunity to change the lens of how we see our classrooms.

R Chapter 2, "Responding Rather Than Reacting," explores happiness, the power of adopting gratitude habits into our daily lives, mindlessness, and the benefits of rest and renewal. We continue with meditation and relaxation exercises, and we close with purposeful planning, this time focusing on the end of our day.

E Chapter 3, "Epigenetics: Ever Heard of It?," introduces a complex term—

epigenetics—and translates it into practical, clear language so that we understand how the body works with stress and begin to better regulate stressful responses by being aware of our mind-set. This sets the stage for our next chapter, simple self-care.

S Chapter 4, "Simple Self-Care," begins with a work stress self-assessment, then transitions into finding time for self-care, including more present moment practice. The personal practices section has a range of strategies, concluding with a loving kindness meditation.

E Chapter 5, "Ever-Lasting Focus," dispels the myth of multitasking and provides ways to focus our attention and energy as well as cope with information overload. Slowing down and the power of no set the stage for the personal practices section with ten productivity tips.

N Chapter 6, "Noticing the Negativity Bias," takes another scientific term, *neuroplasticity*, and breaks it down into teacher-friendly language. How to adopt a growth mind-set and raise our happiness set point leads into coaching actions that focus on documenting and appreciating the good, as well as incorporating relaxation techniques seamlessly into our day.

C Chapter 7, "Can't We Just Get Along?," explores work relationships and how to deal with difficult personalities. The focus is on creating a collaborative culture by cultivating a complaint/gossip-free environment. Mindful listening and the value of silence are introduced along with appreciative interviews.

E Chapter 8, "Envisioning Endless Possibilities for Education," begins with a portrait of a present teacher and helps us imagine the possibilities that exist once we've established healthy mind-sets. This chapter encourages us to not only dream ourselves, but also to ignite a vision in others.

The following elements appear throughout the book:

Quotes and Affirmations: Affirmations and applicable quotes are dispersed throughout the text.

Research and Reflection: The research is what thought leaders in the field have discovered; the reflection is what I have experienced based on applying the research. I have found the most current reputable research and translated it from theory to practice by demonstrating how it applies to my own life.

Paths to Mindful Teaching: These action-oriented suggestions help readers integrate the theory into their busy days; it's the *how to* bridge the research to action. It takes personal planning to implement these strategies. Anyone can read about a strategy and it can sound good, but no change happens until you take action. The action is where the change happens, not in the reading, thinking, or even the understanding. There is never just one way to do something, and the coaching suggestions are for guidance only. The more you try the various practices, the more you'll customize them, almost like your own individualized coaching plan.

Classroom Connections: How the concepts in the text connect to the pre-K–12 classroom will be shared through supplemental sources, links, and websites related to various chapter topics.

At the end of the book is a section of resources that includes websites and additional resources to support the topic.

I have learned that when we care for ourselves, deeply and deliberately, we are able to care for others—our students, our friends and families—in a healthier, more authentic way. I have used the techniques in this book to become more present in my own life. It takes commitment, but the results are worth it. I invite you to suspend judgment and venture onto a path—approaching your life fully immersed in the present moment.

CHAPTER 1

Practicing Presence

Pause, Plan, and Prioritize

2000—Become less stressed. Don't take on too much. Calm down; your plate is too full. You are too hard on yourself. Listen to people more closely and be more attentive. Slow down, relax, and listen. You're always in a major rush and running late, unapproachable. Take your time; stop rushing around and trying to do too much.

This was some of the advice given to me by my supervisors, family, and colleagues in the fall of 2000. I was on sabbatical from my position as a first-grade teacher. After fourteen years in the classroom, I was exploring teacher leadership opportunities. Enrolled in an organizational leadership program, I was taking a course on leadership and ethics. One of the course assignments was to solicit feedback on my work habits from my supervisors and colleagues. I used a leadership tool called 360 Feedback that allows an individual to understand how others view his or her effectiveness as a colleague.

The professor had given me the report and said, "Don't read it until you get home and you are by yourself." Of course, I ran to my minivan, hopped into the driver's seat, tore open the manila folder, and read the summary report as fast as I could. The feedback I received gave me pause, literally. It felt as if all the air was being sucked out of the window. I found it hard to breathe. There was, of course, some great feedback, but as many of us often do, I was focusing on the negative. What made it worse was that the negative feedback seemed accurate.

The old adage is true: You teach what you need to learn. Apparently, according to my colleagues, I had a lot to learn about slowing down and being present. I shouldn't have been surprised—actually, I don't think I was. I was just disappointed, embarrassed, and at a loss. Presence has to do with deeply listening to others, being open to the moment, thoughtfully choosing who we are and how we respond to life. Although our ingrained habits can limit our opportunities to be present, we can adopt new habits to cultivate them. I realized I needed to be open and consider the feedback that I'd received.

After I brooded for a few days, I decided to take action. Somehow, I was going to develop new habits. I was going to slow down, yet still be productive. To be honest, I wasn't sure it was possible. My life, when not on sabbatical, resembled that of a hummingbird. I functioned on about five hours of sleep. My four-year-old son hadn't slept through the night since he entered this world. I was sleep deprived, and it showed. My lists had lists, and half the time I had to ask my husband if he knew where I had left my list.

However, I was determined to make a change. My one-year sabbatical was ending, and I would be returning to the first-grade classroom in two months; I wanted to return a more relaxed, present person. In pursuit of that goal, I immersed myself in the study of presence. I began by collecting information—data. I paid closer attention to the people around me who seemed to not be frenetic. I needed to know what presence looked like before I could begin to work on being present myself. I wanted a clearer picture so I could focus on not just what to do, but what it looked like. I became a people watcher and started to observe the world around me, deliberately gathering information on aspects of life that were appealing to me. What did people who were not running around like chickens with their heads cut off look like? I watched the nuns and priests in church. I observed children engrossed in play. I paid attention to the people who seemed genuinely relaxed and happy. I started to notice who I enjoyed being with. Some common themes emerged. Those who seemed to be most present were good listeners, they didn't interrupt, and they made others feel like they were important. They didn't seem distracted, nor did they seem to be multitasking.

Next, I started to research. I listened to audio recordings in my car by leading scholars in the fields of stress reduction and mindfulness. I read countless books and articles by academic researchers, psychologists, ancient scholars, and current neurologists. I attended and eventually presented multiple workshops on the topic of presence in school districts, child care settings, and educational conferences.

I learned that cultivating presence is clearly an inside job. All the books and lectures in the world weren't going to change my behavior. I had some inner work to do. I began to pay attention to my thoughts and feelings. I started to notice that my thoughts created emotions that I could actually feel in my body. When my son cried as I left for work, my stomach clenched. Too much to do and not enough time—my shoulders felt as if they were tied in knots. During these times I felt heavy, but I also noticed the times when I felt lighter, like when I took a walk or pushed my carefree daughter on the swing. Identification is the first step when pursuing a behavior change. It was a start; I began to realize there was a true connection among my thoughts and emotions, and that they were being manifested physically throughout my body. I learned that presence leaves clues. I wanted more than anything to feel more at ease. But how in the world could I do that while I juggled work, family, and graduate school? Was it possible to be present amid the chaos?

WHAT'S THE POINT?

My father, a former journalist, would have said, "What's the point?"

What is being *present* going to do for teachers or their students? Why write a book on presence? I answer this question with the five W's and one H from Journalism 101: *who, what, when, why, where,* and *how*. Traditional journalists argue that your story isn't complete until you answer all six questions. So here is my quick summary regarding the point of presence and this book.

WHO NEEDS TO BE PRESENT?

Well, we all do, but this book is written to guide educators to be fully present, first for themselves, then for one another, and ultimately for the students they serve. Presence can make a difference in your personal life and in the lives of your students. Emotionally competent teachers set the tone of the classroom by developing supportive and encouraging relationships with their students. They accomplish this by coaching students through conflicts, encouraging cooperation, and serving as role models for respectful and appropriate communication (Jennings and Greenberg 2009). To do this successfully, teachers themselves need to be able to recognize and regulate their own emotions.

WHAT WILL PRESENCE DO FOR STUDENTS?

Breaux and Wong (2003) assert that if well-trained, competent, caring teachers were consciously *present* in every classroom, we should witness a staggering increase in student achievement, motivation, and character improvement, along with a marked decrease in discipline problems. Teachers who behave in ways that promote their own personal and professional well-being perform better in the classroom and effect better student outcomes (Duckworth, Quinn, and Seligman 2009). A student's formal learning context is largely shaped by his or her teacher (Eccles and Roeser 1999). Klusmann et al. (2008) found that teachers' occupational well-being and quality of instruction were enhanced by practicing "self-regulatory" behaviors (e.g., deep breathing, positive thinking). When teachers lack the resources to effectively manage the social and emotional challenges within the particular context of their school and the classroom, children show lower levels of on-task behavior and performance (Marzano, Marzano, and Pickering 2003).

We can all recall "that teacher," the one who inspired us to learn, the one we knew cared about us. Those teachers brought out the best in us, because they had the best of themselves to give. You can't give what you don't have. Today, more than ever, students need teachers to be emotionally available to support them. I once witnessed a colleague do what I call "hold the space" for a student who was having a meltdown. The teacher was calm, nonreactive, and, most importantly, nonjudgmental. She approached the situation from a place of presence and equanimity. She didn't fuel the fire, and as a result, the student's tantrum fizzled out. A few weeks later, I witnessed the same student have another meltdown, but this time the student was with the librarian. The librarian reacted by raising her voice and telling the student he was a constant disruption. The situation escalated out of control, and the principal and the guidance counselor had to intervene. The first teacher responded, the second reacted, and the student felt the difference. Whether we as teachers react or respond has a great deal to do with our own inner resources. Students are watching us to see how we react. It's no different than the student who falls off a swing during recess and looks to us to see what our response will be. If we panic, the child usually starts crying, but if we respond calmly, the student usually picks him- or herself up and continues playing. Our students are tuned in to our emotional reactions.

WHEN DO WE NEED TO BE PRESENT?

Ideally, we need to be present all the time, but this is easier said than done. This book is essentially a set of practices to encourage self-care for educators. Caring for yourself is key to being able to care for others. This begins with slowing down and turning inward. All of the great wisdom traditions, and thankfully now a great deal of scientific research, advocate for some sort of contemplation practice, which is essentially about being present. Ironically, I've found that to be present takes planning and preparation. Each chapter in this book offers insights and choices about how to do this. I'm still on the journey to presence, and I think I always will be. Presence is like an attitudinal muscle; just like we have to consistently go to the gym to work on our physical muscles, we have to consistently bring ourselves back to the present moment. In both cases, there is no "once and done;" consistent practice is required. But that practice can pay off when we need it most.

Lori, a good friend of mine who taught special education, shared this story with me. Her students were teenagers, primarily young men, with severe cognition deficits and extreme behavioral challenges:

There was one young man in my class who had an extremely difficult road in life. He was a big strong boy, about six feet tall and 180 pounds. Along with his autism diagnosis came limited language abilities and almost constant physical pain from Lyme disease.

This student, Mike, had several episodes of great pain per month. His limited communication made it almost impossible to read when he was in pain or needed anything.

One day in particular, Mike came in rather anxious, so we knew to clear the room and give him space. We had a protocol for behavior management to follow for days like this and so I followed that protocol. Many times it worked, but not always.

On this day, Mike reacted to me by throwing a computer and a chair, and finally being able to reach me, ripping my shirt, biting my arm, and pulling my hair. This all happened extremely quickly and I had help within minutes. Clearly, I was extremely shaken and hurt. However, my student Mike was much worse off.

Michael wasn't physically injured, but once my support staff came in and he was no longer lashing out, he was left crying and confused. His behavior was hard for us to understand but it was much harder for him to understand. Mike was left crying and sitting, rocking on the floor. It was then when I sat down on the floor right next to him. The room was dimly lit and we kept everything quiet around us. It was really important for me to convey the message to Michael that I was OK, that I wasn't mad, and that I was there to help him. We spent quite some time holding hands, taking deep breaths, and reconnecting.

Fortunately, these extreme days didn't happen often, maybe once or twice every other month. However, I will never forget the impact that they left on me. Being mindful, present, and calm allowed me to be able to go back into the room with him, without fear or hesitation. It allowed me to continue my work and gave Mike a chance to reconnect and continue his education.

Making the time to live life in the present means honoring and loving yourself enough to dedicate time each day to nurture your own well-being so that you have the reserves to handle situations like Lori encountered. To serve our students, we must first serve ourselves so that we can have more abundant energy and bring presence to each encounter. When present, we build greater self-awareness and can anticipate and recognize our emotional triggers and how these emotions can affect our teaching. We learn to self-regulate and consciously choose to remain in the present moment. We become more interested in those around us, and we see ourselves in others.

WHERE DO WE NEED TO BE PRESENT?

Presence begins at home and continues in the workplace. To create presence, you have to foster intentionality toward the moments that comprise each day. There has to be a plan so that you enter the classroom not drained and half empty, but fueled and ready to meet the challenges ahead. In the personal practices to support mindful teaching sections of this book, I include processes that help me focus and begin the day with a clear vision of how I intend the day to unfold. There are several variations, but one goal: to flow through the day effortlessly and happily rather than frenetic and overwhelmed. For me to achieve this, presence had to begin in the morning, before I entered the world of work, with its endless tasks, needy students, parent queries, and looming to-do lists. I needed to be clear internally so I could be present externally. When present, I was curious and patient with the needy student, I was more responsive and understanding regarding the parent queries, and my to-do list didn't loom.

WHY PRESENCE?

I believe presence is the path to peace and happiness. Isn't that what we all really want? Observed closely enough, every moment of life is interesting. Sadly, we aren't often present enough to observe small moments, let alone life. We are often trying just to "get through" the day. Even social engagements on the calendar can feel like one more task to complete rather than something to look forward to. In schools, our classrooms are brimming with students who seem more distant than ever. They are used to being constantly entertained by some type of electronic device. We can't compete with electronics, but we can offer them something I believe students are starving for: our focused, authentic attention. We need to show our students how to listen deeply, how to focus on the task at hand, and how to pay attention. This requires presence. First, we need to learn how to do this ourselves.

SO HOW DO WE BECOME MORE PRESENT?

This book provides you with some practices, but honestly, the answer is within you. My intent is simply to point the way. The ability to remain present, calm, focused, happy, and centered is always there. It just needs to be cultivated. Connecting with your wise self is like going home; home is a place we all must find. It's not just a place where you eat or sleep; home is a knowing. Knowing your mind, knowing your heart, knowing your courage. If we know ourselves, we're always home, anywhere. We know ourselves best when we are living in the present moment.

Becoming More Present

Presence is a synonym for *mindfulness*, which has roots in Buddhist philosophy and psychology. *Mindfulness* is a more formal, scientific term; *presence* as it is used in this text is a secular, informal term, intended to be applicable to daily life. Whatever we call it, it's a practice that has been around for a very long time. All humans have had the need to cultivate attention, to focus, and to find emotional equilibrium. As teachers, practicing presence gives us the ability to anchor ourselves so we aren't carried away by the ever-changing challenges of daily classroom life. Being present means we can observe our own internal state before we react to events so that we can respond thoughtfully. Presence allows us to be more aware and to observe with clarity and compassion. If we're anchored in presence, the drama doesn't carry us away. The simple act of being present has the power to change how we approach our challenges, our relationships, our communities, and ourselves.

Being present is simplistic, yet difficult. It's available to us at any moment, and it goes by many names. Athletes refer to it as "being in the zone." For soldiers and first responders, it's "situational awareness." Artists see it as "flow," thinkers consider it "contemplation," and Buddhists call it "mindfulness." The name doesn't matter; it's the feeling of peace and stillness that is important. If we want to foster healthier learning environments, we can begin by first attending to our own self-care and model presence in the classroom.

Even in the midst of presence, challenges and obstacles are inevitable over the course of our careers. We live in an increasingly unpredictable and often overwhelming world. We cannot always control what happens to us; however, we can prepare so that we can respond to what happens in a healthy way. Although we are teachers, life itself is the real teacher. How we meet what life dishes out to us, whether good, bad, or neutral, is essentially how we live our life. How we perceive things is how they will be. If you can reframe and change the way you look at things, the things you look at can change. A class list of students who are flagged as "at risk" can be an opportunity to make a transformation that will change their life trajectory. What may have been perceived as an unfair class assignment from the principal turns into an opportunity to make a difference in multiple students' lives. How we choose to view those challenging students matters. Students need teachers who believe in them and see more than their label. To step back and look at the situation from this stance requires a sense of presence.

When I began the journey toward presence in my own life, I wondered if I was the only one who lacked presence. Maybe it was just me? Was I alone in feeling rushed and overwhelmed? I found that I was not alone, and the feeling of being overwhelmed and overworked reached far beyond educators. The Families and Work Institute, a nonpartisan research organization, found that nearly 40 percent of the American workers they surveyed, from the top to the bottom of the socioeconomic ladder, reported feeling overworked. It's not just the current workforce. Brigid Schulte (2015), author of *Overwhelmed: Work, Love and Play When No One Has the Time*, interviewed a senior director of employment research and practice at the Families and Work Institute. According to a report on overwork by worker demographics from their database, nearly one-quarter of retired people, those sixty-two and older, said they felt "flattened" by all the tasks they needed and wanted to do in a day. I could resonate with the word *flattened*; it described how I often felt. When I asked other teachers if *flattened* was a good description for the daily blur, they added, "flattened, and then backed up on, and run over about seven times."

WHY FLATTENED?

We are flattened because the teaching profession has changed and become more challenging in the past three decades. Students are coming to school unprepared, exhibiting major behavior issues as early as preschool. There is a lack of clarity regarding how to translate the standards into actual teaching; too much content; not enough time or resources; changing curriculum; escalating class size; increased student behavior issues; more paraprofessionals who need supervision; additional duties such as cafeteria, recess, and bus line; all leaving limited time to plan and be creative. Some parents don't want their children tested because they are afraid of them being labeled, others do want their children tested because they feel their children are gifted and aren't challenged. Limited time to make real-life appointments or phone calls or converse with colleagues. No time to go to the bathroom.

This initiates a spiral effect. Classroom management becomes compromised, the climate of the classroom becomes less than optimal, and teachers become emotionally exhausted. Burned-out teachers are less likely to demonstrate empathy toward their students and have less tolerance for disruptive behavior. As teachers, we can have difficulty regulating our own emotions, let alone those of our students. When student behavior is problematic, it's essential to remain professional and objective, but this requires the ability to manage our own emotions. Unlike other occupations where workers can take a break when they're experiencing strong emotions, as teachers we are often literally unable to leave the room. Often the only way to manage emotions when surrounded by students and other support staff is to suppress or repress any uncomfortable feelings, which then puts a strain on the stress responsive system. Suppression and repression are the most common ways we push feelings down. Hawkins (2012) explains that repression happens unconsciously whereas suppression happens consciously. When we can't suppress our emotions, it's like driving a car with one foot on the accelerator and the other on the brake at the same time. The pressure of suppressed feelings can be later felt as irritability, mood swings, tension in the muscles of the neck and back, headaches, cramps, menstrual disorders, colitis, indigestion, insomnia, hypertension, allergies, and other somatic conditions. These symptoms lead to emotional exhaustion, and the vicious cycle continues.

BREAKING THE CYCLE

We can start breaking this cycle by making sure we are in the right profession. At the university, I counsel potential postbaccalaureate students who are contemplating transitioning into the field of education. All are career changers, having already earned an undergraduate degree in a field other than education. There is one common denominator among them: their first degree or career doesn't fulfill them. The change in their demeanor when they realize they can choose again is life altering. It often makes me wonder if the inverse is possible. Are there teachers who chose education by default, or without thought, and now would give anything for a second chance to choose a field different than education? If this is you, you probably know it, and you are not a *loser*, unless you are literally *losing time* doing something that doesn't make you happy. The only thing worse than teacher burnout is a teacher whose flame was never really lit. You deserve better, and so do your students. Get a notebook, start brainstorming occupations, hire a career coach, interview people in other occupations, read books on career options, explore what you'd do if you knew you wouldn't fail. We all have gifts we are meant to share with the world; don't squander yours on a career that doesn't fulfill you. What you are really supposed to be doing is what makes you happy.

However, before you start packing up your classroom, be sure you aren't in a role in education that you've outgrown. There are many ways to be an educator. In my career, I've been a classroom teacher, an instructional coach, a supervisor, a director of organizational and professional development, a consultant, and a professor. All were roles in education, but each had its own unique skill set, so I never got stagnant in my job. If you are a teacher and it's your twentieth year teaching first grade, you need to keep in mind that for your students, it's their first time in first grade. If you know you are in the right place, doing what you love, then you need to look for ways to make the very most of your job. A good place to begin is by examining your priorities and paying attention to how you spend your days.

PRIORITIZING

One cannot collect all the beautiful shells on the beach. One can collect only a few, and they are more beautiful if they are few.

—ANNE MORROW LINDBERGH

Most of us have the enviable opportunity to make choices based on our priorities of how to spend our time, with whom to spend it, and how we might offer our talents to the world. Making choices is what it means to be an adult. We choose how to spend our time and with whom, inside and outside the classroom. Truthfully, there are simply too many choices in our fast-paced world. One method I use to narrow down choices is to say no to all the options that don't reflect my highest priorities. It begins by asking a simple question: What will I take off my plate to do this? Notice I did not say, "Where can I make room on my plate?," which is what we as teachers are so used to doing. We are masters of adding; we've done it for so long we don't even question it anymore. More students, more curriculum, more committees, and more accountability. A superintendent would win the support of teachers if his or her mantra were "less is more."

It seems that everywhere we turn, we are being asked to do something: "Can you coach the girls' basketball team?" "Can you host a student teacher?" "Will you conduct a demonstration writing lesson for your grade-level team?" "Can we have the holiday party at your home?" All things we might want to do, but doing *all* of those things just contributes to how busy our lives have become. Being super busy becomes a way of life, and even though we are constantly booked, it can still feel like we are only truly *living* a half-full life. We can be more focused on checking off our to-do lists than actually completing or enjoying a task. We might feel accomplished if we complete the tasks quickly, but there is a huge difference between feeling accomplished and being happy. Accomplishment provides a fleeting feeling of relief; happiness requires no end product to prove our worth. So try to stop and pause before agreeing to do anything, and ask yourself if the task aligns with your priorities. If not, simply decline.

Saying no is a human dilemma each of us faces at home, at work, and in the world (Ury 2007). Saying no means giving up the goal of being everything to everyone. We can't give 100 percent of our attention to all areas of life simultaneously. Saying no requires clarity about what we want to say yes to.

I created a prioritizing tool (see page 27) that consists of a set of questions that I ask myself when pressed to undertake something new. Here is how I used the tool to "just say no" when asked to join the assessment team:

Does this task or commitment align with my highest priorities?	Y/N No. I don't believe in many of the assessments nor do I have the time it takes to prepare and administer them.
Does this task or commitment draw on my strengths?	Y/N No. I am more of a big picture thinker than a data analysis, detail person.
Does this task or commitment energize me?	Y/N No. In fact, absolutely not.
Do I have the time to do this task or commitment?	Y/N No. It takes place after school, which would mean getting someone else to pick up my children, and we'd miss yet another family dinner together.
What will I *not* be doing if I take on this task or commitment?	Going for a walk with my children after work. Preparing a healthy dinner.

When we take the time to ask ourselves these simple questions, making decisions becomes clearer, and we can look forward to planning the yeses we've agreed to.

PURPOSEFUL PLANNING: HABITS, ROUTINES, AND RITUALS

What is the use of running when we are not on the right road?

—GERMAN PROVERB

As my sabbatical started to wind down, I realized that in a few months I'd be returning to the classroom. Because I wanted to return refreshed and less frenetic, I decided to routinize a good portion of my day, especially the morning, which is when I felt the most rushed. I noticed that those who seemed the most present did not appear rushed. Quite honestly, I couldn't imagine how they survived. How did they get it all done? When did they find the time? I found that those people had solidified purposeful habits. Most of our lives are just a mass of habits strung together, but we can be unaware of them. The important concept to understand is that each habit on its own means relatively little, but strung together, the way we organize our thoughts and work routines, they can have enormous implications on our health, productivity, financial security, and happiness (Duhigg 2012). I began keeping a journal, making daily entries, and looking for patterns. I noticed that the less rushed I was, the fewer mistakes I made, and the calmer I felt inside.

Research suggests that approximately 40 percent of our behavior is repeated almost daily. A routine is a string of adopted habits. Establishing habits eliminates the need to make a decision or to have self-control. A habit is something you just do, whether you like it or not. This saves effort and time and reduces the number of decisions needed in any given day. Habits, scientists say, emerge because the brain is constantly looking for ways to save effort. Left to its own devices, the brain will try to make almost any routine into a habit because habits allow our minds to ramp down more often (Duhigg 2012). This makes our brains more efficient, and we can conserve energy easier. I clearly had a need to conserve energy.

I was tired of starting my day feeling behind before I'd even begun. I began to plan purposefully for the next day the night before. I noticed that my brain was always scanning the environment for what I had overlooked or forgotten. Did I respond to the parent e-mail? Had I filled out my own child's school emergency form? Had I entered the grades online for parents to view? Where did I leave my to-do list? The endless background of nagging thoughts drained me of the energy to be present. I realized there literally was too much to do; it was not humanly possible to get done all that needed to be done, unless I prioritized, let some of it go, and created routines.

One of my challenges was that I thrived on change and new experiences. I considered myself spontaneous, but I recognized the benefits of putting routines in place in the areas where I needed to be efficient rather than creative. Quite a few of the habits I adopted were things I did not necessarily want to do, but I made them my new normal and no longer thought of them as optional. Habits such as getting up at an early hour, eating the same thing for breakfast, and leaving my desk at school organized for the next day became simply part of my routine.

I noticed that adopting habits limited the choices and, consequently, the time spent on making routine decisions. The less I had to think about my daily routine, the more space I had in my mind to devote to decisions and circumstances that weren't habitual or that required my best thinking.

It's estimated that a teacher makes anywhere from a hundred to a thousand decisions on any given day. Reducing the number of decisions we make before we arrive at work by establishing routines keeps energy in reserve to deal with the unexpected. The unexpected could be the new child you get on your roster in February who doesn't speak or understand English or the parent waiting outside your classroom who wants a private conference two minutes before students arrive. It could be the child who projectile vomits on your lesson plan book or your shoe. There are endless scenarios of the unexpected, which makes establishing routines in advance all the more necessary.

When I scrutinized my habits and routines, I became aware that I had adopted some bad ones, most involving pushing the limits on the amount of time I had to get places and complete things. I never built in an extra minute, which made me feel anxious and stressed while driving or rushing to complete a task. I knew it was bad when I caught myself speeding to see the sunrise, knowing exactly how long it would take to get to my favorite bench, to witness the sunrise at the exact time my iPhone told me it would emerge. Wow.

Research indicates that our brains don't distinguish between good habits and bad habits. Once a habit is formed, the neural pathway that controls it endures in our brain forever. It is nearly impossible to eliminate the neural pathway of an existing habit, but we can convert the existing bad habit into a good one. That's why quitting habits can be difficult, but forming good habits can be extremely beneficial.

CONVERTING BAD HABITS INTO GOOD

When I started analyzing my typical morning, I realized I had a horrible habit of just barely making it to work on time, with little room for error. I vowed to get up an hour earlier. I already was getting up at 5:45 a.m. to exercise, but I felt like I never had enough time in the morning. Getting up earlier meant going to bed earlier. Next, I started planning what I would do with the additional sixty minutes in the morning. I knew that how I began the day usually set the tone for the way the entire day. I routinized my mornings, beginning with what I did when I first opened my eyes. In the past, I had a habit of beginning my to-do list in my head before my feet even hit the floor. Instead of looking forward to the day ahead, every morning I would agonize over how I would manage to get it all done. I added this to the list of bad habits that needed an overhaul.

Instead of thinking about what went wrong yesterday, or all that I had to do in the day ahead, I took a few minutes to tune in, get quiet, breathe deeply, and enjoy the moment before I started the to-do list. Next, I envisioned the day as a blank canvas, and I wanted to be the first to paint on it. If I waited too long, other people's agendas, my own worries, and endless tasks would take over the canvas, leaving little room for my own priorities. Erasing other people's "strokes" took too much time and energy and distracted me from my own best clear thinking. Things would only get worse if I exhausted myself before I even got out of bed. Sometimes I repeated the affirmation "Everything will get done; there is enough time in this day for everything I need to complete" as a reminder that somehow, someway, I do manage to make it through each day. Many people make fun of affirmations, but the truth is, we're saying affirmations all the time. Everything we think and say is an affirmation of sorts. Start listening to yourself and notice what your first words or thoughts are as you begin your day. If you expect others to be kind to you, it would help to start the day by being kind to yourself.

INCORPORATING RITUALS

A slightly different spin on the concept of a habit is the term *ritual*, which I think of as a habit charged with personal meaning that may be somewhat spiritual. I decided to establish rituals that reflected my highest priorities. I wanted to have more meaning in my everyday life. A ritual that I easily embraced was that of expressing gratitude.

When we focus more on what we want and what is missing from our life than on what we are grateful for, it can be easy to take the things that are working for granted and spend time thinking about the problems in life. We really need to reframe and refocus. I have heard repeatedly that what you appreciate, appreciates. Rather than focusing energy on problems, make a conscious choice to focus attention on what is already working. Make gratitude a ritual. This doesn't mean there won't still be challenges. By noticing the good in our lives, we are likely to find that we are happier and more present. Much of what we worry about has already happened or is something we anticipate happening in the future. For the most part, the present moment is just fine.

I began every day by identifying five things to be grateful for. When I first opened my eyes, I was grateful for the chance of another day. I realized that simply being alive was an act of grace. Then, I thoughtfully gave thanks for at least five things in my life. I made a rule: no gratitude repeats from the prior day. Here's a sample from a typical day:

- Thank you for this wonderful pillow, and my warm bed.
- Thank you for the coffee I can smell brewing.

- Thank you for my husband, who made the coffee and who is downstairs unloading the dishwasher.
- Thank you for my cat, who is literally sitting on my head waiting to be fed.
- Thank you for the chance to face another day.

I vowed to do this every morning before my feet hit the floor. I can tell you now, ten years later, it is a ritual that I wouldn't begin the day without.

To be honest, some days when I wake up, I simply can't clear my head. It's cluttered with worries and my looming to-do list, the typical culprits that take me away from the present moment. When this happens, I quickly record my to-do list in my daily calendar, then put it aside and begin my gratitude practice. Chapter 2 offers additional ways to incorporate gratitude into our daily lives.

REALISTIC ROUTINES

A simple routine is to refrain from beginning the day by checking e-mail. Our inbox is usually just a to-do list of other people's agendas. Stephen Covey years ago advised readers to "put your big rock in first." I prioritized my early morning big rocks as gratitude, exercise, stillness, and healthy food. If absolutely necessary, I open my e-mail and scan it for "emergencies," which mean they cannot wait one or two hours for a response. No emergency, no response; I flag the e-mail and shut it down until I've taken care of myself first. The put-your-mask-on-first mantra has become cliché but it is so true. You have to believe that taking care of yourself isn't selfish; it's actually serving others.

The goal is to allow positive thoughts to build momentum. There is momentum in thought. If I could start to create positive thoughts, and hold on to those thoughts long enough, they would take hold and become a habit, which would turn into a belief. Beliefs are the lens through which you perceive the world. Negative beliefs reinforce limitations; positive beliefs invoke possibility thinking. The most important thing to know about beliefs is that they can be changed.

STILLNESS

Another habit we can put into place is to begin each day with some form of stillness or meditation. Over the past decade, mindfulness and meditation have become more prominent in the mainstream media. Meditation is a concept most people have heard about. The differences between understanding or reading about meditation and actually doing it are enormous. It is often called "meditation *practice*," and the word *practice* is intentional. It's something that you have to practice over and over again. However (and this is important), there is no right way to meditate. There are useful pointers to help you, but there are no hard-and-fast rules.

For me, meditation is when I connect with my wise self and can actually hear the still voice inside. I think of it as my personal guidance system. This time can look different for everyone. It may be prayer, meditation, visualization, or simply gazing at something in nature.

When I first started meditating, I thought I would win an award for the world's worst meditator. My mind ran wild and I wondered if possibly I needed some type of sedative to be able to meditate. Only one thing gave me consolation. I had read in Jon Kabat-Zinn's (2013) book *Full Catastrophe Living* that mindfulness is not about forcing your mind not to wander. It is more about being aware of when the mind is wandering, and, as best as you can and as gently as you can, redirecting your attention and reconnecting with what is most important for you in that moment. I took solace in the fact that I was definitely aware of my mind wandering. Later, when I took part in the Mindful Based Stress Reduction (MBSR) clinic, the facilitator echoed these same sentiments. MBSR was developed by Jon Kabat-Zinn, founder of the Center for Mindfulness (Kabat-Zinn 2009). Kabat-Zinn began his work decades ago by applying mindfulness meditation training to help people cope with medical conditions that traditional medicine was unable to cure, like chronic pain. Numerous rigorous studies have found that MBSR promotes well-being, reduces stress, and enhances cognitive functions, including attentional skills (Chiesa, Calati, and Serretti 2011; Keng, Smoski, and Robins 2011).

I once asked one of my meditation teachers what I should do if I didn't have enough time to meditate. "Oh," he said, "that is easy—meditate." The truth is, to establish the practice of sitting yourself down and being still when you have a million things to do can feel like torture. It initially seems like the biggest waste of time ever. Often, once you sit down with the intent to quiet your mind, it's as if your brain wakes up and begins the most massive to-do list you could ever imagine. Or, it starts to play back all the past events of your life, in no particular order. Notice that both of those paths either take you back in time or have you anticipating time. Neither allows you to be fully present in the moment. Fifteen minutes of quiet contemplation can feel like three hours in a straightjacket. In this book, I provide suggestions for how to infuse different contemplative practices into your daily routine that you actually look forward to. I've experienced the benefits of stillness and still managed to accomplish the to-do list. Actually, it astounds me that I can get more done by doing less. But it works. I do realize it seems counterintuitive to add something to your life when I've been advocating to minimize your task list, but this is one addition that can create more space in your day.

TIME: WE ALL GET THE SAME TWENTY-FOUR HOURS

Making the time to live life in the present means honoring and loving ourselves enough to dedicate time each day to our own well-being. If we cannot be kind to ourselves, how can we hope to be kind to others?

When people say to me that they don't have the time to devote to daily exercise, meditation, or preparing healthy food, I understand the concern, but I know better. When we make time for a daily practice of prayer, contemplation, meditation, and eating healthy, we have much more energy and more balance, and we feel healthier. Counterintuitively, these things don't take time, they give time.

We all get the same twenty-four hours. For some reason, it can feel that we have a little less time than everyone else and that our calendars have no white space. We need to remind ourselves that we keep our own calendar. As teachers, our weekly hours are consistent. Although the hours after work are often filled with meetings and preparing for the next day, we still have some choices about our evenings.

I began to take stock of where my time went and I found that a great deal of my after-work hours were devoted to taking care of family members. I arrived home to the second shift of an already filled day of caring for others. It was like working a "double" five days a week. I also noticed that I spent a great deal of my waking moments feeling horrible that I didn't spend more time with my own children, and as a result, I had a constant running sense of guilt if I ever did anything for myself.

The time when I wasn't at work felt fragmented, as if I was doing three to five things at once. No wonder—I usually did *attempt* five things at once. Rarely, if ever, did I give any task my undivided attention. I put my children in the bathtub, cleaned the toilet, folded and put away the clothes, wiped the filthy baseboards, and on a good day I might treat myself and floss my teeth. My time was scattered, often interrupted, and I was constantly switching from one role to another. I was on role- and task-switching overload.

The psychologist Mihaly Csikszentmihalyi has documented how human time has become fragmented and the toll that was taking on what he maintains is the "peak" human experience, a state he coined as *flow*.

Csikszentmihalyi (1990) conducted a time study that sought to understand how people perceive what they are doing at any given moment; he called it the "experience sampling method." In his studies, he found that fathers do one and a half things at a time, contrasted with mothers, who do about five things at once. And to make matters worse, women are caught up in "contaminated time," which he described as thinking and planning two or three things more. So they are never fully experiencing their external or internal worlds.

I scrutinized my routines to determine if I ever did one thing at a time. What I found was interesting. The one and only task I ever seemed to do alone, fully present, and uninterrupted, was exercise. I consistently exercised every morning at 5 a.m. That had become a habit that turned into a routine. I wondered how I was able to tear myself out of a warm bed day after day. There is a definitive process to establishing a habit. According to Schultz (2006), new habits are created by putting together a cue, a routine, and a reward, and then cultivating a craving that drives the loop.

Unbeknownst to me, I had established all three. Each night I laid out my exercise clothes and sneakers next to my bed in plain sight (cue and routine), and I always got an endorphin rush when I exercised (reward). Just looking at my sneakers triggered a craving for the reward to come.

Just as we all get the same twenty-four hours, we all get the same chance to be the director of the movie called *Our Lives*. Rather than being a character, be the director. Establish routines to ensure you are investing your time wisely, in things that matter most to you.

As we journey through the chapters, we continue to incorporate routines that enable you to create more good habits.

Personal Practices to Support Mindful Teaching

I hesitate to say this, but the truth is, you won't become more present by reading this book. Reading alone won't change a thing about your life. Reading and thinking about what you've read won't change it either. Reading, thinking, and creating a plan—still no change. You have to take action. It's just like losing weight. You can read about how to lose weight, and you can think about all the healthy foods you would like to cook and the foods to eliminate. You can plan out an exercise routine. None of that will do anything until you take action. Theory doesn't change a thing; it's the practice and action that make the difference. So the application is where you take action. In an ideal world, you would have a coach to hold you accountable. If possible, consider finding an accountability partner, maybe a mentor or a colleague.

PRIORITIZING TOOL

This is the decision-making tool I shared earlier. These are questions to ask yourself before committing to anything new.

Does this task or commitment align with my highest priorities?	Y/N
Does this task or commitment draw on my strengths?	Y/N
Does this task or commitment energize me?	Y/N
Do I have the time to do this task or commitment?	Y/N
What will I *not* be doing if I take on this task or commitment?	

I've found the last question to be the most powerful: recognizing that to add one more thing to my plate means something I am already doing will most likely get eliminated or will receive less attention. If our plates are already full, we really shouldn't be adding anything.

BUCKETS: FUELS AND DRAINS

Tom Rath (2004) describes how even the briefest interactions affect your relationships, productivity, health, and longevity. The theory is to increase the positive in your life while reducing the negative. (Note: Rath went on to write several children's books that illustrated this same concept that are used in many elementary schools today.) The idea is that positive actions fill your bucket. Cheryl Richardson (1999) adapted a process for prioritizing from one of the first personal wellness coaches, Thomas Leonard, who had a tool called Clean Sweep from Coach University. Richardson's process is called Fuels and Drains. Richardson advocates that before you fill your bucket, you need to reduce the things that might drain your bucket. I merged Rath and Richardson's ideas to create a tool to establish routines. In this chapter, we focus on the morning routine.

Listed in the left-hand column of the following table are some drains I often hear from colleagues. After reading all the statements, identify one area that you want to focus on until it becomes habitual. All of these drains have one thing in common: time, or more accurately, lack of time. I don't know a practicing teacher who doesn't crave more time. It's important to not try to tackle all the areas at once. You want to focus your attention on one thing at a time. You are prioritizing to see results. Change begins in small increments. Accept that there will always be areas to work on; it's called life. If you start by making a long list of drains, you may get discouraged and give up. The more you focus on one action at a time, until it becomes a habit, the more successful you'll be and the better you'll feel. It isn't good if you procrastinate about doing what comes next. This is anxiety in lieu of action. This rudimentary action tool is meant to be simple. Experience has shown me that it's the simple, small actions that often make a significant impact.

DRAIN	CUE, ROUTINE, REWARD
It takes me forever to find something to wear in the morning.	Choose your clothes the night before for yourself and anyone else you are responsible for. Reward yourself at the end of the week with a half hour to do absolutely anything you want to do—sleep, read a book, or take a bath.
I never have time to eat healthy food.	Limit your choices for breakfast and lunch. Make your breakfast the same every day—a smoothie or healthy oatmeal or cereal, something that takes seconds to prepare. Allow yourself to have one small treat every evening if you've eaten healthy all day. Pack lunch the night before. On Sunday, grocery shop and make three meals for the week. Throwback Thursdays are for leftovers. Reward yourself with a brand-new healthy cookbook.
I'd like to exercise but I can't seem to find the time.	Record in your calendar what time you are going to exercise and what specifically you will do. Treat these times as scheduled appointments. Reward yourself with a healthy smoothie after each workout.
Quiet time to meditate or be still is the first thing I eliminate when I'm rushed.	Start with four minutes each morning. You can find four minutes. Every morning, no exceptions. Try to do this at the same time every day. Possibly right after a shower (cue) so you can be uninterrupted. The reward will be increased concentration and clarity.

PURPOSEFUL PLANNING TO BEGIN THE DAY
Plans are worthless, but planning is everything.

—DWIGHT EISENHOWER

In her 2015 book *The Sweet Spot*, Christine Carter reports that "a large meta-analysis of 85 studies found that when people make a specific plan for what they'd like to do or change, and anticipating obstacles, they do better than 74 percent of people who don't make a specific plan for the same task" (60). In other words, making a specific action plan with a contingency plan dramatically increases the odds that you'll follow through.

Small actions lead to the large improvements in our daily lives. Focus on one thing, but know that even though you are only building up one habit, you are building up the willpower you will need to take on more. You may want to work on one drain for two consecutive weeks. You can customize this process for yourself. What is important is to take stock, notice what's draining you, and formulate a plan to launch into the day fueled rather than drained.

Unfortunately, we often have the best of intentions, but we get busy, and our own self-care gets relegated to the back burner. One way to combat this is to predetermine the cue, routine, and reward for each focus area. Duhigg (2012) elaborates on this process in his book, *The Power of Habit: Why We Do What We Do in Life and Business*. Dughigg explains that habits consist of a simple three-step loop:

> *First, there is a cue, a trigger that tells your brain to go into automatic mode and which habit to use. Then there is the routine, which can be physical or mental or emotional. Finally, there is a reward, which helps your brain figure out if this particular loop is worth remembering for the future. Over time, this loop . . . becomes more and more automatic. The cue and reward become intertwined until a powerful sense of anticipation and craving emerges. (2012, 68—69)*

Duhigg adds that once you've managed to implement new habits for a month or two, to avoid backsliding into old ways in times of stress, it's important to have a strong belief that the change is possible and a solid support system. Surround yourself with positive reinforcements.

PRESENCE PAUSE: REMEMBER TO BREATHE

When we are present, there is something in us that feels compassionate and strong, patient and wise, indomitable and of great value. This something is who we actually are. It is the "I" beyond name, without personality—our True Nature.

—THE WISDOM OF THE ENNEAGRAM, 37

Even if you didn't make time to start your day with gratitude, stillness, or movement, you can still incorporate present moments throughout your day. One of the mistakes we often make is to give up if we haven't begun the day in the way we had intended. Don't make that mistake; remember, you can begin again at any point in your day. That's why throughout this book I provide a menu of choices; you need to do what works for you.

Just pausing can allow you to make a better choice. I've found that incorporating some presence pauses during everyday tasks assures that I remember to do them. For example, my computer log-in passwords are always triggers to breathe, or slow down. Here are some examples of passwords I've used: *clarity, breathe, peace, happiness, inhale, exhale, smile, be happy, presence.*

Have you ever noticed that you hold your breath when you sit down at your computer to answer e-mails? The vast majority of the population does the same thing—forgetting to inhale (or taking shallow breaths) after logging on. I've heard it referred to as "e-mail apnea." This can trigger the body's fight-or-flight response, increase anxiety, interfere with digestion, and, when done day after day (while never really making a dent in those 3,000-plus e-mails), compromises your overall health and immunity. Try pausing to deeply inhale and exhale to stay calm and clearheaded as you work through those endless e-mails. There are many breathing techniques, but the vast majority of us will benefit from making sure that we simply exhale for twice as long as we inhale. Or simply take a deep sigh every time you click on a new e-mail. Believe it or not, sighing is good for us!

Try pausing right before and right after undertaking a new action, even something as simple as starting the car or washing your hands. Such pauses take a brief moment, yet they have the effect of decompressing time and centering you. Just noticing how often we are hurried and frenzied heightens our awareness of how important it is to take a second to simply breathe. If you're at all like me, you may feel that you truly don't have a second, that to pause when we are already late is sheer lunacy. But if you knew that pause might add years to your life, wouldn't it be worth it?

When I am trying not to react to a stressful situation, I employ a strategy that I devised using the first four letters of the word *presence*:

PRES

P: Pause (this needs to become habitual)

R: Relax (or reframe if I'm trying not to react to a stressful situation)

E: Exhale—a reminder to breathe

S: Stillness, another reminder to do nothing for just a moment

I witnessed a teacher use this process in the midst of a difficult parent conference. She had asked me to join the conference, anticipating a difficult exchange. Before the conference began, I reminded her of the PRES strategy. The parent began the conference by demanding that her child be promoted to the next grade, explaining that her child was bored and wasn't being enriched enough. Before the teacher responded, she paused, relaxed her shoulders down away from her ears, and exhaled. This provided the few seconds of stillness that her mind needed to frame her thoughts and thoughtfully respond. The pause calmed her defensive reflexes and allowed her to see the situation from the parent's perspective. She was able to respond to the parent, rather than react or become defensive. It's amazing how a brief pause can improve communication.

Classroom Connections

We can incorporate present moment awareness to tasks that are already a part of many educational programs or systems. Presence can be cultivated anywhere, and by practicing in the classroom, we are beginning to cultivate the ability to sustain attention in an intentional way. We're actually practicing presence.

When you wash your hands, when you walk into your classroom, when you're waiting for students to line up, instead of indulging in thinking and multitasking, take these opportunities to focus on one thing at a time and to be alert and present.

ZOOM OUT/ZOOM IN

Once when I was observing a student teacher, I videotaped her lesson. Midway through the lesson, as she was demonstrating how to do a subtraction problem, I noticed the second grader directly in front of me playing with something in his desk. I zoomed in, and found that he had an entire battlefield of army men staged and engaging in combat during the teacher's subtraction lesson. He had blue and green army soldiers, as well as slips of paper crumpled up for the toy soldiers to dive behind.

After the lesson, I asked the teacher what percentage of the students she felt were engaged during her lesson. Her answer was absolutely 100 percent. I asked her specifically about the student I had witnessed playing army; she was adamant that he, too, was engaged throughout the lesson. If it hadn't been for the video, I doubt she would have believed me. The takeaway here is that as teachers, we really don't know who is actively engaged. Even if our students are looking directly at us, we don't know what's going on in their heads.

The Zoom Out/Zoom In activity is like looking through a camera, first with a wide angle and then switching and zooming in. It's best if done with a partner. I've done it with student teachers, cooperating teachers, and supervisors. It usually makes it quite apparent that we all notice different things and our perspectives are different.

This is a great activity for two pre-service teachers or a mentee and mentor to do together. It's a way to cultivate presence, focus, and attention.

Zoom Out

Determine a classroom to observe with a partner. Both participants should observe with no particular focus, just scanning the room, taking notes on what you notice. Compare notes, and notice how different and possibly similar your perceptions are of what occurred.

Did you both notice the same things?

What was your perception of the things you noticed?

What type of student caught your attention?

Zoom In

Repeat the activity; now focus on a student you "didn't see before." What do you notice now that you missed before?

Repeat again, this time focusing on the teacher. Notice all the micro moves the teacher makes to navigate and manage the classroom. Compare notes with your partner.

There is a vast difference between informally "looking" and systematically observing with a focus. Refocus on the student you didn't see in the first exercise. This time, observe his or her interaction with peers and the teacher. How many times does this student volunteer, talk to a peer, and stay on task?

JUST LISTEN

One way to become more present is to close your eyes and just listen. Once again, observe the classroom, but this time keep your head down, and just listen. Deeply listen: take in the sounds in the hallway, any noises outside the windows, and the background noise in the classroom.

What did you hear that you might not have noticed before?

How do you think the sounds in the classroom may affect students?

FOUR-CORNERS OBSERVATIONS

If you always observe from the same vantage point, your perspective remains the same. This time when you observe, move through four different corners of the classroom. Notice what stands out at each corner. What do you see at each vantage point that you wouldn't have noticed if you remained in one spot?

SEEING WITH FRESH EYES

As you enter the classroom, look at everything as if you are a student entering the classroom for the very first time. Take it all in, and notice what stands out.

- Is it visually appealing?
- Are there too many distractions?
- Can you get a sense from the visual displays what the focus is in the classroom?
    - Are there more posters about writing, math, social studies, science, or social emotional awareness?
- Does the teacher have personal mementos in plain view?
    - Can you tell what the teacher values by simply looking at the room?

PRESENT LESSON PLANNING: TUNING IN AND LETTING GO

Designing lessons based on the standards and needs of the students is a vital component of success in the classroom. Most would agree that there are more standards than we have time to teach, and just as in our daily lives, there is more to do than is humanly possible. Again, the need to prioritize and integrate is essential. For many teachers, a plethora of initiatives, including Common Core standards, have contributed to the "overwhelm" that teachers are experiencing.

Although lesson planning is a component of most teacher preparation programs, what isn't taught is when it's best to let the plan go. Part of being a teacher who is present is recognizing the cues from students that let you know it's time to let go of the plan. This doesn't mean you don't plan. It means the opposite: you plan so that you are comfortable enough with where you are going that you can let go of the way to get there and be responsive to what is right in front of you.

The letting go happens in the midst of teaching. You may be searching for a way to make a concept clear, and in your struggle to make the learning happen, you overlook what is right in front of you. Once I observed a teacher who was struggling to define what snow was to a student who had never seen snow before, while just outside the window snow was falling. Although that's an extreme example, it is characteristic of how we can be oblivious to the opportunities that are all around us. The questions that students ask, or the unplanned ideas that emerge not from your brain but from your intuition, are opportunities to be in the moment. Trusting that still, quiet voice inside you is where the magic happens. Those moments can't be planned, and you have to be tuned in to yourself and present to notice the opportunities.

Always prepare, know your intended outcome, do your best, and be open to the possibilities that emerge.

One of the difficulties of being a novice teacher is that you have no idea what will work best when you teach a lesson for the first time. It gets a bit easier the second time if you have the opportunity to teach the same content again for another group of students, but there is no guarantee that what worked once will work again, because the variables change. The variables are the students.

You also haven't experienced the full year of content and curriculum to know where your students need to be, so you don't always see the opportunities to integrate content. This will come with time—each year does get easier.

In the following chapter, we explore how presence provides an opportunity to reframe and see situations from a different lens. The present will always be what it is, but how we perceive the moment is up to us. There is a saying: "Why do you think they call the present a gift?" It means there is always a benefit to the present moment, but you have to have the right mindset to see it. Next, I share how, through recognizing my own reactivity and mindlessness, I was able to perceive situations differently.

CHAPTER 2

Responding Rather Than Reacting

Recognize Mindlessness and Restore Gratitude

2001—I cannot believe this is happening. What made you think things would be different? You are still in a rush. Nothing has changed; in fact, it may be worse. You can't even tie laces tight enough to keep shoes securely on your own child. How can you be a teacher? Everyone is going to see that nothing has changed; you are still frenetic.

This time, the words weren't from my colleagues—they were from me. It was my first day back from sabbatical. I had gone to extreme lengths to obtain permission to arrive ten minutes late at the elementary school where I worked as a first-grade teacher. It was the first day of school for both me and my kindergarten son. I had promised him I'd put him on the school bus for the first time. I had also promised my principal that I would be there before my own students arrived at school. I had everything perfectly planned: everyone's clothes selected the night before, lunches packed in advance, and a healthy oatmeal breakfast prepared in the crock pot. I had taken the time to start the day with gratitude, exercised, and meditated. Everything had gone like clockwork. I put my six-year-old son on the bus for the first time, then zoomed in with my camera on his hesitant wave as the bus pulled away.

What I saw next was a sure sign of things to come. Lying in the street was his sneaker, just one. When I look back, this was an appropriate beginning to a school career of endless lost projects, missing clothing, and forgotten lunches, but at the time, it put my nervous system on overload.

In this chapter, we identify and plan for the things that drain our energy. We think of energy as the actions we take, but the actions we don't take can deplete our energy as well. Maintaining balance in our life requires that we eliminate the drains so we can make room for "fuels" that restore and energize us. Once again, we are focusing on very simple things that we all encounter in our everyday lives.

I chased the school bus to the next stop and delivered the slippery shoe. My son again had both his sneakers, but this minor incident put me behind by ten minutes I did not have; I arrived at work sweating and with my heart beating wildly. This was my first day back after my sabbatical. Welcome back to the overwhelm; let the daily blur begin. I felt as if all of my best planning, my intent to slow down and to be present, was going downhill before I even got started. I felt as if nothing had changed, and I was the same rushed teacher who I had read about in my 360 Feedback report a year before. I began a stream of negative accusations to myself, ranging from "I'm the worst mother in the world" to "I'm a failure as a teacher."

And then I recalled something else the feedback had indicated: "You're too hard on yourself." Maybe it's because I had exercised, had found some time for stillness, and was feeling prepared. Whatever the reason, what happened next was the beginning of a major shift for me. I stopped the negative accusations against myself midstream. I let it go. I was able to observe my thoughts, and thank goodness some sane part of me realized that those thoughts weren't true. My thoughts weren't reliable. They were actually unreliable, not to mention mean. Psychologists would call these "cognitive distortions." Like many bad habits, we don't notice them when they are happening, and the thoughts they bring are inaccurate. If we can't stop in the midst of the stream of negative thoughts, we end up believing them and acting as if the thoughts are true.

I became mindful and alert to the toxic patterns of thought that were robbing me of my ability to do my job happily and well. I actually named the critical voice in my head after someone who was always critical of me. Then, every time that incessant doubting voice would rear its nasty head, I was able to recognize its ridiculousness, and simply "fire" it.

Stress can distort our thinking in a variety of ways. Here are some common ones:

Overgeneralization: Involves taking one situation and making a general rule about other situations without testing the accuracy of that rule for different circumstances. Key words such as *never, always, all, everyone,* and *nobody* often indicate the habit of overgeneralization. Example: "I'm always late and everyone notices."

Global Labeling: The habit of applying stereotyped labels to whole classes of people, things, behaviors and experiences. Example: "Administrators are so judgmental."

Focusing on the Negative: Selective hearing or seeing that only notices what is negative. Example: "I always mess up. I can't do anything right."

Catastrophizing: A type of focusing on the negative that we think will happen in the future. Example: "My students will never be on grade level. I'm going to lose my job."

Polarized Thinking: Puts everything in terms of extremes, also called "black-and-white thinking." Example: "All of my students are struggling academically."

Self-Blame: Puts you at the center of the universe and then blames you for everything that goes wrong there. Example: "I am sorry that my students didn't do better on that assessment. I don't seem to be teaching them very well."

Personalization: Also puts you in the center of the universe, but makes you feel like you're always under critical observation. Example: "I'm the only teacher who can't understand this data analysis process."

Mind Reading: The habit of assuming that everyone thinks the way you do—projecting your feelings onto them and then proceeding as if your projections were facts. Example: "They will all know I'm a horrible teacher."

Control Fallacies: Either we think we are in control of everything or we think we are in control of nothing. Example: "Nothing I do can make a difference."

Emotional Reasoning: Relies on feelings to interpret reality. You don't use your intellect to examine the accuracy of your emotions. You don't recognize and challenge the judgmental self-talk that may be driving the emotions.

Recognize a Reframe Is Possible

I used my intellect, and stopped and noticed my thoughts, and by some grace was able to stop midstream and reframe. I took a deep breath. I had managed to arrive at work on time and my son was safely at his school with two shoes on his feet. I realized that everyone had started the day with a healthy breakfast, had left the house happy, and at this moment, we were all just fine. I took a moment to accept that I had done a lot right that morning. The careful planning and preparation and routines I had put into place had helped. And then I laughed, out loud. Only my son would lose his shoe boarding the bus for the first time. It was so him, and I loved him for who he was, missing shoe and all. I learned an important lesson that day: the ability to reframe any situation is always there. It's something you can access at any time, but you have to be present enough to remember that the possibility exists.

I had begun my day intentionally taking the time to be still and remember all that I had to be grateful for. This was purposeful; I was having a bit of difficulty thinking about my reentry into the world of work. I had also exercised and meditated. It was a good start, and obviously something was working because I had managed to stop the stream of negativity before it spiraled out of control.

I was also fortunate that missing shoes, forgotten lunches, and homework left on the counter were easily retrieved. I lived around the corner from the elementary school where I worked, but somehow I often still managed to make that two-minute commute stressful. These were the days I fell into doing one more thing before I left the house, just one more chore. None of the "one more things" needed to be done, and they certainly weren't worth the stress I then felt as I raced to school. The world wouldn't end if I didn't switch the clothes from the washer to the dryer, unload the dishwasher, wipe off a counter, or clean a sink, but I felt like I had to leave the house in order. Note to self: it will never be in order, and I would have been better off having a few extra minutes to spend in my classroom. As it was, my nervous system was often on high alert before I even arrived at school.

What are we stressed about? We're afraid of making mistakes, of parents not wanting their child in our class, of not being perceived as good at what we do, of being judged by colleagues or administrators, or of speaking up for what we believe is right. We can't get ahead and we can't keep up with the never-ending amount of work. We're incredibly concerned about the students in our classes—the child who is struggling academically, the student whose parents are separated or getting divorced, the kid who may not be safe at home, the child you know is being bullied. The worries seem endless.

We are living in a constant undercurrent of anxiety masked by a superficial act of being calm. A typical teacher experiences multiple stress responses per day, many of them stemming not from real threats to our lives but from thoughts about imaginary threats that will most likely never come true.

So how do we monitor and control those perceived threats? The first step is to simply become more aware of them. I once heard a speaker say that his own mind was like a bad neighborhood: he wouldn't go there alone. I can relate. One way to combat this stream of negative dialogue is to replace the unconstructive ruminating and anticipating subvocalizations with awareness of what's going right.

Begin by becoming more aware of the words that you and others use. You'll start to spot patterns of rumination or the tendency to catastrophize a situation. If you want some practice, just spend some time in any faculty room during lunch. It gives you pause to consider how much our bodies may be affected by the words of others. Denton (2014), an author from The Responsive Classroom curriculum, wrote an excellent book that shows how teachers can use language, specifically words and tone, to create classrooms that offer safe, trusting climates full of students who are mindful of their words and actions. Johnston (2004) reminds us that the way we interact with children and teach them to interact with others shows them what kinds of people we think they are and gives them practice to live up to our expectations. The real challenge is to remain present without judging when you notice these patterns. When I know I'm going to encounter some negative people, or when I catch myself thinking less than positive thoughts, I remind myself that I can hold the space for positive "possibility thinking."

The psychologist Barbara Fredrickson of the University of North Carolina reported that positive emotions are physiologically beneficial because they "undo" or "unknot" the harmful effects of negative emotions. According to Fredrickson (2013), undoing means replacing one set of emotions (normally negative or unpleasant states that feel bad) with contrary ones (positive or pleasant states that feel good). Positive emotions thus correct the negative emotions by restoring physiological and emotional balance.

HAPPINESS: HOW MUCH DO YOU WANT?

In my quest to slow down, I realized that I not only wanted to be present, but also wanted more happiness in my everyday life. Doesn't everyone?

Shimoff (2008), in her book *Happy for No Reason*, cites research finding that we each have a happiness set point—the genetic and learned tendency to remain at a certain level of happiness, similar to a thermostat setting on a furnace. However, we can alter our happiness set point. In the past two decades, scientists in the field of positive psychology have identified neurotransmitters of happiness and where happiness is located in the brain. Happiness isn't an abstract emotion; it's a physiological state that can be measured. Lykken (1982) found that approximately 50 percent of our happiness set point is genetic and the other 50 percent is learned. Even more significant, Lyubomirsky, Sheldon, and Schkade (2005) found that only 10 percent of our happiness set point is determined by circumstances such as our level of wealth, marital status, and occupation; the other 40 percent is determined by our habitual thoughts, feelings, words, and actions. This is why it's possible to raise your set point.

I began a practice of predetermining my happiness set point before I started my day. When I woke up, I chose on a scale of 1 to 10 how "happy" the day ahead would be, with 10 being the absolute best and 1 the worst. It was unbelievable how directly this number affected the quality of my day. Also interesting is that I noticed I had a hesitancy to choose 10, as if too high an expectation would curse the possibility, or a 10 day wasn't something I deserved. In the beginning, I chose the number 7 a lot, and then I moved to 8 to 9, and the results have been consistent. I tend to have the "number" day I plan for. I'm working toward a constant stream of 10s. If I wake up and realistically look at the day ahead of me, the workload, the meetings, the appointments, the whole picture, I know when it really is most likely going to be a 7 day unless I consciously do something about it. I have a plaque on my wall that says "Do one thing everyday that makes you happy." I find the more specific plan I have, the better the result. Many days that I anticipated being difficult to get through have been better due to this simple exercise. Our thoughts really do impact our experience.

I encourage you not to dismiss these exercises if they feel hokey or silly. Incorporating these exercises can move you in the right direction; however, your happiness set point won't change unless you make a concerted effort to change it.

We know from numerous studies that happier people tend to define their happiness on their own terms rather than compare themselves to others and think about how they're always falling short. Measuring our worth based on what everyone else is thinking and saying about us is pointless. I once heard that in life 30 percent of people will love you, 30 percent will hate you, and 30 percent couldn't care less. I've no idea what the other 10 percent are thinking, but I do know those who are the happiest are too busy living to notice.

Interestingly, my friends and colleagues who are happiest often have the most challenging life situations. My longtime friend with two Down syndrome children appreciates every milestone they reach and has a positive approach to each day that reminds everyone around her to celebrate the small things. One of the most empathetic teachers I know lost her son to cancer. She cherishes every child she has an opportunity to teach; instead of focusing on her own loss, she gets up every day determined to make a difference in the life of a child. Another teacher I work with was recently diagnosed with multiple sclerosis. She's a twenty-seven-year-old mother of two young children with a husband who is a recovering alcoholic. I recently received an invitation to her "cane naming and decorating party." She can no longer walk without a cane, and she wants to be grateful to her cane rather than resent it. When I asked her how she could be so positive, she replied, "What choice to I have? The only choice I can make is how I respond to this situation." When we become more aware of the transience of things, we tend to appreciate and savor the moments we have.

We all have hardships; often the only choice we have is how we respond to the challenges in our lives. One of the habits that support a better outlook is gratitude.

RESTORE GRATITUDE
No act of kindness, no matter how small, is ever wasted.

—AESOP

You become what you think about all day long. You can't be stressed and relaxed at the same time. It goes back to being intentional about how we begin the day. You have the greatest potential of having a peaceful day when you start the day with grateful thoughts and keep that momentum going. The thoughts you think, repeated over and over, become your mind-set. Choose to be selective about what you focus upon. Focusing on what you have to be grateful for is a way to commence your day with a positive mind-set.

In the previous chapter, I shared my gratitude routine of bringing to mind five things every day that I was thankful for. This simple routine had a profound effect on my overall being. To understand why this worked, I began researching the concept of gratitude.

So, why would anyone not want to focus on being grateful? It's simple; we forget. We get busy, and we simply don't notice. I was a prime example. When I was rushing, I tended to miss the bright hues of the autumn leaves or the beautiful sunset, or even neighbors who waved as I rushed by in my car. I was in a constant state of distraction, looking down instead of out. When we are distracted, rushed, hurried, we can't feel grateful or satisfied. The world is full of distractions and seems to alert us to everything we don't have. (Chapter 5 explores how to eliminate distractions.) The opposite of distraction—presence—provides us with the opportunity to savor and appreciate the small moments.

When we make the choice to live a life of gratitude, we open up new pathways in our brains. In the same way we strengthen our muscles when we exercise, we can strengthen our brains, too. Grateful thoughts transmit positive energy throughout our entire bodies (Emmons and McCullough 2004). The more we practice thoughts of gratitude, the more this positive energy flows. We become more optimistic and resilient, and we have more compassion for others. By activating the mind-body connection, gratitude can help us shift from negative to positive states. Being grateful can make us healthier. A thankful thought doesn't just remain in your own mind; it flows, circulates, and expands.

Gratitude is in the present. Being present takes commitment. Gratitude allows us to appreciate the moment at hand. It shifts our attention away from what is missing to what is here now. We learn to be grateful for the little things that were right there all along. Little things like the sunshine on your face, a warm shower, and a smile from a colleague, if noticed, can shift your mood. Begin by saying thank you to the present moment.

We can choose to notice anything we want; if we are looking for imperfection, we'll find it, but if we choose instead to notice perseverance and hope, the imperfections fade and we instead notice the opportunities for growth.

Something else unexpected happened as a result of my gratitude practice. I started to be grateful for the experiences that were most difficult, the places in my life where I had really messed up. I began to see the grace in those experiences, and I began to understand that life is actually unfolding purposefully, even though I don't have access to the master plan. This awareness continues to help me to this day. I found that it was in the times of utter despair that I was broken open and became more authentic, more caring and giving.

The most caring, compassionate teacher I ever knew had two sons, both with multiple sclerosis. Every day before she went to her own classroom, she wheeled both her sons to their classrooms. I never heard her complain, and both the boys were full of smiles and always joking around. They taught us about acceptance and reminded us that we had so much to be grateful for. She was a reminder to our entire school community that there is joy to be found in any situation.

Robert Emmons, a leading scientific expert on gratitude, argues that intentionally developing a grateful outlook helps us both recognize good things in our lives and realize that many of these good things are "gifts" that we have been fortunate to receive. By making gratitude a habit, we can begin to change the emotional tone of our lives, creating more space for joy and connection with others (Emmons and McCullough 2004).

There are amazing studies that focus on gratitude. One that received a great deal of controversial press was an experiment conducted by Dr. Masaru Emoto (2005). He used high-speed photography to show that crystals in frozen water had dramatically different forms depending on the energy that was directed at the water. Dr. Emoto had people gather in a circle around a container of water. Some were directed to send feelings and use words such as love and gratitude, while others focused on feelings of hate and negativity. The containers with love formed beautiful crystal formations; the containers with hate formed random, haphazard, not-so-beautiful formations. It's important to note that our bodies are composed of 70 to 80 percent water.

In a study by Seligman and colleagues (2005), groups of people were asked to practice a gratitude exercise every day for one week. Even though the exercise lasted just one week, at the one-month follow-up, participants were happier and less depressed than they had been at baseline, but by three months they had returned to baseline. Why? Most had discontinued their gratitude practice. Once again, this indicates that the changes you make must become habitual.

The Greater Good Institute in Berkley, California, has sessions focusing on new trends in social-emotional learning and contemplative practice in education and fostering the well-being of students, teachers, and school leaders. An entire day of this institute is devoted to gratitude. The institute provides social-emotional learning tools that benefit both students and teachers and cultivate a positive school climate.

Juliana Breines (2015), a researcher and writer for the Greater Good Science Center, notes that much of the research on happiness could be boiled down to one main prescription: give thanks. Across hundreds of studies, practicing gratitude has been found to increase positive emotions, reduce the risk of depression, heighten relationship satisfaction, and increase resilience in the face of stressful events, among other benefits.

Practicing gratitude is really a decision to give up the lack mentality of focusing on what you don't have. It also encourages you to look more closely at everything you have judged as "negative" and ask what the gift or the lesson is in every situation. For example, the gift of your unhappiness is the chance to be happier. If you can change the way you look at things, the things you look at can change, but you have to be intentional and look for the opportunities rather than deficiencies. If you are mindlessly drifting through life, you'll miss the opportunities.

RECOGNIZE MINDLESSNESS

Have you ever had the experience of running through your day without accomplishing anything, and yet you are exhausted? It's what I call the mindless blur—you survive, but barely.

Unless we are present enough to notice our own frenetic unproductive pace, pause, get present, and intentionally recalibrate ourselves, we most likely will continue to run around mindlessly wondering why we feel exhausted. Many of us look like trees that have never been pruned. Our branches are straggly, with shoots sprouting in a thousand different haphazard directions. A vine without grapes bears no flowers, no fruit, no wine. The goal in this phase is to prune, so that the limbs remaining have a purpose and can bear fruit.

My goal was to be more present, more mindful. I had countless examples of my lack of presence. Here's a list drawn from real life that two colleagues and I came up with in less than a minute of brainstorming:

1. You arrive at work and you have no recollection of the commute.
2. You don't recall if you took your vitamins.
3. You find your keys in the refrigerator.
4. Someone tells you something and you aren't paying attention but you nod yes and look like you are paying attention. Later when they bring up the subject, you swear they didn't tell you anything.
5. Your meal is over and you don't recall eating it.
6. You make a trip to the store and forget why you are there.
7. You have no idea where you parked.
8. You arrive at work on Labor Day.
9. You finish your shower and have no idea if you used soap or rinsed the cream rinse out of your hair. Your body was in the shower, but your mind had already started the day; in fact, you spent your shower in your classroom (in your mind).
10. You realize while watching a television show that you've seen it before, but many scenes are ones that you don't recall.

Speaking of television: It's an escape, and used sparingly can be a good way to unwind, but when you are examining your time for extra minutes, consider how much time you spend in front of the television. If it's a deliberate choice, wonderful. However, if we just turn it on for background noise, we can be bombarded with countless "thoughts" that can influence our state of mind.

Much of the world gets up, gulps two cups of coffee to get caffeinated, and then listens to the flood of negativity on the morning news. These people are then on a trajectory that is dominated by the thinking of the world, which is fear-based. Our systems, if we aren't careful, can be wired for fear. There is an ongoing undercurrent of anxiety running all day long. If we begin our day watching the local news, we are subject to all the stories that capture the crimes that have occurred while we slept: the fires, missing children, horrific crime scenes, home invasions, drunk-driving arrests, and dangerous weather. We are bombarded with stories that can't but help but trigger a stress response. Even though they aren't actually happening to us, they send alarms to our brains and nervous systems, perpetuating a constant subliminal undercurrent of fear.

Fear can be programmed into our minds before we even leave our homes.

If we arrive home from work to watch the world news, the television barrages us with images of war, violence, corrupt politicians, diseases, hurricanes, tornadoes, earthquakes, blizzards, floods, unemployment, religious intolerance—the list is endless. In between those are the commercials that flood our minds with the impending need for prescription drugs to combat a myriad of diseases—including cancer, heart disease, Alzheimer's—and then of course antidepressants to deal with it all. The media and pharmaceutical corporations are programming our minds, and we hardly notice because we are in a semimindless trance.

I am very careful about what I watch and listen to. I screen the images and messages that I allow into my subconscious mind. I mute commercials, turn away from violent images, and don't let myself get swept away by devastation and destruction stories. I look for stories of hope, love, and compassion, things that inspire me—and if I can't find them, I turn the set off.

REST AND RENEWAL

May the sun bring you new energy by day; may the moon softly restore you by night; may the rain wash away your worries; may the breeze blow new strength into your being.

—APACHE BLESSING

You can tell when people are well rested: their eyes look brighter, and they don't have telltale dark circles or bags underneath their eyes. Now, when I'm in schools, I try to notice the eyes of the faculty and students. My unscientific analysis is that there are a significant number of sleep-deprived individuals roaming the halls.

Dongen and colleagues (2003) have conducted scientific studies to prove the benefits of adequate rest. They found that even moderate sleep restriction can seriously impair waking neurobehavioral functions in healthy adults. Their research suggests that "sleep debt" is best understood as resulting in additional wakefulness that has a neurobiological "cost" that accumulates over time.

We can't underestimate the importance of a good night's rest. Those of us who are sleep deprived aren't functioning on an optimal level. Imagine how much more productive and joyful we would all be if we got enough sleep. I would estimate that at least a quarter of the conflicts that occur in classrooms happen because someone needs a nap; this includes the teacher and administrator. Getting enough rest, just like any self-care practice, needs to be intentional, and once again it helps to have a routine.

I learned that paying attention to what you do right before you go to sleep can be as important as the sleep itself. What do you watch, listen to, read, or think about right before you close your eyes? Do you do a daily review of everything that went wrong, or do you start to worry about all that you have to do the next day? Consider being as intentional as possible about the last few minutes before you drift off to sleep. Strategies such as giving thanks for all that went well during the day, reading something uplifting, reciting a prayer or mantra, or just visualizing something beautiful are all opportunities to end the night on a positive note. What we take into our subconscious mind matters, so be selective about what you program into your mind in the moments before you drift off to sleep.

Many people (including myself) say they fall asleep easily, but awaken in the middle of the night, unable to fall back asleep. Few things in life are more frustrating than knowing you need sleep, trying to sleep, and being unable to fall asleep. You lie awake, anxious and feeling as if you've been injected with amphetamines, and then the rumination begins. It usually begins with the thought that once again you are not getting enough sleep. You start to calculate the number of hours you have slept and how this will affect the day ahead. Realizing you will have to face yet another day that you hobble through exhausted, you begin to panic. The to-do list continues to cycle through your head, and you try to decide whether to get up and just start your day, or continue to attempt sleep. You then start counting how many hours it will be until you can get home and back into bed. The irony is that you are in bed now. Once again, you are suffering from a lack of presence.

There are a few things you should *not* do at this point.

The absolute worst thing you can do if you awake in the middle of the night is turn the television on. I speak from secondhand experience; my husband is a frequent offender. He wakes at about 4 a.m., can't sleep, and retreats to the family room, where he flips through television stations for two hours. Trust me, he isn't well rested. Another thing to avoid is eating. Unfortunately, I speak from firsthand experience. I used to be a middle-of-the-night eater; thank goodness I eliminated this habit.

Still, my sleep is often interrupted. I devised a solution that works fairly well for me and also has some positive benefits. I put SleepPhones on and hit play on my iPod with the intent not to sleep, but to meditate. Meditation is defined in often-conflicting ways. Some directions ask you to clear all thoughts from your minds; other directions include mantras or visualizations—basically making *more* thoughts in your mind. The simplest way I can describe it is that meditation is a combination of concentration and relaxation.

I remain lying down. I've now eliminated the pressure to fall back to sleep. I now have the intent to meditate for an hour or more. Ironically, I often fall back to sleep. If I don't, I'm still getting the benefit of meditation. Nagendra, Maruthai, and Kutty (2012) found that meditation increases the production of beneficial brain chemicals including pleasure-causing endorphin, as well as a number of others proven to slow aging and increase longevity and well-being. And here is the research that spurs me on: the need for sleep decreases, yet aliveness, vitality, and energy increase. So to me, this means that even if I don't fall back asleep, I will actually need less sleep. That thought alone often solves my sleep rumination issue.

Other options if noise interferes with your sleep are earplugs or white noise machines. See resources at the end of the book for a list of options. Ideas for a good night's rest include keeping the bedroom dark (no electronics) and monitoring what you eat before bedtime.

In addition to impacting your stress level, lack of sleep can lead to weight gain. Pick (2011) explains that your body understands lack of sleep as another one of those emergencies that causes it to hold onto every calorie as though it may be the last. And if weight gain isn't enough of a deterrent to get a good night's rest, consider how lack of sleep affects your relationships with others. Pick (2011) notes that when you are tired, your intense, impulsive emotional brain is likely to perceive more emergencies, with less of a chance for your calm, rational brain to weigh in. Your amygdalae (two almond-shaped organs that are part of the primitive brain) go on high alert and stress hormones are triggered, and as a result, you have a hard time thinking clearly and keeping things in perspective.

My favorite strategy to support a better night's sleep is sunshine. Yes, a little sunshine goes a long way. This finding made my day. I've always loved the feeling of sun on my face. Keeping in mind that you need to protect your skin with sunscreen when you go outdoors, let's look at some of the surprising benefits of sunlight. Dr. Michael Murray (2013) posted the following information on his blog:

When sunlight hits your eyes, your optic nerve sends a message to the gland in the brain that produces melatonin (a hormone that helps you sleep); the gland decreases its secretions of melatonin until the sun goes down again. In other words, exposure to sunlight during the day increases the natural production of melatonin at night. Low levels of melatonin production are linked to poor sleep quality, especially in older adults.

Discovery Health reports on research that shows that the time of day when people are exposed to the sun is also important. Morning sunlight is even better than sunlight later in the day. Morning light improves sleep because it helps to regulate and reset our circadian rhythm (our natural clocks). The best time of day to get in the sun is between 6 and 8:30 a.m. because that's when our body's clocks are the most responsive to the sunlight. And, for an even bigger boost, try to stay directly in that morning sun for half an hour. As a teacher, I didn't always find this possible during the week, but I make sure to take advantage of sunny days during the weekend, even in the winter. I live in the Northeast so our winters can be cold, but I have found sitting outside, bundled up, on a cold winter day extremely rejuvenating.

As teachers, we can't afford to be overreactive; we need to be just the opposite: calm, clear, and able to maintain equanimity in the midst of chaos. We can't be calm if we're tired and wired. So, what do we do if we haven't had a good night's sleep? How can we get through the day without falling apart?

STILLNESS, BREATH, SUNLIGHT, AND SEATED STRETCHES

If I haven't had a good night's sleep, I make time for some stillness, specifically meditation. Horowitz (2010) is one of many researchers who found that meditating only twenty minutes a day improves stamina, boosts energy, and improves response time, motor skills, and other physical responses—all things that can diminish if you are suffering from a lack of sleep. Meditation trains the brain as if gray matter were a bundle of muscles. You work those muscles and they get stronger.

I also look for opportunities to restore during the day, and I don't mean napping. What educator has time for a nap? During the school day, the chance for rest is nonexistent. So how can we rest during the day without actually sleeping? Incorporating some deep breaths into your day can help. I use the following process throughout the day.

Inhale deeply. Exhale for longer than usual, possibly twice as long as your inhale. Allow all the tension to leave your body. Repeat this mantra: "Inhale peace; exhale stress." Continue for two or three breaths. Feel the ease of letting go. Repeat this whenever you are having difficulty remaining alert. It takes a little practice for the routine to become habitual, but when it does, you will notice the benefit. This strategy is a bit shorter and easier to remember than the PRES (pause-rest-exhale-stillness) strategy in Chapter 1.

If you teach in an elementary school, an ideal time for renewal is after lunch and recess. The students need it, and most likely so do you. I know many teachers who put on relaxing music and allow the students to choose a quiet reading and or writing activity.

Transitions can be a challenge for new teachers (or any teacher). Students' focus and attention can be compromised in the process of ending one lesson and beginning another. I incorporate a variety of transition techniques in the classroom with the intent to provide students with an opportunity to mindfully pay attention to the body so that the mind can recalibrate to the classroom setting. I find that before transitioning into the next structured activity is a perfect time to have students recalibrate, set an intention for their afternoon, and do a four-minute presence pause. I tell my students that an intention is a determination to act in a certain way that you can design—it's what one intends to bring about. It's purposeful and intentional.

A first-grade teacher with phenomenal classroom management always had a sign on her door after recess that signaled that the students were engrossed in yoga. You don't need to be a yoga practitioner to incorporate relaxing movement into the classroom. Just spending some time doing seated stretches and mindful movement is extremely beneficial, for you and for the students.

The next section provides you with some more tools to help regulate your nervous system and restore when you are feeling depleted.

Personal Practices to Support Mindful Teaching

BODY SCAN

I established a routine of quiet reflection early in the morning and just before going to bed. Those were definitely times when centering myself was beneficial. But I quickly realized that most of my stressful thoughts happened in the midst of the day. I started experimenting with taking just one minute per hour throughout the day to focus on my breath. It was rejuvenating and worth the sixty-second investment, so I started to incorporate a quick body scan throughout the day to help myself refocus. Here are the simple steps I use. I find this strategy helpful before a faculty meeting, parent conference, or back-to-school night. The process takes less than three minutes.

To use your attention to find your breath in your body:

- Starting from your feet, move your attention through your body and notice your experience. Scan for tension in your feet, lower back, stomach, shoulders, face, jaw, forehead, or wherever you hold tension in your body.
- As you scan each area, breathe into the area, releasing tension and bringing in new energy.
- Expand your awareness to your entire body and feel the breath move from your head to your feet.

HEART COHERENCE TECHNIQUE

The heart coherence technique is from the HeartMath Institute, which is on the cutting edge of research and technology in the area of the heart's influence on health and happiness.

You can do the quick coherence technique anytime, anywhere, and no one will know you're doing it. I have taught countless colleagues and student teachers how to do this before a formal observation. In less than a minute, it creates positive changes in your heart rhythms, sending powerful signals to the brain that can improve how you're feeling. You can apply this technique when you feel overwhelmed or you simply want to practice increasing your coherence. You can also use quick coherence whenever you need more coordination, speed, and fluidity in your reactions.

Step 1: Heart Focus. Focus your attention on the area around your heart, in the center of your chest. If you prefer, the first couple of times you try it, place your hand over the center of your chest to help keep your attention there. If your mind wanders, just keep shifting your attention back to the area of your heart.

Step 2: Heart Breathing. Breathe deeply, but normally, and feel as if your breath is coming in and out through your heart area. Focus on the area of your heart. This helps your mind stay focused and your respiration and heart rhythms synchronize. Breathe slowly and gently until your breathing feels smooth and balanced, not forced.

Step 3: Heart Feeling. As you maintain your heart focus and heart breathing, activate a positive feeling. Recall a time when you felt good inside, and try to reexperience the sensation. One of the easiest ways to generate a positive, heart-based feeling is to remember a special place you've been to or the love you feel for a close friend or family member or treasured pet. This is the most important step. Once you've found a positive feeling, you can sustain it by continuing your heart focus, heart breathing, and heart feeling.

FOURTEEN GRATITUDE HABITS

If we take the time, no matter how crazy and troubled we feel, we can find something to be thankful for.

—TERRY LYNN TAYLOR

Think of gratitude as a habit to cultivate so that it becomes your new normal. When you look for things to be grateful for, you see more of them. When you create an intention to focus on something, you see more of it. What has been right in front of you all along suddenly becomes clearer and more prominent. Following are some gratitude habits. Choose one or two to incorporate into your day.

1. In the previous chapter, I shared how I begin every day with five things to be grateful for. I have incorporated different ways to do this. Sometimes I go through the alphabet, each day focused on things that began with the letter of the day. For example, day one is *A*. I list as many things as I can think of that I'm grateful for that begin with *A* before I get out of bed, and all day long I mentally add to my list. A variation on this: at night, I mentally go through the entire alphabet, *A* to *Z*, thinking of one thing for each letter that I'm grateful for.

2. This technique comes from Brother David Steindle-Rast, a Benedictine monk and the founder of the Network for Grateful Living, who has written several books about gratitude. In an interview with Marci Shimoff (as cited in Shimoff 2008) Brother David shared an exercise for increasing feelings of gratefulness in his life. Each morning, he chooses a theme for the day to focus on. For example, if he picks water, every time he feels, sees, or interacts with water in any way, he notices and appreciates water and gives thanks for the role it plays in his life. So, while brushing his teeth, watering his plants, or simply drinking water, he has a heightened awareness and is more present. My favorite focus is the sun. Every time I feel the warmth of the sun on my face, see a sunrise or a sunset, I am instantly filled to the brim with gratitude. On the days when there is no sunshine, I keep in mind that it's still there, and I find that I look forward to its reappearance more than usual.

3. Imagine If is a modification of the Mental Subtraction activity on the Greater Good website (http://greatergood.berkeley.edu). Bring to mind someone or something that you are grateful for. Create a picture in your mind of this person or thing. Now imagine if the person or thing were no more. Sounds horrible, almost a cruel exercise, but it can put things into perspective really quickly. I have used this when I am feeling a bit annoyed by someone's actions. It's amazing how quickly you can exchange annoyance for gratefulness.

4. Recall a difficult time. This may sound as if it would have the exact opposite effect of gratitude, but if we reflect on the trials we've faced, we often realize that it is in the difficult times that we grow the most. The contrast in our lives helps us savor and appreciate when things are good. By recalling the tough times, we become less inclined to take all the good in our life for granted. This does not mean to ruminate on the event. Feel what emerges, but then move on. It's healthy to feel emotions, but overthinking and replaying events serves no purpose, and it's the opposite of being in the present moment. The point of this exercise is to visit the past fleetingly, but to then return and live in the present.

5. Abstinence activity: Abstain from something that you love for four days. Notice how much more you appreciate whatever it is that you abstained from when you reintroduce it back into your life.

6. Say "thank you" when things go right. Don't take the moment-to-moment blessings for granted. Stop and appreciate what has occurred, and don't just *say* thank you, mean it, and feel it, and even better, record it.

7. Express to others verbally what they have done to make you feel grateful. Be specific; tell them what they did and how it made you feel and why.

8. Put your gratitude in writing. Take the time to send a short text or e-mail, or better yet, a card or note that will be a tangible reminder for someone else that his or her act of kindness counted. If you interview for a job, send a formal, written thank-you note, not just a text or an e-mail.

9. Reach out—literally. Hug someone who you feel grateful to have in your life. Touch activates the vagus nerve, and can release oxytocin, a neurochemical. An appropriate, friendly touch, such as a pat on the back, has a dual benefit. Students feel more confident and are more likely to speak up in class when they feel comfortable; appropriate touch can foster a feeling of mutual trust and helps create a nurturing environment.

10. Find a gratitude mantra, prayer, sentence, anything that you can repeat throughout

the day. I purchased a bracelet that every hour makes a very quiet buzz and vibration. It's called the Meaning to Pause bracelet (and can be purchased at http://www. mcssl.com/store/meaningtopause/). It reminds me to stop what I'm doing, soak in the present moment, and give thanks for what I have. It takes seconds, but it keeps me focused on what's important. When you hear the buzz, you could actually do any number of things, such as take a few cleansing breaths, text a family member an uplifting message, take a brief stretch break, drop your shoulders, breathe and relax, drink a glass of water, or close your eyes and visualize someone or something that makes you smile.

11. Create a happy file. Every time a parent, student, colleague, friend, or family member gives you a sincere thank-you, keep it, add it to the file, and revisit it on the days when you are struggling to remember the good in your life. I have one of these files at work and one at home.

12. Notice others being kind to one another, and be grateful that there is still so much good in this world. The opening scene from the movie *Love Actually* depicts this concept more beautifully than I can ever describe.

13. When you can't sleep, count your blessings. Substantial research indicates that grateful people sleep better and spend less time awake before falling asleep.

14. End your day by recording in a gratitude journal three things each day that you are grateful for.

If you could choose just one of these practices, and make it habitual, you would begin to actually rewire your brain to notice what's good rather than what's bad.

Joe Dispenza (2012) writes about Hebb's rule: the neuroscientific principle that "nerve cells that fire together, wire together." Dispenza explained that if you repeatedly activate the same nerve cells, they eventually learn to fire in unison. Over time, those neurons develop a long-term relationship; they become "hardwired." To initiate change in our lives, we need to do new things and think new thoughts that spark new neurons and create new neural connections—and do it often enough to develop new habits.

PURPOSEFUL PLANNING: ENDING THE DAY

Just as we were intentional about beginning the day, it helps to have purposeful routines to close your day.

DRAIN	CUE, ROUTINE, REWARD
I feel overwhelmed with the amount of information that enters my life in the form of mail, books, magazines, and e-mail.	Sort your snail mail every day into four areas: bills, important information, coupons, and trash.
	Have a large manila folder for coupons and transfer the coupons to whatever you carry when you are doing errands.
	Reward yourself by subscribing to one magazine a month—possibly *Organized Living* or *Clean Eating*.
I have unreturned phone calls, e-mails, or other form of communication that needs attention.	Do it, delegate it, or delete it. Vow to touch a piece of paper or an e-mail only once and act on it.
	Reward yourself by calling someone from your past who would be surprised and delighted to hear from you.
I watch too much television.	Use discretion. If you have a favorite television show, record it so you can fast forward through the commercials. Start noticing how much time you spend watching TV. Learn to cherish silence instead of television as background noise.
	Reward yourself by going to or renting a classic film that you have never seen.
I do not get the sleep I need to feel fully rested.	Before you go to bed, prepare your music player with a meditation track and have your earphones ready, so all you need to do is hit play if the sleepless rumination begins.
	Reward yourself with a new meditation or song to add to your music library.

Classroom Connections

"WRITE 'EM UP BOX"

Young children can be extremely reactive and very egocentric; it's a normal part of their development. I can recall the line of students at my desk after recess. Each student had a litany of complaints and injustices. One of my goals as a teacher was to have students solve their own problems; my being the jury and judge after recess wasn't supporting that principle. Another goal was to have students integrate writing across the curriculum as much as possible. So, I devised the "write 'em up box." If students had suffered an injustice at recess, I told them to write up their experience (or draw, if they were preemergent writers) and put it in the box. That's it. I did not respond to each injustice unless it was a major concern. Ninety-nine percent of the time, the students felt better by just writing down their feelings and thoughts. It's the same concept as journaling.

GRATITUDE JOURNALS

Have students make their own gratitude journal and incorporate this into the morning routine. If they begin their day with documenting one thing they were grateful for, it could help shape their outlook. One year, we turned the journals into gratitude books that students gave their parents for Thanksgiving.

MORNING EXERCISES

Many teachers I know simply turn on music in the classroom and let the students move to the beat. Music can shift our energy and boost our mood; it's also another effective transition tool. Consider conducting opening procedures outside. Remember the summer camps that began with calisthenics? They knew what they were doing. Spending time outside in the fresh air and incorporating movement primes the brain for learning. When I was teaching phonemic awareness, the research substantiated that gross motor movement can help solidify new information. Our class often went outside to learn various concepts.

ACKNOWLEDGE THE WEARY

Keep in mind that you may not be the only one who is tired. When I taught first grade, after recess about one third of the students would fall asleep during my read-aloud. I let them sleep for about twenty minutes. They would usually wake refreshed and ready to learn. We've all experienced trying to stay awake when we're exhausted and our eyes feel heavy, and it's a horrible feeling. It certainly isn't a time for optimal learning. We can't control our students' sleep habits, but we can acknowledge their learning state and make accommodations. When weariness became habitual for a particular student, I would document and contact the parents or guardians so that they were aware.

CHAPTER 3

Epigenetics: Ever Heard of It?

Enjoying Experiencing Life: Making Epigenetics Work for YOU

2002–2004—I was in the role of "teacher on assignment," a fancy title that actually meant I was a literacy coach, the first in our school district. My professional life had fallen into place in ways I could never have imagined. The Organizational Leadership program I had been enrolled in during my sabbatical had been full of business professionals who had coaches to support them in achieving their goals. It struck me that teachers also needed coaches—confidential colleagues to assist with new initiatives, provide support to help teachers design instruction, help fine-tune instructional delivery, and analyze and reflect on their students' progress. Amazingly, that was my role now, and I felt completely "on purpose." The role had its challenges. I was assigned to ten schools, and there were never enough hours in the day to do all that needed to be done. I realized that I wasn't the only one overwhelmed; we had an epidemic of overworked, overextended, exhausted teachers in our district.

The assistant superintendent and I were brainstorming next steps in a professional development plan when my cell phone rang. My stomach clenched. The phone calls were beginning to become more frequent, and the situations more serious. My mother had been recently diagnosed with Alzheimer's. Inside, I knew my mom wouldn't want me to share her situation with anyone. However, I was starting to get phone calls from her caregiver that she was wandering and wouldn't open the door to let the caregiver in, among other things. I was afraid I'd be called away from training during my workday and I wanted to prepare the assistant superintendent for the possibility. My father was also debilitating fast; he had pulmonary fibrosis and his prognosis wasn't good. I didn't want to whine or seem weak by sharing my family's health challenges, but I knew there were soon to be days when my work life would be interrupted. Juggling a new position, graduate school, two school-age children, and declining parents, I felt pulled in multiple directions. I took the phone call in the hallway, and kept my situation private, at least for the time being.

I share the above not to unburden myself, but because I know that most teachers will at some time in their life have to show up for work while part of them is somewhere else—possibly with an aging parent or a sick child, sibling, friend, or spouse who needs them. We so often have to divide our time, emotions, and energy, which brings enormous guilt. It also takes an incredible toll; there is even a name for it: compassion fatigue.

I learned from experience that keeping your emotions inside and not sharing your struggles is not the answer. You need a support system and some close friends, colleagues, or a partner to confide in.

Mingled with the complexities of being a caregiver is also the fear that you may have inherited the same faulty genes your parents had, and one day you will ultimately face the same demise. For me, the two genetic ghosts that plagued my thoughts were pulmonary fibrosis and Alzheimer's disease. Pulmonary fibrosis means your lungs slowly close until you can no longer breathe, and a diagnosis of Alzheimer's means fading away gradually, forgetting everything and everyone. If I were a product of my parents' genes, the joke I told myself was that I'd most likely forget to breathe.

Then, I read about epigenetics, and my worldview and self-prognosis changed.

WHAT IS EPIGENETICS?

Your genetics load the gun. Your lifestyle pulls the trigger.

—DR. MEHMET OZ

Bruce Lipton (2008), a stem cell biologist, uses clear and recognizable language to explain this unfamiliar concept. *Epigenetics* is a daunting word that simply means "above the genes." It is the science of how environmental signals select, modify, and regulate gene activity. This science of epigenetics reveals that our genes are constantly being remodeled in response to life experiences. Although we don't get to choose our genes, the science of epigenetics is showing us that we may be able to influence how and if our genes are expressed. Many of us have the belief that genes control us. However, our lifestyle, the choices we make, and the thoughts we think are as important as our genes. The signals that control genetic expression are not in the genes but come from the environment. Genes don't turn on and off; genes are blueprints. According to Justice, "genes account for about 35% of longevity, while lifestyles, diet, and other environmental factors, including support systems, are the major reason people live longer" (2000, 63). As Dossey reports, "several studies show that what one thinks about one's health is one of the most accurate predictors of longevity ever discovered" (2006, 21).

Science is beginning to reveal what many of us have assumed for years: our lifestyle and responses to life events affect our well-being.

Lipton (2008) explains that our life experiences can affect our cells, our DNA, and even the way our brain develops. Epigenetic medicine is a field that every teacher, parent, and student needs to be aware of and take seriously. Unfortunately, the majority of the population has never heard of epigenetics. Many of us feel that we are victims of our genes with no way to escape our predestined fate, or we rarely think about it and just hope for the best. However, that is not the case, and the resources to learn more are easily accessible, not just buried in scientific journals.

In 2010, *Time* magazine published an article by John Cloud, "Why DNA Isn't Your Destiny," explaining this scientific concept that you can alter how your genes are expressed:

> *At its most basic, epigenetics is the study of changes in gene activity that do not involve alterations to the genetic code but still get passed down to at least one successive generation. These patterns of gene expression are governed by the cellular material—the epigenome—that sits on top of the genome, just outside it (hence the prefix epi-, which means above). It is these epigenetic "marks" that tell your genes to switch on or off, to speak loudly or whisper. (2)*

Consider your own thoughts about your health and about the diseases that are in your family. What did your grandparents or possibly your parents die from? Have you been told you inherited these same genes? Do you have an image of what a seventy-five-year-old looks like? Is it someone who is vibrant, eyes sparkling full of adventure, or is it someone hunched over, sedentary, and slowing down? Your beliefs can literally be affecting your future. Several studies show that what we think about our health is one of the most accurate predictors of longevity ever discovered (Idler and Kasl 1991). My advice: start reading about healthy, happy centurions and envision yourself living to a ripe old age. Find a role model or mentors who are a decade older and inspire you. I have been extremely blessed to have wonderful mentors who had more experience than me and were willing to impart their wisdom.

If you have an accident, or develop a disease, practicing healthier thought patterns will allow you to be better equipped to handle the curve balls life throws you. In *You Are the Placebo*, Dr. Joe Dispenza (2014) shares numerous documented cases of patients who reversed cancer, heart disease, depression, crippling arthritis, and even the tremors of Parkinson's disease by believing in a placebo. Similarly, Dispenza tells of how others have gotten sick and even died after being misdiagnosed with a fatal illness. Belief can be so strong that pharmaceutical companies use double- and triple-blind randomized studies to try to exclude the power of the mind over the body when evaluating new drugs.

HOW IS THIS RELATED TO EDUCATION?

Teaching is recognized as a stressful occupation (Kyriacou 2001; Lambert and McCarthy 2006). Unfortunately, stress can cause us to feel tired and fragile, which compromises our immune systems. When our immune systems are down, we are more apt to suffer from illness. When their primary teacher is ill and substitutes are used, students' learning outcome can be affected. Parents don't relish the fact that their child has a substitute, administrators often have difficulty securing quality substitutes, and it's a budget nightmare. Healthy teachers are good for the entire system.

SADLY, STRESS BEGINS EARLY

One of the things we can control is how we respond to the stress in our lives. If our genes can change expression depending on our experiences, we want to engage in different activities and strategies that help us create stress resilience.

We need to reassess our lifestyle choices, determine what's good and what's bad, then avoid the bad and take in more of the good. One thing to take less in of—stress. Unfortunately, at every school I entered, from preschools to higher education, I encountered educators lamenting over the amount of stress present in their lives. It really struck home when I overheard the following conversation at a preschool from a group of three-year-olds who were playing at various centers. The teacher rang a bell, which meant that the children should rotate centers. Three children were in a heated debate at the block area. It went as follows:

Susie: Tommy, you have to clean up your blocks and move to the painting center.

Tommy: *You* can't tell me what to do. I don't have time to paint, I'm still building, and I want to finish making this castle. I need more time. You are *stressing me out.*

Jane: I'm telling the teacher, Tommy. You know you can only build until the bell rings and then you have to go and paint, and if you don't paint you won't get snack and then you won't be able to go outside and play. You are running out of time to get done.

Susie: Tommy, you need to *move!* We can only have two here at the blocks, and I'm *so stressed* I can hardly think of what to build. *I just can't take it anymore.*

Jane: Tommy, you are *always* so slow. You're a mess.

Tommy: I want to go home. I want my mom.

A few themes should be immediately apparent here. The first is the ridiculousness of the time limits we impose on children. The second are the words and phrases that sadly were used very appropriately by these very young children. The three-year-olds were bullying and complaining, with the correct language and intonation. "You are stressing me out," "I don't have time," "I'm so stressed," and "I can't take it anymore" aren't the words we want to hear from healthy, happy children. Where did they get this language? I don't know for sure, but I can speculate: they are mimicking the adults in their lives. These preschool children will be entering the K–12 system in just a few short years, and they are already verbalizing that they are stressed and overwhelmed.

Deepak Chopra (2013) asserts that controlling the level and amount of stress in our lives can cause epigenetic modifications and alter gene activities. I left the preschool on a mission to consciously choose how to respond to the multiple stressors in my own life and help others do the same.

STRESSFUL STRESS STATISTICS

I plunged into the research on stress. I read countless articles about how to manage stress, regulate stress, and become stress hardy. I learned there are many different kinds of stress— good stress, bad stress, chronic stress—and about the long-term effects of stress. The reality is, this entire book could be only on the topic of stress, or I could fill an entire library on the topic. The amount of research and information on stress is staggering. Most is depressing.

The American Psychological Association (2013) describes stress as a feeling of being worried, overwhelmed, or run down. I could relate. In the APA's report on stress in America, they include results from research finding that 75 percent of Americans surveyed reported experiencing at least one symptom of stress in the past month. In addition, 20 percent of respondents felt that they were experiencing extremely high stress. However, 42 percent of those surveyed said that they were not doing enough to manage their stress. One in five people admitted to doing nothing at all to help relieve their issues. Stop and take in that statistic for a second. Only one out of five sought to relieve stress. Why would we not try to relieve our stress? Could it be we are proud of our stress? Does saying we are stressed prove that we are busy, productive, and valuable? This gave me my first clue about what needed to shift. If we really understood what stress did to our body, wouldn't we start to explore ways to manage and reduce it?

HOW THE BODY WORKS WITH STRESS

Most of us aren't even aware how much stress rules our lives, but our bodies tell the real story. Stress affects people in many different ways. It often creeps up when we feel overwhelmed or pressured to accomplish something in a short amount of time.

Stress triggers an alarm in the brain, telling our bodies that something is wrong. When the fight-or-flight response calls in the nervous system to respond, hormones are released, jolting the body into action. Muscles become tense, breathing increases, and the pulse quickens.

The hormones that surge when we are stressed have a purpose, but the problem is, they were designed for real life-or-death situations. That adrenaline surge you feel when you think you've sent your e-mail to the wrong person, or when the principal asks to talk to you about your evaluation, is real. The problem is those hormones were meant to be a healthy survival mechanism that triggers the fight-or-flight stress response when your life is in danger. Your body can't tell the difference between being chased by a tiger or having a fearful thought about an e-mail or your evaluation. Whether you're about to be a tiger's lunch or you're having a fear-based thought about an imagined future, a stress response is activated and the body is filled with stress hormones like cortisol and epinephrine.

This wouldn't be a problem if our bodies were only in stress response once or twice a week, because stress responses are only meant to last ninety seconds beyond when the threat to your life is over. But this is not what happens. Modern-day humans experience more than fifty stress responses per day—most of them stemming not from real threats to life but from thoughts about imaginary threats that will most likely never come true.

Start to notice when you get sick. It's often *after* a stressful event. It's a phenomenon that's often referred to as "the let-down effect." It is a pattern in which people come down with an illness or develop flare-ups of a chronic condition not *during* a concentrated period of stress, but *after* it dissipates, explains psychologist Marc Schoen, an assistant clinical professor of medicine at the University of California–Los Angeles and the author of *When Relaxation Is Hazardous to Your Health* (2001).

The body is beautifully equipped with natural self-repair mechanisms that know how to prevent infections, but these mechanisms are turned off every time the body is in stress response. If we engage in negative thinking, then the chemicals produced in our brain will depress our immune systems.

Toxic stress creates numerous mental and physical issues such as a weakened immune system, leading to a host of problems, as well as increased feelings of anxiety or depression. According to the Centers for Disease Control and Prevention, 80 percent of visits to the doctor are believed to be stress-related. The critical factor associated with stress is its chronic effect over time. Chronic stressors include daily hassles and frustrations.

When chronic stress goes unreleased, it suppresses the body's immune system and ultimately manifests as illness.

WORKPLACE STRESS

Workplace stress has reached epidemic proportions. Stress in the teaching profession is considerably higher than the workplace average, with more than 89 percent of teachers experiencing stress, anxiety, and depression at work and more than 50 percent feeling severely stressed (National Union of Teachers 2013). The Mindfulness in Schools Project in 2014 reported that a survey on occupational stress, published in the *Journal of Managerial Psychology* in 2005, ranked teaching as the second most stressful profession out of twenty-six occupations analyzed, second only to ambulance driving. The report went on to state that stress levels appear to be rising inexorably and that teachers have an increased risk of suicide and premature death (see also Bowers 2004; Howard and Johnson 2004).

Chang (2009) describes the teacher's day as a relentless storm of interactions with colleagues, students, and parents that routinely involve uncertainty and actual or potential conflict. To negotiate these conflicts successfully, as teachers we must learn to be flexible. We can do this by shifting our attention, making moment-by-moment decisions, and carefully regulating and managing our thinking, behavior, and emotions in the direction of positive states of mind. Many of the strategies in Chapter 4 focus on regulating our thinking and emotions, which can result in increased motivation, enthusiasm, and self-belief, while still managing distressing mind states such as frustration, lack of control, anger, and fear.

Any veteran teacher can attest to the fact that teachers are bombarded by persistent, moment-by-moment emotional demands for which a novice teacher is simply not prepared.

No teacher preparation program can adequately train a new teacher for the onslaught of decisions, problems, and unforeseen events that he or she will encounter in any given day.

Most teachers I know mask their stress, but they still show signs of being overwhelmed when the level of stress becomes too high. Signs that teachers are experiencing "role overload" can include forgetfulness, unclear thinking, and lack of emotion regulation. A reading specialist I knew lost her filter at faculty meetings when her student caseload became excessive. She threatened to quit during a routine discussion about bus duty. Later when I checked in on her, she broke down in tears describing how she had too many students to see and left each day knowing she hadn't seen enough of any of them. There is actually a clinical term for this, *depressive guilt*; it comes from feeling you are hurting those you care about most because you simply don't have the resources to give enough.

I've watched countless teachers become frustrated when the students acted out, testing their limits. I once consoled a new teacher who doubted her choice of profession on day six of the school year. A seven-year-old had refused to line up for art. The teacher took it personally and got into a battle of wills rather than examining the root cause of the child's refusal to line up. It turns out, he had never been to an art class and he was afraid of the unknown. Both teacher and student were struggling to adapt to their new roles.

Countless teachers struggle to retrieve the right word to articulate a concept clearly when they are being observed. I didn't realize other teachers had this issue until I began observing my colleagues. Many had difficulty recalling a common word, or the name of a student, a clear sign your brain has been temporarily hijacked. Recalling all the times I worried about my own memory loss, I now realized this was not a sign of early Alzheimer's, but, rather, stress. I was multitasking, not taking enough brain breaks, functioning without enough sleep, maintaining a poor diet, and simply not being present. I remember once I spent about twenty minutes frantically looking for my phone while I was on my phone with a distraught friend. And all those times I misplaced my phone possibly were the universe's way of trying to get me to slow down and unplug from all the e-mails, texts, and voice mails.

Have you ever tried to talk about how stressful teaching can be with your noneducator friends or family? In my experience, they can be quick to point out that most teachers have summers off, receive multiple days off during the school year that coincide with traditional holidays, and have a workday that usually ends by 3 p.m.

What those friends and family don't see are the hours teachers spend outside of the classroom planning lessons, grading papers, answering e-mails, attending committee meetings, meeting with parents, analyzing data, and creating engaging activities for students. This list could go on and on.

When I'm consulting in schools, I find very few teachers who are living a balanced life. I met with a focus group while writing this book and asked group members what caused their stress. Their top ten stressors were as follows:

1. Lack of time to teach all that is required
2. Unrealistic testing expectations from federal, state, and local administrations
3. Colleague conflicts
4. Challenging students
5. Difficult parents
6. Constantly changing curriculum and standards
7. Lack of adequate resources
8. Unnecessary meetings
9. Scarcity of public support for professional expertise
10. Safety (many remarked this is a new worry)

TO STRESS OR NOT TO STRESS

Individuals vary widely in how they respond to stress. The same stressor may be manageable for one person and overwhelming for another, depending in part on perception. Another factor is control. Stress is much less likely to be harmful if people have some control over the situation. A tight deadline is stressful but manageable if you have the ability to meet it. If not, you feel helpless, and the stress is more likely to be harmful. Most people don't realize that a little bit of stress, the manageable kind, isn't such a bad thing. When we stretch out of our comfort zone a little bit, we are trying on a new mind-set, a new way of thinking about things. However, extreme or chronic stress is never good. But moderate and short-lived stress—like that associated with an upcoming exam or preparing for an observation or presentation—can improve cognitive performance and memory.

This makes sense. We all know that a small amount of stress, such as worrying about a back-to-school-night presentation, produces just enough anxiety to prompt you to clean your classroom, review your notes, and prepare. This manageable stress can actually occasionally improve organization, performance, and memory.

It's also true that a happy event, like a wedding or celebration in which you are the focus of attention, can cause stress. Different people have different triggers that cause the stress response. The idea of speaking in front of a group or being observed while teaching can cause many people anxiety; others make a living this way and enjoy nothing more than being in front of a crowd. So it's not always the event or situation that creates stress, it's our reaction. Actually, it's our mind-set. And keep in mind that what you are thinking, feeling, and believing impacts others.

MIND-SET

The greatest weapon against stress is our ability to choose one thought over another.

—WILLIAM JAMES

Stress is not just about what happens to you, it's also about what you say to yourself about what happens to you. Research in the field of cognitive behavioral therapy has established that your thoughts, beliefs, and attitudes—not the events and situations in which you find yourself—create and cause your emotional reactions and your behavioral responses (Burns 1989).

A great deal of stress comes from what we think (mind-set) and what we experience (condition). These factors are entwined, and how you react behaviorally and verbally can have a lasting impact on students (Dweck 2006). If your mind-set about your work condition causes a negative emotional response, you bring that mind-set to work each and every day with you. Over time, chronic negative thoughts turn into beliefs and habits, which create chronic stress, which have a devastating effect on our health. Studies show that the emotions that originate in our minds impact our bodies. As Sapolsky (1994) explains it, "If you repeatedly turn on the stress response, or if you cannot appropriately turn off the stress response at the end of a stressful event, the stress response can eventually become nearly as damaging as some stressors themselves" (16).

Think of how you feel when a student disrupts the class. You feel as if you've lost control. Your body tenses up, which makes your digestive organs become rigid; your heart rate increases; and you may feel your jaw and facial muscles contract.

Understandably, this can make us feel upset. But if we spread that feeling into the classroom, we've become agents of negative epigenetic change, unknowingly activating negative feelings and anxiety in other students. If we can catch ourselves, make a conscious choice, and be present, we can make a conscious intervention. Maybe we take a presence pause, visualize the good in the problematic student, or simply count to ten.

Dunham and Varma (1998) cite numerous studies showing a clear relationship between the stressors that can occur in teaching and physiological symptoms. They list the following stress-related symptoms for teachers (in descending order):

- physical exhaustion/fatigue
- skeletal-muscular tension/pains
- heart symptoms and high blood pressure
- headaches
- digestive disorders
- respiratory difficulties
- sleep disturbances
- voice loss

If our mind-set can help regulate stress, then we aren't powerless victims of it. The truth is, most stress is a choice. Our own minds' negative thinking fuels stress. You can't bring me a bucket of stress. If I asked a group to create a visual representation of stress, I'd get as many different pictures as there were people in the group. Our perception of events creates a feeling that we have labeled stress. So rather than managing our stress, we need to change our perspective and manage our thoughts about how we interpret and think about the challenging incidents that occur in our lives. Often, advice to manage stress involves removing us from the stressful situation. In the example of the disruptive student, that isn't an option, nor will that work long term. If we try to just push through the stressful day or workweek in anticipation of the weekend or vacation, we end up missing the majority of our lives. Instead, we can develop and practice skills in an intentional way that enables us to be fully present. This is the ultimate goal of the remainder of this book.

THE REAL QUESTION: HOW CAN WE LIVE MORE FULLY PRESENT, JOYFUL LIVES?

The real voyage of discovery consists not in seeking new landscapes but in having new eyes.

—MARCEL PROUST

I know from personal experience that all of the stress in our lives isn't worth it. The cumulative effects of overextension and exhaustion can affect our health. At your funeral, I guarantee no one will comment on how responsive you were to e-mail and text messages. When you are gone, people will remember the good times they had with you, the meaningful things you did in life for others, and what made you special. They will remember how you made them feel. They will remember when you were truly present in their company. We all know what presence feels like, and it feels good. So shouldn't we invest the time and energy to learn how to be more present? Our students know presence when they experience it.

Asking the right question can be a catalyst to a shift in perspective, which can set into motion new thoughts, which can become actions that turn into habits, which can lead to profound change. Rather than asking ourselves how to manage the stress in our lives, we need to ask, How can we live fully present, joyful lives and make a difference?

Our lifestyle choices and our responses to life are what matter. Now that you understand the basics about epigenetics, you realize that your choices today not only affect the present, but also impact the future. This book empowers you by fueling you with information, but it's up to you to make choices that allow you to live a more fully present, joyful life. What you are thinking, feeling, and believing is changing the genetic expression and chemical composition of your body on a moment-by-moment basis (Church 2008).

A LOOK AHEAD

In this chapter, we explored the field of epigenetics and the ramifications of what this means for our present and future health and well-being. In Chapter 4, we discuss a range of strategies that can help us adopt a healthier lifestyle. For example, we need to stop multitasking; we explore that in Chapter 5 ("Ever-Lasting Focus"). In Chapter 6 ("Noticing the Negativity Bias"), we explore how to retrain our brains to refocus on the positive—on what's working, and on what we enjoy in our work—walking away from stressful situations as soon as possible. Chapter 7 ("Can't We Just Get Along") explores how to arrive at work fueled with energy and a positive mind-set that allows us to "envision endless possibilities for education" (Chapter 8).

Each chapter continues to have informal and formal practices to choose from. Formal practice are regular exercises that strengthen our ability to incorporate informal practices, which help us establish an attentive presence while in the midst of our typical teaching day. Weaving presence into our everyday lives will not only help reduce stress, but also increase health and overall well-being. The more present we are about our choices and interventions, the higher our chances of reducing the effects of stress. Remember, if we change the way we look at things, the things we look at change.

Personal Practices to Support Mindful Teaching

SHOULD TO COULD

I've made a conscious effort to eliminate the word *should* from my life. I think it has a connotation of guilt. You *should* eat right, you *should* exercise, you *should* call your sister-in-law. The word *should* makes everything unappealing. There is nothing in this book that you *should* do. There is a great deal that you *could* do, but the choice is yours. It begins with believing what you do will make a difference. Why else would you change your ingrained habits? As teachers, we are role models. We can model for our students how to take care of themselves by caring for ourselves. We can send a clear message to students that when they feel good enough about themselves, they treat others with respect, kindness, and compassion. Using strategies to better regulate our emotions, we can model these skills for our students. The way we live our own lives sends a louder message than any words we use. As teachers, we know students learn best by our example.

As we become more present, we have greater capacity to pay attention to our students, and we notice things we might have overlooked before. We begin to hone our five senses so that we see the clues our students are leaving for us about how they learn best.

You'll notice there are no new strategies in this chapter. Instead, I urge you to revisit Chapters 1 and 2 and determine not what you should do, but what you could do that would make a difference in your overall health and well-being.

RENT A STRATEGY

At a Mindfulness in Education Conference, the facilitator, Laura Weaver, shared a variety of strategies from the book she cowrote, *The 5 Dimensions of Engaged Teaching* (Weaver and Wilding 2013). Weaver said, "These strategies are for rent if you want to try them out." This is exactly what I want to say to you. Rent a strategy, don't buy into it. Try it on, and if it's for you, then maybe you will adopt it.

If you can change one thing a week, try to adopt one strategy; that adds up to fifty-two positive changes in a year. If you want to take it slower, one new strategy a month could literally change your life. Start where you are, but commit to something. Being present is perhaps the hardest thing you'll ever attempt to do, because it's work that never ends. So rather than work, let's think of it as a game, an eternal challenge to remain present. Remember, your life depends on it.

Before we move forward to Chapter 4, which is full of new strategies to choose from, let's revisit Chapters 1 and 2.

- Have you incorporated any purposeful planning to begin your day? How you begin your day is usually how the day will be.
- Have you tried the presence pause on page 29?
- Has your sleep improved?
- How often do you use the heart coherence technique (page 50)?
- How many of the fourteen gratitude habits have you tried?
- Have you incorporated any of the end-of-day purposeful planning strategies?
- Have you paid attention to where you are being mindless?

CHAPTER 4

Simple Self-Care

Time Analysis

2005-2007—I was now in the role of the language arts and social studies supervisor, and my transition into administration had been anything but smooth. I supervised five new literacy coaches and multiple reading specialists; most weren't happy. Now, finishing my second year, it was time to ask myself if the stress of the job was worth the unhappiness it was creating in my life. I realized all jobs bring some stress, but the constant strain of being in an environment that was in such opposition to my core beliefs and priorities was taking a tremendous toll on me.

As I stood in the self-help section of the local bookstore, I glanced around nervously. I did not want to be seen. Self-help implied lack, the need to fix, that something must be wrong. I thought there should be a category titled "Nothing drastically wrong, but reaching to feel better. I needed some type of self-assessment to see where I should focus." As usual, nothing I found seemed to be what I was looking for, so I configured my own self-assessment. The two broad categories were lack of time and role dissatisfaction. I decided to take a month to focus on creating time for my own self-care and build ways to restore and feel rejuvenated into my day. I would then reassess my role from a centered, hopefully rested perspective.

I reminded myself once again that although I wished for more time, we all get the same 24 hours, 1,440 minutes, or 86,400 seconds each day. I thought I had put everything into place to be time efficient, but I realized I needed a new planning tool so I could reassess how I spent my days. Actually, I needed to return to an old tool. I had been the college geek with the Franklin Covey Planner, a system that enabled me to record, track, and analyze how I spent my time (see Resources section). In the age of electronic calendars, I had abandoned that system and replaced it with my iCal. I decided to return to my former planner, and within a week after logging and analyzing my time, I was able to spot where I had been "losing time." I also found that writing the things I would look forward to each day in my favorite color was a wonderful visual. It's amazing what the right tool for the right job can do.

Next, I decided to take an honest look at my role satisfaction. The following assessment can help you determine what some of the more prevalent stressors are in your workplace. We have to pinpoint the areas that are problematic before we can start to find solutions.

WORK STRESS SELF-ASSESSMENT

	NEVER	SELDOM	SOMETIMES	OFTEN
Do you feel your teaching/supervising aligns with your philosophy of teaching?				
Do you feel like you are always rushing to get to places or get things done?				
Do you lose sleep ruminating about your job or the events of the day?				
Do you wake in the middle of the night thinking about all that you have to do?				
Do you dread getting sick because it is too difficult to plan for a substitute or cancel a meeting?				
Do you feel others don't appreciate or realize how hard you work?				
Do you feel isolated, with few people to consult with or talk about your job?				
Do you feel overwhelmed by the paperwork and reports that are due?				
Do you have endless phone messages and e-mails to respond to?				
Do you spend more time than you'd like worrying about students, parents, or colleagues?				
Do you feel your job doesn't make good use of your talents and skills?				

	NEVER	SELDOM	SOMETIMES	OFTEN
Does your work consume your life, rarely allowing time for you to pursue outside interests?				
Are there creative projects you'd like to explore, but cannot because you're simply too overwhelmed?				
Do you feel guilty taking time for leisure activities after work is done?				
Do you ever contemplate looking for a new job or changing careers?				
Totals				

If you have checked *sometimes* or *often* in five or more areas, you would most likely benefit from investing some time in your own self-care.

FINDING TIME FOR SELF-CARE

As we discussed in Chapter 3, the stress response—that constant feeling of anxiousness—was never meant to be an everlasting condition. Our body was designed to respond to challenges and then release and relax. Students need us to be at our best. To do this, to come to school feeling prepared and vibrant, we need to take time for ourselves before we start taking care of others. Caring for ourselves physically, mentally, and emotionally can help anchor us in the present moment. This means we bring our best self to work each day.

Integrating self-care practices into our daily routines takes purposeful planning. The bottom line is that you have to want to make wellness a high priority in your life. Self-care isn't selfish; it's actually self*less*. We are better equipped to serve our students, colleagues, friends, and family when we have invested the time to learn how to best care for ourselves.

OUR NERVOUS SYSTEMS AT A GLANCE

There are two complementary aspects of our nervous system designed to maintain balance. The *sympathetic nervous system* mobilizes energy through a number of glands and organs, including the adrenals. It controls the body's responses to a perceived threat and is responsible for the fight-or-flight response. It causes our heart to beat faster when faced with a challenge. It's the feeling you get when the principal walks in and your classroom is chaotic and you feel out of control. I can feel this system gear up when I'm driving and get lost and I start to sweat. Your sympathetic nervous system causes your adrenal gland to produce epinephrine and cortisol in preparation for fight or flight. Your amygdala revs up, causing you to feel stressed and on high alert.

The *parasympathetic nervous system* stores energy and allows the body to relax and prepare for the next challenge. It is responsible for the body's "rest and digest" function. It allows our heart rate, blood pressure, and breathing to be in a more relaxed state. These two systems are meant to work in tandem. However, if you feel exhausted, you may be spending too much time in high alert (sympathetic mode) and may not have allotted yourself time for restoration (parasympathetic mode). How to restore and bring balance to these two systems is the question. Once again, it is about being present to the choices we make on a daily basis.

PRESENT MOMENT PRACTICE

In looking at my work stress self-assessment, I realized it didn't highlight what I loved most about teaching—the students. Taking the time to really make a difference, to go above and beyond to support a student, always made me feel more on purpose. It actually was a form of self-care. We've all heard that by serving others, we are often serving ourselves.

One of my former first-grade students, Tommy, provided "presence practice" on a daily, actually moment-to-moment, basis. Tommy was never absent, always restless, and easily distracted. He interrupted frequently, never got the concept of "an inside voice," and was always causing students around him to lose their own focus and attention. Tommy and I practiced together how to bring our attention back to the present moment. We began by practicing direct, focused awareness, which basically meant we timed how long he could focus on an activity. I helped him to understand that attention, just like physical exercise, requires practice. As the year went on, he began to self-regulate. He would catch himself before he interrupted a peer or veered off task, and he did his best to steer his way back to the present moment. He also jokingly reminded me of when I interrupted or multitasked unconsciously, and we both became more reflective and self-aware. Tommy was a reminder that not only are we watching our students, but they are very carefully watching us.

Our own presence brings forth others' presence. Notice when you are 100 percent "there" for someone else. They feel it, you feel it; it's a connection like no other. When you offer others quiet, peace of mind, and gentleness, a tranquility will emerge. Those teachable moments when we know we've helped a student to "get it" happen in the midst of presence.

There is such wisdom and clarity when we remain in the present moment, although remaining present can be elusive with the multitude of distractions in our midst. When present, we attune to how we are actually feeling. We feel things in our hearts, not our brains. When facilitating stress reduction workshops, I often ask participants to point to themselves; almost everyone points at their heart, not at their head. In the book *Presence: An Exploration of Profound Change in People, Organizations, and Society*, Senge (2004) notes that in cultures around the world, when people want to indicate a point that has meaning to them, they gesture toward their heart.

The adage is true: "follow your heart." As educators, we have been trained to use our mind, to analyze, to make decisions analytically. Although our mind is a powerful tool, it needs to be tempered with the intuition we feel from our heart. I've learned that when my head says yes and my heart feels no, I am best served by following my heart. It's a way of feeling our way through decisions rather than solely thinking them through. To do this, we have to be present in the body. Racing through our days without checking in to how we feel physically is common. However, be forewarned: when you tune in, what you may find is exhaustion.

THE FALLOUT OF FATIGUE REVISITED

In Chapter 2 we explored rest and renewal. If you haven't done anything to improve your sleep habits, noticing the fallout of fatigue may prompt you to make this a priority. We all realize the importance that adequate sleep plays in our own self-care, just as we have seen evidence of the impact that good nutrition has on our mood, mind, and metabolism. Both sleep and nutrition are key components of good self-care, and once again, mountains of scientific evidence points to the importance of establishing optimal eating and sleeping habits.

It's common to respond to a lack of sleep by overeating or making poor dietary choices. How many times have you arrived home from work, stood in front of the refrigerator, and inhaled everything that was edible? Were you conscious? Or were you running on empty and trying to fill up as fast as possible? What happened to all those healthy eating intentions? As the day goes on, our willpower slowly wanes. Duhigg (2012) reports that over 200 studies have found that willpower isn't just a skill, it's a muscle, and it gets tired as it works harder. No wonder I lost all my resolve to eat healthy every day at 4 p.m.; even my willpower muscles were tired. Not to mention that a lack of sleep seemed to be related to an increase of hunger and appetite.

Not enough sleep can also contribute to depression; cause forgetfulness; lead to injuries and accidents on the job; impair attention, concentration, and judgment; age your skin; and lead to a whole host of potential health problems.

If you wake up feeling tired or notice that you are always simply exhausted by the end of the day, something is off-balance. Life is meant to be enjoyed, not endured. You may be sleep deprived. Those who have taken the advice in Chapter 2 about the importance of rest and renewal seriously may now be experiencing the benefits of sleep. Epstein and Mardon (2007), authors of *The Harvard Medical School Guide to a Good Night's Sleep,* describe the benefits experienced by those who have made the conversion from sleep debt to regular sufficient sleep:

- **Alertness/performance.** When you're well rested, you feel vigorous throughout the day.
- **Memory, concentration, and creativity**. Think of all that free time you'll have to think and plan creatively when you aren't searching for your keys for the thousandth time.
- **Better health**. Research has shown that short-term sleep debt is associated with health problems such as headaches, colds, and stomach discomfort. Teachers are notorious for working through minor illness rather than creating substitute plans.

When I thought of all the times I'd dragged myself to work feeling awful, I realized I'd have been better off investing my time in creating some healthy sleep habits.

In her book *Are You Tired and Wired,* Marcelle Pick (2011) explores the emotional component of being tired and wired and the need to meet other people's needs, expectations, and demands at our own expense. She describes how these feelings trigger a physical response that causes a cascade of hormones and neurotransmitters whose side effects include weight gain, blood sugar dysregulation, and numerous other physical side affects, as well as memory problems and the inability to concentrate, irritability, anxiety, and depression. If you think you want to learn more about adrenal dysfunction, this is the book for you. Keep in mind that a book provides information, but to apply that information you have to tune in and be self-aware.

SELF-AWARENESS

Self-awareness can free us from unconscious patterns that have become habits. Those habitual thoughts can become our dominant m.o. (modus operandi), which means instead of self-care, we might be self-sabotaging. It helps to remember that we created our own habits. If we created them, we can change them. Rebalancing our lives one day at a time requires us to examine our daily habits and pay attention to the decisions we make when we are at our worst. Personally, everything goes south when I'm tired. Having the self-awareness to recognize my exhaustion and then mustering some self-compassion when I realize that I am behaving ridiculously is a step toward more compassionate self-awareness.

Initially, although I had the best of intentions, I noticed that a nasty taskmaster in my head would point out all that I had to do whenever I contemplated doing anything for myself. The idea that somehow I would find the time during the course of the day or evening to devote time for myself wasn't close to practical—it seemed ludicrous. However, starting with just a moment at a time, it was feasible. A place to begin was by becoming more self-aware of my inner dialogue.

I started to become really cognizant of how brutally uncompassionate I was toward myself. I thought of self-care as indulgent behavior for the rich and idle. It was time to not just examine, but also break up the patterns of unconscious thoughts that just weren't true. Negative emotions and negative self-talk can be as toxic to the body as eating the wrong types of food. I realized I wasn't alone; my colleagues were also heavy negative self-talk abusers.

One night after parent/teacher conferences, I saw a colleague in the classroom next door sitting alone in the dark after the last parent had left. I know she had stayed up late the night before categorizing student work samples, analyzing test results, and completing conference reports and report cards. She said, "I feel like I've been chewed up and spit out. I have no business teaching, I'm not good enough to help these students progress, I'm a lousy teacher."

This was one of the best teachers in the school, one parents requested and other teachers respected. I listened to her beat herself up about how awful she was while she binged on the mints she had left out on the table for parents. She was inhaling sugar and negativity simultaneously on an empty stomach in a sleep-deprived body. When I pointed this out to her, she laughed, then cried, and then laughed again. We walked out together and the next day she was back to her former optimistic self. The problem is, we don't always have someone to point out the obvious, and when we're in the midst of negative mind chatter, we're usually alone. This means we have to be aware and catch ourselves before we tumble down the path of self-condemnation.

Self-care requires conscious choices. I recalled what I had learned from Chopra and Tanzi (2015): your genes are eavesdropping on every choice you make. Chopra also says that "the issues are in the tissues," which would explain why often the physical symptoms we experience occur as a result of the emotional toll on our bodies.

Something interesting happens when you invest the time and energy into caring for yourself. You instinctively start to care more for others, and you become more aware of their needs and emotional states. Your own increased presence creates more presence for others. This often reconnects us to our initial reason for choosing the vocation of education. For many of us, it was to make a difference, to connect with students and families, and to prepare students to be productive members of our society. Somewhere, in the midst of aligning standards with objectives, designing curriculum, and creating assessments, we lost sight of our purpose. It can feel good to remember. Moving through our days with purpose helps us approach tasks in a more thoughtful manner.

What is the primary purpose of your work? Thinking about that, getting grounded before you begin your day, will determine how you move forward. Peel back the layers of *why* you are doing what can seem like mundane tasks and remember the real purpose. For example, when writing lesson plans, do it with the intention of keeping your students engaged and curious. Think about an individual student and consider whether you are addressing his or her specific need. Make it personal rather than simply going through the motions of putting objectives and standards on paper. By designing a more creative lesson, it's not only our students who are more engaged—we are, too.

Unfortunately, according to *The MetLife Survey of the American Teacher* (MetLife 2013), teacher satisfaction in 2013 had declined 23 percent since 2008, and 51 percent of teachers reported feeling under great stress several days a week. Only 2 percent of teachers reported that they were *not* experiencing stress on the job. When teachers lack the resources to effectively manage the social and emotional challenges within the particular context of their school and classroom, children show lower levels of on-task behavior and performance (Marzano, Marzano, and Pickering 2003). Skills and good pedagogy aren't the primary resources that most teachers lack, nor are school supplies, leveled books, or administrative support (although all these can be factors). The primary resource we lack is the ability to nurture and care for ourselves. Taking care of ourselves before we sign up to take care of others needs to be a priority. Instead of dragging yourself into work when you have a sinus infection and can hardly function, keep reminding yourself that countless others will benefit from you taking better care of yourself. Teachers are natural nurturers; they are often the primary caregivers for an aging parent, a sick neighbor, and every stray animal that crosses their path. This drains them physically and emotionally.

Sadly, we cause some of our own emotional drains. The solution to this is some self-compassion.

SELF-COMPASSION

If one going down into a river, swollen and swiftly flowing, is carried away by the current—how can one help others across?

—THE BUDDHA

Studies show that self-compassion buffers stress and increases resilience and self-worth. We can't have compassion for others unless we can treat ourselves with compassion.

Often, as teachers, we can easily have compassion for the students in our class, but we struggle with the ability to direct this same compassion inward. I can't think of a better way to care for ourselves than to refrain from the negative commentary that seems to turn on when we've made a mistake.

A simple exercise to allow you to be more compassionate to yourself is to notice the judging voice you hear in your mind when you've made a mistake. Then, quickly bring to mind a student who is trying his or her best, but is having a difficult time. Put your hand on your heart, envision yourself as that child, and shift the compassion to yourself. Inhale deeply, and exhale fully. You are training yourself to see your human behavior, flaws and all. Being kind to yourself can raise the oxytocin in your system, which allows you to refocus and concentrate as the stress levels decrease. If you see yourself in a positive light, you will be more inclined to see others through that same compassionate lens.

The key is to remember that you have a choice, but you have to catch yourself before the stream of negative insults progresses too far. Learn to question your negative thoughts, and recognize that they just aren't true. The story lines we create behind events often add unnecessary drama and limit our self-acceptance.

I was making copies in the office of a middle school one day when out of nowhere a teacher skidded up to the copy machine, papers flying everywhere, and exclaimed, "I'm going to be late for my class, you gotta let me jump in!" I moved aside, and as she loaded the machine she began describing her morning. "I think I left my lunch on top of my car, it must be scattered all across Route 3. *I am such a scatterbrain.* I forgot to put the sandwiches in my kids' lunch; all they have are pretzels and cookies. *I'm a lousy parent.*" As she continued, the copy machine jammed (I swear, even machines can pick up on our negativity). Start to notice how many of your colleagues not only are racing through life, but are racing through and reaming themselves simultaneously.

Have you ever sent a mass e-mail and just as you hit the send button noticed a typo? Rather than calling yourself an idiot, think about it. Does that action really mean you are incompetent, or just that you're in a hurry? Reframe that voice and acknowledge that mistakes happen; bring compassion to that critical voice. Nobody is going to see anything in us that we don't see in ourselves. So take stock and see the good in yourself. You'll be amazed at how this really does affect how others perceive us.

DON'T TAKE YOURSELF SO SERIOUSLY

It wouldn't hurt to add some humor to your day. Northrup (2015) highly recommends laughter. The benefits include reduced inflammation, lower blood pressure, greater immunity, improved memory and circulation, and better blood oxygenation. Laughter also reduces pain by increasing your beta-endorphins, which are feel-good neurotransmitters. Rather than yelling at yourself, try laughing. I once butt dialed the superintendent by mistake (does anyone ever butt dial on purpose?) while reading a book to my then three-year-old son titled *The Gas We Pass*. When I realized what I had done, I was full of self-recrimination, positive that I had just ruined my career. Then I started envisioning the school board meeting where I'd be fired for butt dialing while reading a book on flatulence. Sometimes you just have to laugh.

TAKING CARE OF THE MOST IMPORTANT FACTOR IN STUDENT LEARNING: YOU

When we truly care of ourselves, it becomes possible to care more profoundly for other people. The more alert and sensitive we are to our own needs, the more loving and generous we can be toward others.

—EDA LESHAN

Over and over again, the research shows that the most important factor in student learning is the teacher (RAND Corporation 2012). Teachers spend more waking hours with a child than most parents do. We need healthy, happy, *well-rested* teachers to be positive role models for our students. Socially and emotionally competent teachers are able to be present to support students and create a classroom climate that is conducive to learning. Students naturally gravitate to teachers who are clear minded, centered, and happy.

There is actually a biological component to this attraction. When students observe their teacher displaying a particular emotion, it activates nerve cells in their brains called *mirror neurons* causing students to spontaneously experience a similar emotion (it's called a neurobiological response). This explains why when we enter a classroom with the teacher who is genuinely content, balanced, and happy, the students usually are as well. One of the most fun-loving, happy teachers I know rarely has discipline problems. He is too busy making the room come alive and presenting material in a compelling fashion. Often when I walk by his room, you can hear the students laughing; he has this wondrous ability to infuse his teaching with humor. The students are motivated and inspired to learn.

I've also noticed those who weren't born on the sunny side of the street often struggle to maintain control. Their students seem to be bathed in a lukewarm learning environment, and they all seem trapped in mundane routine.

So how do we help the lukewarm classrooms become more alive? We focus on the lukewarm teacher and help them remember what they used to be fired up about.

In his 2006 book *Crazy Busy,* Edward Hallowell says that one of the keys to positive emotions is maintaining your connections to what matters most to you. Select what you care most about and deploy your time, attention, and energy to these priorities. Finding time to dedicate to your priorities isn't going to magically happen—you have to make the time. As teachers, we are notorious for making time for all kinds of other commitments; consider this a nonnegotiable one.

Make an appointment with yourself. Odd concept, I know—but it works. Some advance planning is essential. Allocate time every Sunday night to do some weekly and long-range planning. See the Sunday Meeting Self-Care Plan on page 84. Take control of your calendar, which actually represents your priorities. Begin with planning something that you will do just for yourself. I tried yoga. It didn't go so well, at least not at first.

YOGA CLASS: THAT WAS THEN

I know, the last thing you want to hear is, "Just do yoga, it will help." I won't tell you that, but I will share my own experience: Everyone seemed to be telling me, "You need yoga," so I forced myself to buy a mat and attend class, but I really struggled. My mind raced and I questioned whether the entire activity was just a waste of time.

The voice in my head sounded something like this:

> *What the heck am I doing lying on this mat, I should be doing cardio. This isn't burning any calories; it's just a waste of time. Thank god the instructor is incorporating some abdominal crunches; at least maybe I'll get some results out of this. Based on what I ate last night, if I do 200,000 crunches, I might do some damage control. Why don't they play music here, it might help this constant monologue in my head. Ugh, what am I going to wear when I get home? Shoot, did I pack fruit in Craig's lunch? Oh who cares, he probably just throws it out anyway. I've got to get that boy to eat healthier, maybe that will help him pay attention more at school. Wait, I missed another cue, why are all these people turned toward me? Crap, I don't have any idea what that instructor just said, this is nuts. I am definitely sneaking out during Savasana—it's like getting to go*

back to bed and then some annoying bell rings and we have to get up and start all over again. Besides, if I stay, all I'll see is that clique of happy people getting coffee together afterward. Who the hell has time for socialization in the morning? Don't these people work?

And that was on a good day.

Somehow, I stuck with yoga, but truly, that was a very typical class for me. Don't worry; you are not going to read about how perfect my yoga practice is now. My inner voice is still questioning and chattering, but with much less frequency. Now when I notice it, I redirect myself.

It started happening when I started letting go. There is a tortuous pose called *Supta Eka Pada Rajakapotasana* (also called One-Legged King Pigeon Pose), which is essentially a one-legged stretch that is a hip opener. When you are in this pose, your head is down on your mat, and no one can see you. I took advantage of being anonymous, and often, for no good reason, tears would stream down my cheeks as I lay there. I later read that your hips tend to be a place where we store negative emotions such as stress and guilt. Makes sense. Surrendering any negative feelings or feeling of guilt seemed to create space, not only in my hips, but also in my mind.

YOGA CLASS 2008—THIS IS NOW

Breathing in and out, we start to pay attention to our breath, regulating our inhales and exhales—this helps us conquer the hills of life. Our breathing can help us manage our fears when we're off the mat.

That's the kind of direction instructors give in yoga, and truth be told, they're right. As my yoga practice evolved, so did my ability to handle the chaos of life. When asked what type of yoga is best, my answer is simply the one that feels right, and where you feel no judgment whatsoever about your personal practice. Yoga should be the one place where you can always be 100 percent your authentic self. Yoga is one of the longest surviving practices of holistic health care in the world. It is practiced by a variety of cultures and widely acknowledged for its effects on mental and physical health. Through various postures and breathing, the process of yoga oxygenates the blood, helps to calm the nervous system, improves circulation, improves flexibility, and releases tension. These results are dependent upon the ability to focus and concentrate as you move through the various yoga poses. The more you have to concentrate on the poses, the less time you have to think about anything else, which helps slow down the mind chatter.

Do I still have moments of reactivity and act in ways I regret? Yes, but I'm better than I used to be, and that's all we can ask of ourselves. I am more aware of my triggers and emotions, and because of that I forgive myself a little more easily when I mess up. So, I can't promise that you'll love yoga and see immediate benefits, but I would say it's worth trying.

Those happy people who socialize after yoga? I now call some of them my friends. Joining them is typically the best part of my day. I'm now part of the "breakfast club." Close connections have a positive impact on quality of life and strong social support increases the odds of living longer by 91 percent, according to a review of 148 studies by Holt-Lunstad, Smith, and Layton (2010). Even if you don't choose yoga, finding a healthy activity will help you foster meaningful connections with people who are also trying to improve their self-care.

In a May 2016 issue of *Yoga Journal*, Melinda Dodd cites the following benefits to practicing yoga:

- According to *Frontiers in Human Neuroscience*, yoga helps to keep our minds and bodies in peak condition, which can make engaging with those around us easier. (I thought about how when I feel better about my body, I'm less self-conscious.)
- Some studies suggest that yoga optimizes the workings of the vagus nerve, a cranial nerve or a bundle of fibers that extends from the top of the spine through the respiratory system and gastrointestinal tract and affects your heart rate, breathing, and other physical processes. As your yoga practice grows, you may see improvement in sleep and digestion. (I do sleep better the nights after I've done yoga.)
- With regular yoga practice, you also may find that you're more adept at regulating stress, controlling emotion, and directing attention. (I have definitely made progress, but can't be sure which healthy habit it's a result of.)
- Yoga provides practice in tuning into your breath, which can prevent irritability and help stave off conflict. (I definitely have learned to use my breath when faced with a conflict of any kind.)
- Yoga positively impacts your mood, psychological functioning, and focus. (I have to admit that on days when I do yoga I'm in a better mood and seem to focus on one task at a time.)

I have no doubt that if I was writing a book on yoga, I could find countless studies and research to support the wellness benefits of it, but I'm not, so I'll end my "try yoga" mantra here with one concluding thought. I was on a search to become present. I had found there was no better place to practice being present than on my mat. However, the real presence practice takes place when I'm off my mat; life is guaranteed to provide endless opportunities to bring yourself back to the present moment. One of those practice opportunities occurs in classroom transitions.

INTENTIONAL TRANSITIONS

We all know how important transitions are in the classroom. It always amazed me how chaos could erupt in a moment's notice when students transitioned from being seated at their desks to moving to the carpet. When teaching how to engage learners at the university, I emphasize the importance of thoughtful transitions; it's classroom management 101. So much can go wrong in the transition. The entire day can go south in a second. Transitions are trouble waiting to happen.

Kindergarten teachers spend the first weeks of school modeling how students should stand up, sit down, push their chairs in, line up, hang up their school bags, walk in the hall, board the bus. They know all too well what havoc erupts when one student disrupts the flow. Teaching a group of five-year-olds how to walk in a straight line and get on the right bus home is an art form. Any elementary teacher whose student has missed the bus knows the chaos that ensues from deviating from that effective transition. Middle and high school teachers know that most of the drama ensues during the transition from one class to another. Early in my career, I was assigned hall duty; my job was to monitor hallway havoc. Trust me, transitions can be trouble.

It occurred to me that just as a novice teacher doesn't always thoughtfully envision and plan classroom transitions, I rarely took the time to contemplate the transitions in my own day. Transitioning from one meeting to another, I often was in a hurry. Transitioning from work to home, I brought work home with me instead of leaving it where it belonged. Our days are made up of countless transitions, and just as we invest the time to meaningfully and intentionally transition our students, we want to intentionally transition ourselves throughout the day. This means pausing between classes and meetings; we make mistakes when we go too fast. If we pay attention, we can feel when something is off. We have a built-in guidance system, and to take advantage of this, we have to slow down.

If you feel the class unraveling, it doesn't hurt to hit the pause button. Most students now have water bottles at schools. Have everyone take a three-minute break to rehydrate, while you put on some relaxing music or a music video. Seventy-five percent of Americans suffer from chronic dehydration (Ericson 2013), which negatively affects our mood and cognitive processes. The effects of dehydration are real and especially detrimental to students and teachers who are trying to think clearly. Incorporate a few deep-cleansing breaths. While students are breathing and rehydrating, you are visualizing how to get everyone back on track. Once the three minutes are up, describe your expectation to your students and proceed calmly.

We make our last transition at the end of the day, before we go to sleep. Think back over your day, and forgive yourself for anything that you aren't proud of. Acknowledge that you did the best you could, and let it go. Ruminating over every single misspoken word, missed opportunity, or lapse in judgment will only disrupt your sleep. After you've forgiven yourself, set an intention for a restful, peaceful night of sleep. Intentions are the starting points of what you want to unfold. They are a determinations to act in a certain way.

Be intentional about your intentions and your transitions.

Personal Practices to Support Mindful Teaching

SUNDAY MEETING SELF-CARE PLAN

There are many fine things, which you mean to do some day; under what you think will be more favorable circumstances. But the only time that is yours is the present.

—GRENVILLE KLEISER

- Take thirty minutes and commit to a Sunday meeting with yourself.
- Start with your calendar. Once you review your calendar for the week ahead, you may realize how little free time you actually have left; hence, you might need a refresher from Chapter 1 on the power of saying no. No wonder we're all so darn tired—we most likely overcommit on a weekly basis.
- List in bold the appointments you have that are nonnegotiable (work, meetings, personal appointments, family events, graduate school, etc.).
- Schedule your top two personal priorities for the week. Revisit the prioritizing tool from Chapter 1 to help narrow down and focus. For example, I wrote in times for exercise and some sort of stillness. These priorities seemed to stay fairly consistent. I penciled in when I would exercise and meditate. This reserved two hours of each day. Simply the awareness of how much time I actually needed was life altering.
- Plan what time you will go to sleep. This sounds like overkill, but it's important. The only time I could find to exercise was 5 a.m., which meant I had to go to bed

by 9 p.m. or I was a dishrag. Part of my self-care was getting on a schedule and restoring some of my energy reserves. Exercising in the evening resulted in my being too wired to fall asleep. This was counterproductive, so I had to make some deliberate compromises. I happen to fall into the small percentage of people who tend to be most comfortable going to sleep at 9 p.m. and rising early, but if you are a night owl you'll need to take that into consideration. We all have different sleep rhythms and requirements; find what works best for you and stick to it.

- Delineate how much time after the regular workday you need to prepare and plan for the following day. I found if I scheduled thirty minutes every evening of uninterrupted time, I was better able to accomplish a task than if I were juggling between cooking dinner and helping with homework.
- Next, list in your favorite color ink a weekly mini-retreat (this is an activity that you absolutely promise to do for yourself). A few of my examples: taking a walk in the arboretum, leisure reading, or baking my favorite dessert.

SCHEDULE A MINI-RETREAT

The way you live your days is the way you live your life.

—ANNIE DILLARD

When you think of the word *retreat*, you might envision being far removed from home, in some type of secluded setting, being spoiled and having a time-out from the reality of everyday life. Most educators I know might get this opportunity once a year—if they are lucky.

Anything we do for ourselves that isn't necessary will often be relegated to the end of a to-do list or the first to be crossed off a calendar. The next thing you know, fifteen years have passed, and you have been busy surviving, not thriving.

So why not schedule a mini-retreat once a week?

What you do during this time is simple—anything that makes you happy. But here's the catch: do it alone. This isn't happy hour, or a power walk with your friend. This is your time, with yourself, to get quiet, slow down, and retreat from your typical life. Very few teachers I know have someone who nurtures them—that's their role. It's time to turn that inward, to personally restock and refuel.

In her wonderful book *The Artist's Way*, Julia Cameron (2002) calls this time "The Artist's Date." Cameron described this as a block of time especially set aside and committed to nurturing your creative consciousness.

I know you may be thinking: "I'm not an artist, I'm an educator." This type of thinking is precisely why you need some solitude, to quietly reconnect with your inner artist. I have no doubt that within every one of us is an artist who has been covered up by life. We live in a noisy world, constantly bombarded by sounds and interruptions. Creativity requires some stillness.

There is an art and a science to teaching. We need to remember that although we have a great deal more brain research about how students learn best to inform our teaching, some aspects of teaching are more creative and intuitive.

Each day we have opportunities to learn things about ourselves as we discover talents that we didn't realize we had. As we challenge our students to take risks and grow, we are growing and learning right along with them.

Pretend someone painted a beautiful portrait of you when were two years old. The eager, mischievous smile, eyes twinkling, arms extended waiting embracing life—then that child got "painted over" with all the trials and tribulations of everyday life. Think of this retreat as being devoted to that lost, forgotten child. Sometimes it's easier for us to nurture ourselves if we envision that former small child; it makes it OK to devote some sacred special time.

Here are some ideas, but remember: only you know what's best for you.

MINI-RETREAT SUGGESTIONS

- A morning of yoga, followed by the farmers market where I buy anything that smells good, followed by a walk where I eat whatever I bought and don't share or tell anyone. It doesn't get much better than this for me.
- I bought something called a Mini-Buddha Board (www.buddhaboard.com). On this board, you paint with only water. The image you paint darkens and then slowly fades away. Its purpose is to value the present and bring out the creative side that exists in all of us. There is a kids' version of this called Water Wizard, and it's a great addition to the art center in a primary classroom.
- In the early morning, even though my to-do list is endless, I find someplace where the sun is peeking in and I read a magazine. For some reason, reading a magazine to me seems so forbidden; it's a luxury in which I seldom indulge.
- Walking barefoot on the grass grounds me in a way I can't quite explain, but that I know is truly restorative.
- Lying on my back gazing at the sky, just looking at the clouds, is one of my favorite things to do.

- I like to pet my cat. My cat knows when I'm present, and when I'm not. I've seen dogs and their owners be more present than most humans.

SPECIAL OCCASIONS

Envision special occasions as opportunities for mini-retreats. It's expected that we celebrate holidays and birthdays, so why not make the most of them? My sister and I used to roll our eyes at how my Dad wanted so badly for us all to gather and celebrate his birthday in a special way. We both had young children at the time and we had the mind-set that birthdays were for children, not grown-ups. Now that my own children are grown, I have changed my tune. I really regret that I didn't recognize the importance of celebrating in a more thoughtful way. Any time you can be with those you care about is really a special occasion and should be celebrated.

NOTICE THE RHYTHMS OF THE YEAR

Just as our days have a natural rhythm to them, so does the school year.

There is a cycle to the year that becomes predictable once you experience it a few times. Where I live on the East Coast, we have a traditional school year that lasts from Labor Day to mid-June, with summers off and various holidays in between. There is the dread of returning to school after the leisurely days of summer, paired with the excitement of September and a new class. November brings the first cycle of report cards and parent conferences, making it often often a stressful time. December brings a weeklong winter break.

We simply endure January and February. March, for a multitude of reasons, is often when everyone falls apart in schools due to standardized testing and another round of report cards and conferences, not to mention that it's typically gray outside. April and May bring the hope of summer and increased daylight. June is time to wind things down and shift into summer mode.

Notice the rhythms of the school year so that when they occur you know why and can be a bit more compassionate to yourself. By putting into place some of the strategies in this book, you can replace the "gray of the day" with more bright spots.

A veteran teacher in her fortieth year of teaching swears that the last hour before you leave for a holiday break is the best hour of the break, and everything goes downhill from there. Most of the teachers I know can relate; vacations and weekends seem to fly by but the workweek can feel eternal. If we don't change this perception, we will spend our lives only minimally in the present. Sadly, sometimes it takes an injury or an illness to make us realize how good we have it.

INJURIES AND ILLNESS

Stop acting as if life is a rehearsal. Live this day as if it were your last. The past is over and gone. The future is not guaranteed.

—WAYNE DYER

We certainly don't schedule injuries and illness. There is no good time to be sick or injured, and unfortunately, it is rare, if at all possible, to escape injuries and illness in the course of life. I know that when I have an injury or illness, I usually worry more about how it will affect my ability to work than I do about the actual illness.

However, I no longer go to work sick. I learned my lesson when I retired from the school district, leaving behind hundreds of unused sick days. I recalled the days I limped into work with a broken foot, the days my throat hurt so bad that I could hardly speak, the countless times I worked through a bad cold, the times I left my own sick children home and had a grandparent care for them because "I couldn't take off." No one benefits when you struggle to get through your day.

My best advice is to create a week's worth of advance plans. For example, when I was teaching elementary school, I chose a core book that was appropriate for the grade level. I then planned the activities for language arts, math, science, health, and social studies connected to the text. I had enough activities and plans for a week. I then put this under my desk and let one of my colleagues know where it was in case of emergency.

UNPLUG

I try to take one day at a time, but sometimes several days attack me at once.

—ASHLEIGH BRILLIANT

Reframe the notion that you need to be immediately responsive to every text and e-mail. Most of our mistakes happen because we are in a hurry, trying to take care of loose ends before we transition to the next phase of our day.

Make your communication style so clear that no one expects you to be responsive to an e-mail or voice mail after 7 p.m. (or whatever parameter works for you). Parents may have important questions about their child, but most queries can be answered within twenty-four hours. We aren't doctors on call working in emergency rooms. I've heard of very few curriculum emergencies. It's rarely perilous. So stop the cycle of responsiveness that makes work feel never-ending. The blurring of the "never done" doesn't allow us to unwind and relax. Your colleagues may criticize your lack of responsiveness, but truth be told, they might be a little jealous. Also, try unplugging all electronics for a portion of every day. No background news while you prepare dinner, no TV while everyone wolfs down breakfast. It's amazing how much conversation increases when there are no competing distractions.

WALKING

Walking is man's best medicine.

—HIPPOCRATES

It seems like such a simple concept, walking. This simple activity can be the antidote to much of the stress that is accumulated throughout the day.

When we walk, several things happen. Walking improves circulation, can lead to weight loss, strengthens muscles, improves sleep, supports your joints, and lightens your mood. I find walking clears my head and focuses my thinking. Numerous studies have associated walking with a reduction of depression, anxiety, and sadness. Hartman, author of *Walking Your Blues Away* (2006), points out that most assume this is because walking promotes blood flow, which helps increase oxygen and nutrients in the brain, but it may also be because of walking is a bilateral motion. Bilaterality, explains Hartman, is the ability to have the left and right hemispheres of the brain fully functional and communicating with each other. Bilateral activity gives access to the whole brain, enhancing creativity and problem solving.

There are benefits to walking alone, but walking with a partner has its own rewards. As we walk, we often talk about our worries, hopes, dreams, and fear. The stories are shared experiences, and the commonality among them builds trust, relationships, and a sense of not being in this alone.

My daughter and I are frequent walkers. Often we leave the house stressed, and as we walk we take turns sharing the events of the day. By the time we've completed our loop around the neighborhood, we are often smiling, no longer venting, and it seems that everything that was so important just a half-hour ago is now relegated to its proper place.

TAKE CHARGE OF YOUR OWN HEALTH: ONE SIZE DOESN'T FIT ALL

Invest the time finding health care practitioners you like and respect and who have the same philosophy you do about your health. A decade ago I changed my general practitioner and found an integrative doctor, an acupuncturist, a chiropractor, and a massage therapist. I am now in charge of my own health care, and I strategically decide who I see and what I need based on how I feel. I also strategically supplement the resources my physical body needs.

I take a variety of supplements based on what my blood work shows rather than one multivitamin. I want to be strategic and intentional about what I put into my body. Sometimes I think about that purpose as I take my vitamins, or about someone in my life who needs my support.

For example, I take gingko for memory (see University of Maryland Medical Center 2017). As I take the gingko, I think of my son Craig; he tends to lose things. When I take fish oil, I think of my husband, who needs this same supplement for his own healthy heart but doesn't always take it. I'm simply incorporating some good wishes for people in my life as a way to start my day focused not just on myself, but on others that I care about.

LOVING-KINDNESS MEDITATION

I once heard someone say that worrying is a way of praying for the worst outcome. Rather than worry, when I want to send someone good wishes, I stop and repeat the loving-kindness meditation. Loving-kindness, or *metta* as it is called in the Pali language, is unconditional, inclusive love, a love with wisdom. It has no conditions; it does not depend on whether one deserves it or not; it is not restricted to friends and family; it extends out from the self to include all living beings. There are no expectations of anything in return. It comes from a selfless place. The process is first one of softening, breaking down barriers that we feel inwardly toward ourselves, and then those that we feel toward others. It is not a sentimental feeling of goodwill, not an obligation, but it comes from a selfless place. It does not depend on relationships or on how the other person feels about us. In this way, it is similar to the parent-child or teacher-student relationship; it is unconditional acceptance.

When I first heard of the loving-kindness meditation, I thought it was so odd to be sending loving-kindness to myself. I first experienced it at a retreat, and even the title seemed off-putting. It seemed really awkward, but when I sent loving-kindness to someone I loved, I felt better. Then, when it was time to send loving-kindness to someone I was having a difficult time with, I again felt uncomfortable. However, this practice has grown on me. I use it formally and informally. I've grown to cherish every aspect, especially sending loving-kindness to someone I'm having a difficult time with. Following is the full practice that I often do in the morning. I think of this as the more formal practice.

We begin with loving ourselves, because unless we can cultivate this unconditional love and acceptance for ourselves, it is difficult to extend it to others.

May I be happy.
May I be healthy.
May I be free from pain.
May I be at ease.

Then we include someone we love.

May you be happy.
May you be healthy.
May you be free from pain.
May you be at ease.

Next, we repeat the same mantra toward a person we don't know very well, just someone we see occasionally but don't have a relationship with. We then repeat the mantra for someone we are having a difficult time with, and, ultimately, for all things everywhere, living or nonliving. Gradually, both the visualization and the meditation phrases blend into the actual experience, the feeling of loving-kindness.

This is a meditation of care, concern, tenderness, loving-kindness, friendship—a feeling of warmth for oneself and others. The practice is the softening of the mind and heart, an opening to deeper and deeper levels of the feeling of kindness and love. Some days I simply repeat parts of the mantra (informal practice). Just like everything in this book, you can choose whether you want to do all, part, or none of this. But do yourself a favor and start with you, and the rest will surely follow.

Classroom Connections

TALLY YOUR THOUGHTS

Teach your students to reframe their inner dialogue. Keep in mind that if we want our students to talk to their peers and themselves using positive, constructive language, we need to do this ourselves. Practicing what we preach isn't always easy!

Share the fact that psychologists estimate that the average person has 40,000 to 60,000 thoughts per day, and that we are responsible for choosing our thoughts. Set a timer for one minute and instruct your students *not* to think, but to make a tally mark if they do have a thought. This will most likely be eye-opening.

As a class, devote thirty minutes (or less depending on students' ages) to noticing any inner dialogue, and commit to changing any negative self-talk. Remind students that positive words invite more positive feelings; negative self-talk invites more negative feelings.

THIRTY-SECOND LAUGH

Creating a storehouse of videos for transitions is well worth the time. Watching a funny video gives both you and your students the opportunity to laugh and relax. Laughter releases nitric oxide and beta-endorphins into your bloodstream, which boosts immunity. I often select funny kitten videos via YouTube for a quick laugh.

READ—REST—DESIGN—IMAGINE

Our students need the same replenishment we do. If we give them the time to recharge their batteries, they become more engaged. Recharging can be as simple as taking time to draw or listening to music. Many teachers now use mindfulness coloring books as classroom rewards and breaks.

You too can recharge. Write in your journal, reflect on your lesson, brainstorm, imagine what you would do if you knew you wouldn't fail. This is easier said than done. The temptation to grade papers, finish administrative tasks, or prepare for the next segment of the day is overwhelming. Try to make a goal of recharging twice a week and notice if it makes a difference in your day.

PLAY

To this day, one of my favorite memories of school as a child is of all of us sitting on our desks and just throwing a ball around. It was simply wonderful. There are hundreds of indoor games; use these as rewards and brain breaks. A five-minute game break between tough lessons is enough to recharge students and teachers.

The focus of this chapter has been on you. As educators, many of us graduated from college and plunged into the real world of work without having a sense of how to navigate through all the responsibilities and commitments that real life requires. We didn't think much about it, we just did it, and life just happened. We got a job, some of us started families, and in both situations we cared for others. In the midst of all this care, we forgot about taking care of ourselves. To counteract this, we can make a conscious choice to treat others and ourselves with a bit more kindness.

CHAPTER 5

Ever-Lasting Focus

Eliminate Extraneous Distractions

2008—Word had spread quickly that I'd resigned as program director for organizational and professional development. Here I was, near the top of the mountain, and I had looked around and said, "Oops, wrong mountain," and hurled myself off the ridge. I didn't slowly make my way back down the mountain; instead, I made the decision to leave the moment my Dad took his last breath. I realized in that instant that everything I thought mattered so much to me just didn't.

I went home and typed my letter of resignation. I assured the superintendent I would finish three major tasks before I left: the strategic plan, the professional development plan, and preparations for induction. What everyone was calling the biggest mistake of my life I knew was a window to future freedom. I was transitioning to a tenure-track position at a university in the college of education. I would be making less than half of my current salary, but I had no doubt that the price of happiness couldn't be measured in dollars and cents.

MID-MARCH MADNESS

To complete those three monumental tasks I had promised to do before I left, I decided to find a way to stay on task and do the work efficiently. I vowed to "stay until I left." Remaining present while planning for a future I wouldn't be a part of was a challenge, and I realized I needed to learn some strategies to keep me on task. I reminded myself that I would be teaching educators who would need strategies to learn to stay on task themselves and to teach their students. I have always viewed life as one giant curriculum that I have willingly signed up for, and my purpose is to learn as much as I can to share with others.

I took stock of my work habits—if I were grading myself, I would have earned a C-minus. There was plenty of room for improvement.

I began to read, research, and experiment with strategies to increase productivity. A multitude of books have been published on these subjects. Most of the literature pointed to eliminating distractions and remaining focused. I've synthesized the research into ten productivity tips.

TEN PRODUCTIVITY TIPS
1. The Myth of Multitasking

Multitasking is the enemy of focus. It stresses us out and prevents us from doing our most meaningful work. The human brain did not evolve to focus on many things at once; it evolved to focus on one thing at a time.

CHRISTINE CARTER

Wanting to know more about productivity, I purchased Christine Carter's 2015 book, *The Sweet Spot*. Carter's theory is that we achieve more by doing less. Who wouldn't want that? Sign me up. She equates busyness with cognitive overload, explaining in an interview in *Mindful* magazine that "an overloaded brain hinders performance. It impairs our ability to think creatively, plan, organize, innovate, solve problems, make decisions, resist temptations, learn new things easily, speak fluently, remember important social information, and control our emotions."

Cognitive overload affects our productivity. In all of the myriad articles and advice on productivity, context switching is the most cited as diminishing productivity. In its simplest form, context switching is jumping between various unrelated tasks. Context switching is the worst form of multitasking, especially for an overloaded brain. The American Psychological Association describes three types of multitasking:

- Classic multitasking: Trying to perform more than one task at a time
- Rapid task switching: Going from one task to another in quick succession
- Interrupted task switching: Having to switch from one task to another, before the first task is complete; the mother of all time sucks

As I read, I realized I had one major problem—I was a multitasking sage. I was guilty of all three types of multitasking. I could multitask with the best of them. I imagine most teachers would have the same claim to fame. It's what we do, all day long. We can collect field trip money while checking attendance and at the same time listen to why a student didn't hand in his or her homework. During small-group instruction, we monitor our own group, keep an eye on the rest of the class, and know when someone enters the room. Many of us leave school, navigating a stressful commute home, where we land and begin our second job (family). I recall picking my own children up at the babysitter's after school, bringing them back to my classroom to play as I prepared the next day's lesson, and somehow simultaneously playing with them while trying to work. I then drove home to prepare dinner while monitoring home-work and folding clothes and attempting to have an adult conversation with my husband.

Eliminate multitasking? Really? I hesitantly decided to give it a try.

My first attempt at eliminating multitasking was a monumental failure. After a few days of doing one thing at a time, I quickly resumed my former habitual juggling act. Seriously, how bad could multitasking be? Still committed to finding productivity tips, I turned to the work of Ed Hallowell, author of multiple books on distraction such as *Delivered from Distraction* (Hallowell and Ratey 2006) and *Crazy Busy* (Hallowell 2006). I hoped he would provide different ideas about productivity.

I was sorry but not surprised to read that Hallowell concurs that it is neurologically impossible to concentrate on two tasks at once. He explains that what we really mean by "multitasking" is switching attention from one task to another in rapid succession. If both tasks don't take much cognitive attention, you can get away with it. For example, I can staple papers and manage a phone conference. That's not what Hallowell is describing. He is referring to fairly complex tasks, such as composing an e-mail while on the phone—both the conversation and e-mail will suffer because both require cognitive attention. The rule of thumb seems to be that if either of the tasks requires that you be present, then only one task that should be occurring. Hallowell's (2015) latest book, *Driven to Distraction at Work*, is a quick, informative read that expands more on this concept.

Searching for someone to disagree with Hallowell so I wouldn't have to give up multitasking, I looked to productivity experts Tony Schwartz and Catherine McCarthy (2007). Unfortunately, they found that a temporary shift in attention from one task to another increases the amount of time necessary to finish the primary task by as much as 25 percent and that multitasking exhausts more energy and time than single-tasking every time.

The research is clear: any form of multitasking is a giant energy drain for your brain. My brain did not need to be drained any more than it was! I was committed to doing everything that I could to keep my own brain healthy. This time I vowed to *reduce* multitasking instead of eliminating it. I began by paying attention to when and why I multitask; sadly, I realized it was just my modus operandi, an ingrained habit. For example, as I typed this sentence, I seamlessly gave the Pandora song playing in the background a thumbs up, checked on visual thesaurus to make sure I spelled and used the term *modus operandi* correctly, and added a task to complete later to my Trello board. Whew! This was going to be hard work.

I set a goal to reduce multitasking by at least 50 percent. I didn't keep a log (this would have been multitasking); instead, I began to observe my work habits, and I quickly realized how distractible I was.

2. Deterring Distractibility
Things which matter most must never be done at the mercy of things which matter least.

—GOETHE

I took stock of when was I most distracted and apt to task switch. The answer was obvious: when I was "plugged in." I began to observe the way I used my digital tools, or rather, how they used me.

I teach online courses, and to best prepare to teach, I have enrolled in multiple online courses myself. While listening to an online lecture, I am embarrassed to admit I have been guilty of the following:

- Checking e-mail
- Texting
- Tweeting
- Surfing the web to check a source that was mentioned in the lecture
- Ordering a book on Amazon
- Googling the lecturer

- Updating my Netflix queue
- Checking my calendar
- Adding a task to Trello

I'm known for having multiple browsers open, often two screens fired up (laptop and desktop), and my phone and iPad in close proximity.

However, as a result of reading all of the research, I've changed some of my bad habits, and I can honestly say I am more focused and intentional. I have given up most of the disruptive behaviors. I've learned to not have phone conferences or coaching calls in my office, but instead in a spot where I have limited distractions. When I abstain from this task switching, I notice an improvement in my task completion and my ability to sustain attention. I seem to be saving time and producing better-quality work.

Once again, change begins with being observant about our own habits. I realized I needed to create the space to observe my own digital patterns of behavior. While completing all of the final projects at the school district, I had an incredible opportunity to observe my very poor work habits. I also tuned in to what was happening in my mind and body while I was working. My shoulders often crept up to my ears, I held my breath when composing an e-mail message, and I often slumped in my chair rather than sitting upright. My back hurt, and my eyes were often tired.

Here are three good habits that I adopted:

1. Stand and read aloud before hitting send: I learned this trick from John Collins, developer of the Collins Writing Program (see Resources). He points out that the ear will hear what the eye doesn't see, which is why we should read aloud what we write. Standing up to proofread what you have written also sends blood to the brain. Switching between standing and sitting is good for you. Even better, every twenty minutes, stand and move for about two minutes. Movement is important to get blood circulation through the muscles.

2. Listen to Background Music: There are many apps to help with focus while working. According to Hallowell (2015), listening to classical music while writing can alter the part of the brain that would otherwise be distracted. Music has been used across cultures for millennia to put people's minds in specific states: only recently have neuroscientists discovered that this effect is due to the broad impact of sound on neural circuitry across the brain.

Hallowell recommends focusatwill.com, which was developed by a British rock musician turned scientist of sound. It's a new music service based on human neuroscience. According to focus@will, listening can help reduce distractions, maintain your productivity, and retain information when working, studying, writing, and reading. The scientifically tested technology behind focus@will has been shown to alter brain activity toward a state that is more conducive to productivity. I happen to be listening to this music as I write this paragraph.

3. Schedule and communicate specific times to answer e-mail: A colleague of mine uses this autoreply for e-mails:

    In order to maintain optimal efficiency and effectiveness, I respond to emails twice daily, Mon.–Fri. at approximately 7 a.m. ET and 4 p.m. ET. If you require more urgent assistance, please call me at XXX-XXX-XXXX. Thanks for your understanding and cooperation. **This is an autoreply. I will process your email following the above schedule.

    As a classroom teacher, I always communicated when I would respond to e-mails and phone calls. We had a twenty-four-hour communication policy in our district, which I honored, but I communicated with parents in a specific time of day that I had blocked off for them.

If you'd like to explore more strategies to combat digital distraction, I would suggest exploring Levy's (2016) book, *Mindful Tech: How to Bring Balance to Our Digital Lives*. It's an informative guide to being more relaxed and attentive while online.

This type of information is valuable to our own students, too, at every level. A colleague and I have facilitated technology professional learning communities for multiple years. While presenting at conferences on the topic of student teaching and distractibility, it has become clear to me that many educators struggle with this topic. Not only do we as teachers need strategies to combat digital distraction, we also need ways to teach our students what to do when their minds take a mental excursion.

I used to witness students "check out" while reading aloud. Even when their eyes were focusing on each word, as they were pronouncing each syllable, their actual attention was being taken up by thinking about last night's television show or worrying about something a friend had said.

Teaching how to juggle multiple distractions and build an arsenal of strategies to help manage the interruptions isn't often taught in a traditional curriculum, but could possibly help many students acquire more focus and concentration.

3. Focus Your Energy

When you wash your hands, when you make a cup of coffee, when you're waiting for the elevator—instead of indulging in thinking, these are all opportunities for being there as a still, alert presence.

—ECKHART TOLLE

In a 2011 TED Talk, Matthew Killingsworth described a study in which he and a colleague sampled over 2,000 adults during their day-to-day activities and found that their minds were not focused on what they were currently doing 47 percent of the time. The study found that when people's minds were wandering, they tended to be less happy, presumably because their thoughts drifted toward the negative.

Take stock of what gets your attention and how you spend your time. We are literally *spending* every second, and we can make conscious choices about how we do it. When we focus on one task at a time, we're actually more productive in the long run, and we're less exhausted at the end of the day. Everything we do uses energy, and what's undone also depletes our mental energy. Our ability to remain present is drained when our thoughts are tied up with what's not finished.

We are most attentive when we are engaged. I now consciously do first what matters most to me, and as a result I am happier. This doesn't mean that I can forgo the tasks that I don't look forward to so much, but the shift to doing something meaningful first has yielded more overall productivity and presence while completing tasks. When you are doing what you are good at and like to do, the task is more meaningful and your ability to remain present is heightened. Mihaly Csikszentmihalyi (1990) described this as "flow" and wrote an entire book on this concept. He is legendary for his national best seller, *Flow: The Psychology of Optimal Experience*. He defines *flow* as "the state in which people are so involved in an activity that nothing else seems to matter; the experience itself is so enjoyable that people will do it even at great cost, for the sheer sake of doing it" (5). It's important to know your own "flow times," when you are at your most creative and engaged so that you can focus your energy on what matters most to you then. My lessons are significantly better when I plan them in the early morning as opposed to late afternoon.

I have experienced flow when I have prepared and practiced enough that I can let go and rely on my memory to carry me through a task so that I can be responsive to what's right in front of me. When I teach a great lesson, I know it's because I've prepared and can be truly present for the student or students in front of me. Once you've experienced flow, you tend to want more of it, but you can't manufacture it. Flow happens when you are able to let go and just let it happen. Easier said than done. To let go, you need to be prepared, and to be prepared, you need to have been present for your planning by not multitasking.

4. Pay Attention
The education of attention would be the education par excellence.

—WILLIAM JAMES

Attention is focused awareness. Often you have to intend to focus. Attention works best when combined with intention—the two combined can be extremely powerful.

Deepak Chopra describes focus like this:

> *The secret to holding focus is to make it effortless. You relax into a receptive state and you get quiet inside. The experience is allowed to sink in. You are filled with a subtle feeling of curiosity, pleasure, wonder, or love. You appreciate this feeling and allow it to linger. (2013)*

Stop for a minute and envision a classroom full of students. Do you see a great deal of curiosity, pleasure, wonder, or love in their expressions? Do you see yourself taking the time to let new learning linger? If not, when and how can you create the space for this to happen? As usual, it begins with your own experience, so that you will recognize the benefit of re-creating it with your students.

If we would teach our students at a young age how the brain works, and explicitly how to pay attention, they would apt to be more attentive. As educators, understanding how we focus, attend to, and remember new information is the first step to teaching our students to become aware of how they learn best. The next chapter, "Noticing the Negativity Bias," provides a multitude of strategies covering how to harness the power of our brain.

I often gave an assignment before and after students took their first test. Before the test, I asked the students to describe in writing what they had done to prepare for the test. They would write things such as read, make flash cards, and so on. After the test, I asked them to list what they could have done to better prepare. I then provided a brief mini-lesson on a variety of study skills. I included strategies such as how to predict test questions and deal with test anxiety and what to do before and after the test. Most students performed significantly better on subsequent tests. They first had to understand that all studying isn't equal and learn which study skill was best for the task at hand. Teaching students how to keep their attention focused and actively engaged with the material is always a useful mini-lesson.

Rick Hanson (2007) makes the following analogy: "Attention is like a combination spotlight and vacuum cleaner: it illuminates what it rests upon and then sucks it into your brain—and your self." As teachers, once we have students "suck in" the information, the next step is to provide them with strategies to transfer that new information from their working memory to their long-term memory. Often, learning sticks when students have an emotional connection or can personally relate to the content. Explaining why students are learning something is such an easy thing to incorporate into your daily teaching.

Often teachers implore students to "pay attention." Notice the word *pay* in that phrase. Like anything you pay for, this requires effort. When students disengage, most will attempt to reengage, but often they lose focus again within seconds. At this point, asking for them to focus is pointless. Hallowell (2015), describes three factors that in combination create mental focus:

Structure
Novelty
Motivation

Many teachers tend to invest the most time trying to create structure, when what's needed is a bit more novelty. Ask any high school graduate about his or her most memorable school experience and he or she will recall the novel events—like the teacher who taught about Presidents' Day dressed up as Abraham Lincoln, or the time the class went to the local nursing home to deliver handwritten holiday cards. My former first graders from twenty-five years ago remember events like the book jacket fashion show and the garden poetry party. We know from research that our brains pay attention to the novel. Engaging teachers know this and strive to motivate their students with unique lessons.

The ability to control your attention and focus on one thing at a time, filtering out external stimuli and internal mind chatter, is a skill set that needs to be practiced. Attention isn't passive. It's an action that takes place mentally, and if that action doesn't take place, you can be awake without being present. This happens when we are tired: our ability to focus wanes, and we experience attention fatigue.

5. Recognize Fatigue
Our fatigue is often caused not by work, but by worry, frustration and resentment.

—DALE CARNEGIE

When you are focused intently on a task, sooner or later you experience attention fatigue. It's as if your brain says, "Enough, I need a break." It's literally an overworked muscle. You become irritable, distracted, or simply ineffective. It's your body's signal to take a break. Instead of pushing through to complete a task, walk away. I should have learned long ago that it's more beneficial to briefly step away from the task at hand than to continue to spin your wheels in frustration.

While I was writing this chapter, my daughter invited me to go to a winery for a wine-tasting event. I declined; yet again, I had too much to do. The truth is, I was burned out and needed a break, but I was determined to persevere. Even though I was mentally drained, I thought I could resist my tired state and continue to plow through and be productive. She left me with my laptop surrounded by papers, books, and multiple projects. While she was gone, my computer crashed and I got multiple error messages suggesting it had been hacked. I spent the three hours she was gone on the phone with technical support and canceling credit cards. Ugh. When she arrived back home she took one look at me and said, "Have you been outside or even left this room since I left?" I had not, so she dragged me outside. I immediately felt better. If only I had listened to her five hours earlier.

Our bodies know when our minds are fatigued, and exercise can help combat that feeling of mind lethargy. I noticed something interesting while reading and researching information for this chapter. If I read on my Kindle, while on the elliptical machine at the gym, I could sustain attention much longer than if I was simply sitting somewhere comfortably. Even better, if below me at the gym within my line of sight there was a basketball game going on, I could read, and when I needed a break, I would focus my attention on the game below me. However, midway through writing this chapter, I sustained a major back injury. I was unable to exercise, and I found that my ability to think and stay on task diminished substantially. I had no doubt there was a major mind-body connection. John Rately (2008) provides evidence that aerobic exercise physically transforms our brains for peak performance. He explains why getting your heart and lungs pumping can mean the difference between a calm, focused mind and a harried, inattentive one. It makes me wonder about all of the students I worked with who had comprehension issues. They were "word callers" but had no idea what they read. What I wouldn't give now to put them on a treadmill and see if their comprehension improved with some movement. Companies now make desks with stationary bikes and treadmills underneath. I have no doubt that my next book will be written while my legs are in motion.

6. Give Up the Crazy Busy Persona

Remember this rule: the more responsibility you have, the more hats you wear, the more likely you are to become inefficient.

—DAVE CRENSHAW

Did you ever ask someone how he or she is doing, and the reply is, "I'm crazy busy!" or "I'm overwhelmed!" The exchange then goes something like this: "Oh, me too, I'm simply nuts! There is not enough time to get anything done, and I need more hours in the day."

We are competitive about how busy we are, and we wear our busyness as proof that we are productive members of society. The perception seems to be that if you're not insanely busy, you must be slacking off.

When was the last time you asked an educator how he or she was and he or she replied with authenticity, "I'm really good." Most educators I know don't have full plates; they have cracked plates that are heaping and overflowing all over the place. We keep trying to scoop it all up and rearrange it, attempting to hold it all together. There truly is too much to do and not enough time to do it. It's not poor time management, it's overload; it feels as if there is no feasible way to get it all done in a meaningful way that makes you feel centered, present, and good about the quality of what is being done. When I think of educators, the word *frenetic* comes to mind.

But there is always more. Just once, I'd like to check everything off my list and declare, "Done." I would say this has always been my most difficult obstacle to feeling at peace. I never feel done.

How can we stop this feeling of being overwhelmed and never being done? I know one thing for sure: There will always be more to do than we have time for. We are in a profession that offers endless tasks, planning, and preparation. Accepting this is a good first step.

Elizabeth Dickinson (2016) reports that more than one-third of Americans say they don't have enough time in their day to get things done. Gallup polls show that the strain of our hectic schedules correlates with a precipitous increase in anxiety, and that the majority of Americans who report not having enough spare time also say they battle stress. Remember, stress is not something that happens to us, but rather something that develops within our own thinking. If we want to change our crazy busy response and persona, we have to slow down.

7. Slow Down

The good news is that as I started to focus on one task at a time, I felt less frenetic. I was slowly altering my multitasking habit, and I was seeing positive results. However, I realized my pace was still roadrunnerish. Interestingly, even though I tried, I didn't really slow down except when I was injured. I've gotten in the habit of asking my injuries what I'm supposed to learn from them, and I can't tell you how many times I've heard, "Slow down." My experience has been that I will keep receiving the message, in various ways, until I get it.

I found there were some unexpected benefits to slowing down. For example, I have always been sensitive about my memory. The names of people, movies, and places often escape me when I'm in the midst of a conversation. When I'm functioning at a slower pace, my memory and creative thoughts are more efficient. I also seem to teach deeper and explain things better.

How you do anything is how you do everything. You can make every aspect of your day an opportunity to be present. When we hurry, we make mistakes. *Slow down, focus, and do one thing at a time.* This is my daily mantra, and one that I have to continually practice. You can use any routine task to practice. For example, greeting each student at the door, greeting your colleagues in the halls, walking to your classroom. Make these daily mundane acts conscious, instead of unconscious, and you become more present.

In school, we often reward speed. The student whose hand is raised first is apt to be acknowledged as the most decisive and brightest. However, sitting quietly, hand not yet raised, may be the child who is pondering new ways to look at things, who is contemplating, dreaming, and using his or her imagination. When we slow down and increase wait time, what I call "possibility thinking" is given the space to emerge.

The concept of "wait time" as an instructional variable was first introduced by Mary Budd Rowe in 1972 after five years of observation and research. The wait-time periods she found—periods of silence that followed teacher questions and students' completed responses—rarely lasted more than 1.5 seconds in typical classrooms. She discovered, however, that extending these periods of silence to at least three seconds produces significant changes in the classroom:

The length of student responses increases.

The number of unsolicited but appropriate responses increases.

Failure to respond decreases.

Student confidence increases.

Students ask more questions.

Student achievement increases significantly.

To attain these benefits, teachers were urged to wait in silence for three or more seconds after asking their questions and after students completed their responses.

Students aren't the only ones who need a little more wait time. Many of us yearn for a slower pace. When we slow down, a sense of calm replaces the sense of overload and we naturally become more content. We also tend to respond rather than react when faced with a challenging situation. Of all the lessons I've learned, the one that I have to continue to work the hardest at is slowing down.

8. Information Overload
It's not information overload. It's filter failure.

—CLAY SHIRKY

Another reason for multitasking is information overload. In his book *The Organized Mind*, cognitive neuroscientist Daniel Levitin (2015) has quantified how overwhelmed by information the poor human brain is. "In 2011, Americans took in five times as much information every day as they did in 1986—the equivalent of 175 newspapers. During our leisure time, not counting work, each of us processes 34 gigabytes or 100,000 words every day" (5). Our brains are tired, and our bodies may be just as weary. Struggling to keep up with our frenetic pace, we are tired and wired.

In his book *Mindful Tech*, David Levy (2016) describes how we are all continually making moment-to-moment microdecisions about what to pay attention to and what to ignore. The fabric of our day is woven from the accumulation of these microdecisions. The productivity of our day depends on what we choose to do and what we leave undone. If we observe and reflect on the kinds of choices we habitually make and why we make them, we become more present and can start to adjust the behaviors that are not useful.

I now choose carefully what blogs and Twitter users I follow. I don't surf the Internet or check my devices while immersed in a project. I limit what and when I take in new information. My productivity and creativity have increased as I've decreased task switching and the amount of information I take in.

9. Do It or Delegate

Nature does not hurry, yet everything is accomplished.

—LAO TZU

If we can let go and trust that everything is happening for our own higher good and that of the planet, we can go beyond the striving and the goal setting and surrender some of the need to achieve the perfect outcome.

I try to strike a balance between having goals and allowing life to unfold. I like to think that we all have our own individualized education program. We're all on different paths, but there is a commonality among all of us.

When I left the school district, I formed my own business, LJ Coaching & Consulting. I completed an intensive coach-training program that provided me with accreditation from the International Coaching Association. Many of my clients were teachers, and they echoed the same concerns I had heard from teachers when I was an instructional coach: they were overwhelmed with too much to do and they wanted more peace in their life. Don't we all? We have to create the space to slow down, and a component of this is managing our time and tasks.

Most teachers I coached were used to making to-do lists. How you approach the items on your list is more important than the list itself. Writing things down is a great start. Once you write down a task, the next step is to either do it or delegate it. Don't keep moving the item to the next day; it actually drains your energy. It's the incomplete tasks that we remember in the middle of the night. I use the same approach with my mail at work and at home. Every piece of paper I touch is either something I take action on, throw away, or delegate to someone else. If you have piles of paper in your home and work, they are major distractions. Create a system so that you no longer just keep shuffling them from table to table. An uncluttered work environment supports an uncluttered mind. You are creating space both in your brain and in your environment.

10. Revisit the Power of No

It's easy to say "no" when a deeper "yes" is burning inside.

—STEPHEN R. COVEY

Many of us multitask for the same reason: we overcommit. Other people's agendas become ours. I've had this problem. It stems from an inability to say no. As a result, I can easily find myself in a constant state of being overwhelmed and overloaded. Can you relate? If so, here are some suggestions.

First, when asked to do one more thing, ask yourself what on your current plate is going to come off in order for you to do this effectively. This is a good time to revisit the prioritizing tool from Chapter 1 (see page 27). Remember the last priority question: What will I *not* be doing if I take on this task or commitment?

Next, be prepared to decline.

Hallowell has a great phrase to use when you want to decline. Simply say, "I'd love to do that if I had the time, but as it is, I could not give it the attention it deserves so I would not be able to perform as well as you and the task warrant."

I couldn't commit that to memory, so I modified it. I often say, "I'd love to do that but I just can't give it my full attention and I would hate to not devote 100 percent." I'd like to stamp that phrase on my forehead.

As teachers, we tend to be givers. We often volunteer inside and outside of school, and we like to plan and organize events. If you live in a neighborhood and you're a teacher, you're apt to plan the neighborhood activities (guilty). You might teach Sunday school, and make meals for your neighbor. At school, you're asked to be on various committees, and you have a hard time saying no. Thoughtfully choose what you agree to do, and don't overcommit.

Another strategy to help you decline is to give yourself some time between the request and your answer. Again, have a response ready, such as, "That sounds really interesting. Let me sleep on it. Can you check in with me tomorrow?" Here the ownership is on the person requesting; if they don't check in, you're off the hook, unless you sleep on it and decide it really is something you want to commit to, and then you follow up.

I recall hearing Robert Holden, author of *Success Intelligence* (2005), say on a PBS television special, "Some people *go* through life and others *grow* through life." Once you know what you want, say yes to anything related to that priority, and say no to everything else. Can you imagine only saying yes to what you want to do? First you have to get in touch with your intentions, listen to your heart, and get clear about what is most important to your growth.

This doesn't mean it's all about you, but it does mean that you have prioritized what's important, and you are willing to let other things pass by without feeling guilty.

I have one very vivid, memorable event that illustrates this point beautifully.

I had always thought I would stay home while my children were young. Well, life didn't work out that way, and not working wasn't an option.

When my daughter was born, I did not have a permanent teaching contract. I was a long-term substitute, assigned to a kindergarten classroom. It was my first year in a public school, and I was finally making more than the $9,000 I had made teaching at a parochial school. The school district made it clear that if I did not return in a "timely fashion" to finish out the school year, I would be limiting my chances of receiving a contract for the following year. My husband and I needed the benefits and the income that a contract would provide. So, my daughter was born on April 1 and I returned to work five weeks later to finish out the year. It broke my heart, but I did it knowing I only had to work a month and would have the summer off.

Fast-forward four years: I now had a contract and was pregnant with my second child.

My son was born on September 6, and I had promised the school district I would return after the winter break on January 2. As Christmas approached, instead of looking forward to the holiday, I was dreading returning to work. I was joyful beyond words being home with my son and daughter. I had never been happier. I truly felt sick inside with anticipation of leaving them. At my husband's holiday party, one of his colleagues' wives noticed I wasn't myself and asked me what was wrong. When I explained, she said, "Lisa, you don't have to go back. No one can make you." Something clicked in my head and my heart, and I realized that I *did* have a choice. I could stay home the rest of my year. I was a tenured, contracted teacher, and the district had to hold my job for a year. I walked over to my husband and said, "I'm not going back to work next week." I went home and called my principal; I explained how I felt and she understood. Bottom line: I said yes to what I wanted most, and we figured it out. I tutored at night, and I had the best year of my entire life.

I have encountered hundreds of teachers who find themselves in the same situation. Sometimes, we don't realize we have choices. Explore all options; think outside the box. If staying home is what you want, do it. You will never, ever get the days with your own children back.

I listened to my heart, to what mattered most, and today I only regret I didn't do this more often.

Personal Practices to Support Mindful Teaching Aligned with the Ten Productivity Tips

This chapter could have been an entire book, so I've taken each productivity tip and expanded upon the concept to provide more strategies.

1. THE MYTH OF MULTITASKING
Mind Map: Identify Distractions

Take some time over the next few days to begin capturing the myriad distractions that contribute to your feeling overwhelmed. Create a mind map of all the things that distract you. Next, identify the habits that lead you to distraction. Pinpoint the trigger. Once you identify your triggers, have a plan to not succumb to them.

Manage Your Technology

Set a timer and check e-mail at scheduled times rather than throughout the day. Turn off the text and e-mail alert sounds that interrupt you to let you know you have a message. Let go of the idea that you have to be immediately responsive to the world. You will never be present if you are constantly interrupted. My own children have declared that I am no longer the "primary contact" because I don't respond instantly. At first I felt guilty, but I'm now delighted; their father is now in charge! Sometimes I think we are afraid that if we're not immediately responsive, we'll be perceived as deficient. It's just the opposite; we're smart enough to not let other people's agendas highjack our own.

2. DETERRING DISTRACTIBILITY

A distraction that affects our emotional state is the student who is having a difficult time. Did you ever notice that if you have a class of twenty-five students and twenty-four of them are progressing and doing well, you still feel as though you are not doing your job well? This one student can make you wonder if maybe you aren't meant to be a teacher and can take up to 90 percent of your time and energy. Often, the parents of that student take up your after-school hours with e-mails, meetings, and phone calls. This situation would classify as a drain. You can't refuel by replacing this student. You can put into place systems to improve the behavior of the child, but there are no guarantees these will work. When I hold seminars with student teachers, this situation presents itself every semester. My students want answers, and I have to admit that there are no quick fixes, but I always suggest changing the way they look at the situation.

Reframe the Situation

Try to reframe how you see this one student. No matter what you do or say, the student can feel your energy. If you enter the classroom dreading what this student might do next, and you feel tense and full of anticipation of the next outburst, that outburst is primed to occur. However, if you can have an optimistic stance, expect the positive, and let go of worry, the energy might shift. Setting boundaries with the parents and the student is essential. As teachers, we feel responsible for every aspect of the child's progress in our classroom, but the truth is we can't control everything, and we certainly aren't responsible for all student outcomes, academic or emotional. Students come to us with their dispositions already wired. They have acquired habits and ways of being in this world that were established long before they walked into our classroom. Children have had to learn how to navigate through life, and many have learned to manipulate their parents to get what they want. When they behave with us as they would with their parents, and their manipulations aren't successful, they understandably fall apart. What they learned to do isn't working, and they feel frustrated and confused. Our being calm, objective, consistent, and crystal clear about what we expect is key. They need to learn to navigate in the classroom with our rules. It's not a battle of wills, but rather an understandable system with clear expectations that you hold for all students.

It's not just about what goes on in the classroom. How much time, thought, and energy do you devote to this situation when you are *out* of the classroom? Giving this student or his or her parents more of your energy isn't refueling you, or changing what has happened or could happen. Be present to what is in front of you. When you are driving home, pay attention to your driving and the sights along the way. When you arrive home, if you are preparing dinner, pay attention to the food in front of you. If you go for a walk, notice the trees and your surroundings; don't take your difficult student with you. This takes constant diligent awareness, and at the end of the day, we are often tired so it's hard to be vigilant of our thoughts. However, the more you are, the more habitual it will be to reframe when you catch yourself lost in the downward spiral of ruminating.

3. FOCUS YOUR ENERGY

Presence Cues

Visual: I use affirmations to help me focus every day. My workspace is full of present moment reminders. I have a plaque that says "I am present" hanging where I see it every day in my office.

Auditory: In the classic Christmas movie *It's a Wonderful Life*, the little girl says to her father (played by Jimmy Stewart), "Daddy, every time a bell rings, an angel gets his wings!" We can use bells and chimes as reminders all day long. When you start to notice the bells and chimes in your environment, you can train yourself to take a deep inhale and exhale. I hung a beautiful chime outside of my home office, and every time I hear it I stand, stretch, and take a breath.

4. PAY ATTENTION
The Pomodoro Technique

The Pomodoro Technique is a time management strategy developed by Francesco Cirillo in the late 1980s. I use this technique to minimize distractions while working, but it is also a way to minimize mindlessness and build in some revitalizing moments in the day. The technique uses a timer to break work down into intervals, traditionally twenty-five minutes in length, separated by short breaks. These intervals are known as "pomodoros." The method is based on the idea that frequent breaks can improve mental agility. (Learn more at http://pomodorotechnique.com.) DeFreitas & Garrison (2015) describe this process:

> First, choose a task you want to get done; choose something that could be completed in approximately 25 minutes. If your project requires more time, divide it into increments. This process will also help you more accurately approximate how long tasks actually take. Next, set your time for 25 minutes and do not allow yourself to be interrupted while you completely focus on the task during this time. To set yourself up for success, shut off all notifications, email alerts, and turn off the ringer on your phone. When the timer goes off, give yourself a five-minute break to do something you enjoy, preferably something that gets you up and moving. When the break is over, repeat the 30-minute process. Once four pomodoros are completed, treat yourself to a longer break of 10 to 20 minutes. I often will go for a quick walk.

A number of apps can be set to time your twenty-five-minute and four-minute intervals, such as

- the free Clear Focus app,
- the countdown timer on a phone or tablet, and
- an online timer (like the one found at http://www.online-stopwatch.com).

Truth be told, my body knows when it's been twenty-five minutes, but we have to tune into our bodies enough to notice, and then be responsive.

In my role as a presenter, I pay careful attention to the body language of participants. It's easy to see when most need a break. I also need a time-out, so I've learned to protect my own time during breaks. I always announce I have a few quick tasks to complete; then I quickly leave the room and take a *short* stretch. I make sure I'm back before it's time to reconvene the session. I pause before reentering the room and take a moment to set an intention that all the people in the room are getting the information they need, in the way they understand best. I then answer any questions before starting the session again. In the past, I would announce a break and then be bombarded with individual questions, without getting a second of restoration myself.

When I'm teaching at the university, I typically teach a three-hour class. I divide the class into six thirty-minute segments. We take a three-minute break after each segment. Students stay more attentive and engaged, and I am modeling for them the importance of chunking information and providing time to process, reflect, regroup, and transition.

5. RECOGNIZE FATIGUE

To avoid overload, delegation is key. Set a goal to become interdependent, not independent. Assign your students as many of the routine classroom tasks as possible; in your home, delegate to whomever else shares your space. One of my favorite stories to read my own children was *The Country Bunny and the Little Gold Shoes* (1955) by Edwin DuBose Heyward. In the story, the mother bunny of twenty-one children delegates beautifully all of the household tasks so that she can become the first female Easter Bunny. It was hard at first for me to follow this model, but now I'm a convert!

Get enough sleep. Hallowell (2006) suggests the amount it takes to wake up without an alarm clock, which for most adults, is about eight hours.

Consider your food fuel. There are many books on this subject, but I had a major shift in mind-set when I started thinking about how food affected my energy level. I have found that what I eat has a direct correlation to how I feel and the energy I have. The quality of my nutrition has a direct impact on my energy level and productivity. Research shows that diets full of omega-3 fatty acids (think fish and nuts) help us stay sharp and stave off cognitive declines later in life. I store almonds in my car and my desk at work. Also, don't forget to hydrate. Our brain cells need consistent fluid levels to function. When we're dehydrated, our short-term memory suffers, we feel tired, and we have difficulty focusing. Take a large water bottle (approximately sixty-four ounces) to work, add some lemons and mint, or whatever will make it most appealing to your palate, and make it a goal to have it finished before you complete your commute home. I've found that being well hydrated and fueled with healthy food helps combat fatigue. Conscious nutrition has to do with listening to your body's wisdom, and we do that when we are fully present while eating and drinking. Does this mean I never eat a cookie or a chip? Of course not, but I make sure I am fully present so that I can enjoy every bite.

6. GIVE UP THE CRAZY PERSONA
Reframe Your Typical Response

In Chapter 7, I expand on a concept I have used in multiple settings: Mindful Mondays. In this version, we agree to avoid complaining for just one day a week to start. When someone asks how you are doing, vow to only respond with some type of positive response. No "Hanging in there" or "Not bad." Make your response authentic, something that you can actually believe. I tend to say, "Really good." This may take some practice. Then, if talk moves to "ain't it awful" mode, quietly remove yourself from the conversation. You will find you have less to say, so consider this as also adding time to your life.

Mindful Meditation

Throughout this book, I've provided different contemplative strategies designed to help you slow down and be present, but they all require that you devote some time each day to your own cultivation of well-being. If we want to bring our best selves to the classroom every day, we have to carve out time to serve ourselves so that we can bring presence to each encounter. You've heard the saying, "If you want peace, you must be peace." It takes a little practice. My search for presence landed me in mindfulness-based stress reduction class, but I don't think meditation is something you have to take a course in. Most people I know who begin meditating think they are doing it wrong and have anxiety that they aren't good enough. They are waiting for that time when they feel beyond time and space, void of thoughts, in perfect bliss. Good luck. I spend the majority of the time noticing how much my mind wanders, catching it, laughing at myself, and bringing my focus back to my breath or my mantra.

Every time I replace judgment with a return to presence, I am strengthening my mind from drifting. A good meditation teacher will explain this and not make you feel that you are doing it wrong, which is why being guided by someone with a good deal of experience can be really helpful. But you can meditate without taking a formal course. Everyday life is the real meditation. You can sit on a cushion for three hours chanting mantras that make you feel calm and peaceful, but if you then get off the cushion and go out into the "real world" and your life is a train wreck, something isn't transferring. We don't live on a cushion; we live in an increasingly complex world, with multiple triggers. Meditation should prompt us towards a life of mindful engagement. Sitting on a cushion is the practice. It gives us the opportunity to feel what it's like to be in control of our mind by finding moments of stillness. The transfer is bringing that feeling into the everyday moments of life.

I noticed the positive effects from meditation when that student who knew how to push my buttons still pushed, but I no longer was as reactive. I could catch myself feeling frustrated, notice it, and, in that brief gap, release some of my tension.

In the business of life, finding time to meditate may seem like a time drain, but actually meditation can create more time and energy when we need it most. It's like stopping to fill up our cars with gas when the tank is almost empty; if we don't refuel, we'll eventually run out of gas.

We are now learning from careful research that how you focus the attention of your mind can shape the activity and structure of your brain. Several current studies examine the effects of lifetime meditation experience on brain activity. The studies reveal that experience matters—those who were more experienced meditators had different levels of brain activity in the relevant networks. This suggests that their brains may have changed due to repeated practice, a process called *neuroplasticity* (the topic of the next chapter). It's another big word that we should all understand the meaning of. It will change how we learn and teach forever.

I rotate my forms of meditation based on my mood. Following are some of the basic types I use:

Sitting meditation, which involves sitting in a relaxed but erect posture and cultivating awareness of each breath you take.

Body scan, which entails methodically paying attention to each part of your body, from top to bottom. You can often lie down while doing this, but be forewarned, you may just fall asleep. That's OK. Sometimes that's exactly what our body needs. I'm apt do this in bed in the morning before I get up.

Thirty-second vertical body scan, which I use to focus my attention before I teach,

- Begin by centering yourself.
- Feel your feet on the ground. Starting from your feet, move your attention through your body and notice your experience. Scan for tension in your feet, lower back, stomach, shoulders, face, jaw, forehead, or wherever else you hold tension in your body. Often, if I'm about to start a workshop or class, I'll shrug my shoulders. I seem to hold on to tension in my shoulders, so I have to

consciously bring them down away from my ears.

- As you scan each area, breathe into the area, releasing tension, and take a few heavy sighs.
- Expand your awareness to your entire body and feel the breath move from your head to your feet.

Guided meditation, which is led by someone else, either in person or via a recording, will usually (although, not always) have a theme and relaxing music playing in the background.

A book I use in the classroom is *Guided Imagery for Groups: Fifty Visualizations That Promote Relaxation, Problem-Solving, Creativity, and Well-Being* by Andrew E. Schwartz (1997). I find that students who like to daydream absolutely love it. I often read one of the passages before a writing assignment or as a relaxation tool after recess or lunch.

Daniel Goleman (2013) describes meditation from a cognitive science point of view as "the retraining of attention—a bulking up of the neural circuitry that allows you to detach from where your mind has wandered, bring it back to the point of focus, and keep it there."

Mindful awareness in wisdom traditions has been taught for thousands of years. *Time* magazine has declared that mindfulness is now a revolution. Mindful awareness training gives you the opportunity to focus a certain way and helps you let go of judgments and be in the present moment. A kindness and tenderness is embedded in mindful awareness.

7. SLOW DOWN
Present Moment Living

Imagine how different your experience of time would be if you could truly proceed through your day focusing only on the task at hand, the present moment. This means when you are in the shower, your mind hasn't fast-forwarded to the faculty meeting you have in an hour; while driving, you aren't planning your lesson; and while eating lunch, you aren't thinking about what the rest of the afternoon entails. It's not easy. The more I practiced this, the more I realized how seldom I was in the present moment. Even the most mundane things are opportunities to practice. When you are walking, walk; when you are sitting, sit. This is ancient wisdom. Try it for a day; actually, try it for an hour. Just do one thing after another, giving your full attention to what is right in front of you.

Past—Future—Present

Begin to slow down, slow your breath, and let this be your anchor. Slow down your thoughts. As your thoughts arise, if they concern the past in any way, squeeze your left hand, and let them go. If they concern the future in any way, squeeze your right hand, and let them go. Repeat this mantra: "Peace to my mind; let my thoughts be still." If you continue to do this, you notice that you are often thinking about past and future events, but the present moment is hard to stay in. You are trying to cultivate stillness and peace by letting go of the ruminating and worrying. You are essentially training your mind to operate from a quiet, present center.

Micromoments

Anything that you do repetitively in certain situation can be your go-to when you notice you are not feeling at ease.

When I feel that there isn't enough time to get done what I need to complete, I hunch my shoulders up to my ears as I inhale and round them down my back as I exhale and say to myself, "Everything will get done; there is enough time in this day for everything I need to complete."

The release of my shoulders and the breathing may be what calms me down, but having the ritual allows me to feel more in control and less overwhelmed.

A Practice of Silence

Practice radio silence. When you wake, don't turn on anything. Notice the sounds of nature. Tune in and notice the sounds around you instead of adding more noise. This simple strategy can support your nervous system and can ignite curiosity.

8. INFORMATION OVERLOAD

Realizing I could not eliminate distractions, I focused on *managing* the distractions that were unavoidable. For example, when I'm multitasking on my computer and have several windows open, it's almost as if my computer says, "Enough, your brain can't handle all these topics and tasks," and then the cursor starts spinning. You know the one, the image of the ball that just goes round and round, that you watch, sending adrenaline through your veins—it makes you want to physically throw your computer out the window. The computer reacts by doing nothing. Actually it does something, it freezes. I detest that spinning ball, and I used to react by pummeling the keys harder and faster, which only made it worse. After watching it for only seconds I could feel my shoulders hunch and my impatience escalate. Then, the worst happens: You realize that the ball (formal name: "spinning wait cursor," but I call it "aggravation") is not going to stop spinning. The only thing you can do is close your browser, which means losing all information. Anger and frustration are streaming through your body. Finally, you have no choice but to admit defeat, surrender, and shut down your computer. More precious minutes wasted.

I'd like to propose another way.

Inhale Peace; Exhale Stress

Einstein said the definition of insanity is doing the same thing over and over again and expecting different results. So, I have tried a different tactic: I turn away and breathe.

Think of a frozen computer as your cue to turn away from your monitor and take six deep breaths using a positive word on the inhale, and exhaling out a negative word. For example:

1. Inhale *peace*; exhale *stress.*
2. Inhale *relax*; exhale *pressure.*
3. Inhale *focus*; exhale *distraction.*
4. Inhale *surrender*; exhale *tension.*
5. Inhale *presence*; exhale *frustration.*
6. Inhale *acceptance*; exhale *tension.*

Then, turn back to your computer. If the ball is still spinning, it's time to close the browser, and repeat the breath exercise above, accepting that you may have to surrender and accept that you have to restart your computer. This is where it gets really crazy. Shut down the computer, and go for a quick ten-minute walk. Something happens between the time that I am about ready to hurl my computer out the window with frustration and when I return from my walk. I now have to begin again, but what I lost doesn't seem so important anymore. I've gotten a sense of perspective, and it's almost refreshing to start with no windows open on the browser. It's a lesson: we can always begin again.

9. DO IT OR DELEGATE
Delegating Technique

This process is part of letting go. The following example is a to-do list; I have let go of the details of how the things will get done. It's unusual, but it works. Essentially, you set a goal, but let go of the details, believing that the right people, sources, information, and opportunities will be provided.

GOAL: COMPLETE BOOK ON PRESENCE	
In My Control	**Trusting in the Universe**
Complete book by deadline. Write daily, persevere.	Encounter content and sources to make the information credible and interesting.
Enjoy the process.	Encounter reminders to be present and grateful of the opportunity to share this information with others.
Keep chapters concise and engaging. Develop as a writer, continue to improve.	Editors improve my drafts and show me ways to improve writing.
Continue to hold workshops on topic; refine my speaking craft.	The right audiences find me.

10. REVISIT THE POWER OF NO

The biggest obstacle to saying no successfully is a lack of clarity about what we would like to say yes to. We are all faced with myriad choices and endless opportunities. Only by saying no to some of these competing demands for your time can you create the space for a yes. It's easy to lack clarity about what you really want. So the first step in saying no is clarifying what in your life you'd like more of.

In every school I enter, I see teachers who are under increasing pressure, often to do things they don't believe in. The first step in saying no is to get crystal clear about what your priorities and beliefs are. Then, when asked to do something that you'd like to decline, have your no response ready. Here are a few more ways I've said no:

- "No thanks, but I appreciate your asking."
- "I'm not actually comfortable doing that."
- "That wouldn't work for me."
- "I would prefer not to."
- "Based on my priorities and values, that wouldn't be something I'd be interested in."

After you have declined, leave it at that. Don't fill the space with words and apologies for saying no. Stop talking.

Classroom Connections

MODEL PRESENCE

Before you begin to teach a lesson, focus completely on the students. Let go of your intended plan, eliminate all external distractions, and slowly take in the students in front of you. What are they doing? How engaged do they seem? What do they need before you begin your instruction?

Now, the students know they have your total attention. You aren't reviewing lesson plans or adjusting the technology. They feel your presence. Focus on the task at hand. Resist being distracted.

MIND MAP FOR STUDENTS

Have students list their distractions while completing any academic task. This gives both you and them insight into the barrage of distractions they have to overcome.

THE EVER-PRESENT BELL

In many schools, I seem to be bombarded by a constant stream of sporadic bells. I read a story in Hallowell's (2015) book, *Driven to Distraction at Work*, about a Benedictine nun who is a trainer and supervisor of new members of her order. Early in their training, she asks the novice nuns, "Why do we pray?" After several responses, she informs them, "We pray because the bell rings." Every day they gather for worship when they hear the bell: it's simply their ritual; it's what they do. Reading this, I realized the "bells" were an underutilized opportunity. Now, without fail, whenever I hear a bell ring, I smile, take a deep breath, and return myself to the present moment.

I've often thought a wonderful research study would be to train half the students in a school to take a deep calming breath every time they hear the bell. My hypothesis is that if we could measure the hormonal levels of all participants, there would be a decrease of stress hormones in those who were trained to take a breath when they heard the bell. I now begin and end most classes by ringing a chime that I purchased from Responsive Classroom (see Resources).

These kind of repeated mental exercises are like going to the gym, only you're building your brain muscle instead of your biceps. Think of the bell as the weight you add to the barbell—you need some "resistance" to build your focusing capacity.

This might explain why it feels easier to "drop" thoughts as you become more experienced in meditation—and thus better able to focus. Thoughts become less sticky because your brain gets rewired to better recognize and disengage from wandering. If you've ever struggled with rumination—reliving a negative experience over and over, or stressing (unproductively) about an upcoming event—you can appreciate how being able to let go of your thoughts could be a huge benefit. The following strategies and tools can be used as cues to infuse mini-mediation practices. These are ways to take meditation "off the cushion" and integrate them throughout the course of a day.

Singing Bowls: I often use the singing bowl, which emits a polyphonic sound, as a way to get students' attention. I find students respond faster and more calmly to this than all the other chants and catchy phrases I've used over the years.

Inner Vision: When things feel frenetic, prompt your students to close their eyes and look at the field inside. Most will be intrigued at the various colors that may appear and that they never noticed before.

DAYDREAMING STUDENTS

According to Dan Goleman (2013), about half of all our thoughts are daydreams. As teachers, do we allow our students enough time to let their minds just wander? Substantial research indicates that mind wandering could be of real value. Goleman explains that the brain systems involved in mind wandering have been found active just before people hit upon a creative insight. Those with attention deficit disorder (ADD) are more inclined to mind wandering, and many studies show that those with ADD show higher levels of original creative thinking and more actual creative achievement. What we now diagnose as ADD may reflect a natural variation in focusing styles that had advantages in evolution and so continues to be dispersed in our gene pool (Goleman 2013).

MINI-POMODOROS FOR STUDENTS

As a teacher, I divided my entire day into a series of mini-lessons at every level I taught. Depending on the age of my students, I allocated between eight and twenty-five minutes to deliver my content before transitioning the students to an activity that they did themselves, with a partner, or in a group, followed by time for independent practice. This is essentially the Pomodoro technique in the classroom. I used this technique when I taught preschool and elementary school, and I still plan my graduate school seminars, whether online or face-to-face, in this way.

MUSIC

Many people work productively with headphones on which makes me wonder why we ban headphones and music in schools. I know the policies vary, but in the school district in which I worked, students were not allowed to wear headphones or listen to music as they worked. If your policy is more flexible, experiment and see how music affects you and your students.

A Look Ahead to Chapter 6: "Noticing the Negativity Bias"

The next chapter reveals how using our mind can change our brain. This concept is called *neuroplasticity*, and we explore how to engage with it in an intentional manner. It has a great deal to do with how we direct our attention. Think of attention as a flashlight. What we focus on is illuminated and receives our primary attention. What's in the periphery is still there, but doesn't receive the same attention. Through discussing the myth of multitasking, information overload, and recognizing fatigue and slowing down, this chapter has concentrated on how to minimize distraction; the next chapter focuses on how to intentionally *direct* our attention. By incorporating some of the strategies introduced in this chapter, we can actually rewire our brain.

CHAPTER 6

Noticing the Negativity Bias

Nuts and Bolts of Neuroscience

2009—It was the spring of my first year at the university in my role as an assistant professor. In my mailbox were my fall student evaluations, which would ultimately count 50 percent toward my tenure decision. I took them home, not wanting to review them surrounded by colleagues. At home, I sorted through four classes of evaluations. Ninety-five percent of them were excellent. So why did I keep reading the three that weren't glowing? I discarded the good comments in a pile and compiled the handful of the negative comments on a spreadsheet. As I listed them, I became aware of my negative self-talk. "What was I thinking going into higher education? I don't belong here, they probably made a mistake giving me my doctorate, I'm not cut out to be a professor. Ugh, this is a disaster. I'll probably never get tenure, I'll be without a job, how in the world am I going to put my own children through college? Where will I work?"

And down the rabbit hole I plunged.

I went through this same routine when I looked at my consulting evaluations, always scanning for the negative, focusing on the 3 to 5 percent of negative feedback, completely disqualifying the positive feedback.

THE NEGATIVITY BIAS

My reaction to the student evaluations isn't uncommon. Teachers are notorious for being critical about their evaluations or feedback. When I first began as an instructional coach, after observing a teacher, I would begin the postconference with a casual question such as, "How do you think that lesson went?" I quickly realized that teachers never started with what had gone well in the lesson but instead began a stream of comments about everything they had done wrong. I learned quickly to begin a postconference with, "Tell me everything that went right during that lesson." Most found this a difficult question and would try to revert the conversation to what had gone wrong. This is what's known as the "negativity bias," which means that the brain, to help us survive, preferentially looks for, reacts to, stores, and then recalls negative information over positive information. For example, Gottman and Silver (1999) found that it takes at least five positive interactions to make up for just one negative one. So, a negative interaction or incident is five times more powerful than a positive interaction. This explains why we could have twenty positive parent/teacher conferences, but the one that goes south is the one we replay over and over all night long as we try to fall asleep. Rarely do we rehash what went well.

Teachers also tend to ruminate about the one student or parent who is problematic, giving that student or parent far more energy and mental replay than the students and parents who are not problematic.

A lot of us think about problems all day long. We're worrying about our family, we're rehashing a conversation we had with our supervisor, and we're obsessing over something bad that hasn't even happened yet.

And we don't think these thoughts just once, we replay them over. As Rick Hanson (2009) explains in his book *Buddha's Brain,* they are leaving behind traces of neural structure that are negativistic and very self-critical. The classic line in neural psychology is, "As neurons fire together, they wire together"; mental activity actually creates new neural structures (LeDoux 2003). The seemingly immaterial, fleeting flow of thoughts actually changes the brain.

If you, like me, are one of these people, you're probably wondering, "Really? Our brain changes? How so? And what can we do about it?"

First, we need to recognize that the negativity bias is active, and then we need to train the brain to release neural chemicals that create positive instead of negative feelings.

Interestingly, Hanson (2009) states that because the brain and, correspondingly, our nervous system and health, are shaped by our experiences, negativity does not need to be the force in charge. Positive feelings can be exercised to our advantage.

For most of us, our days are made up of mostly neutral or positive events that we don't think much about. However, we often rewind and replay the negative events. These negative experiences are instantly registered and intensely focused on. This is the negativity bias of the brain. Negative events get stored in what's called "implicit memory," where we slowly accumulate residue of negative experiences. How do we counteract this? We need to actively build up *positive* implicit memories that balance this unfair accumulation of negative implicit memories.

We want those feel-good chemicals such as serotonin, oxytocin, and dopamine to start flowing and counter the effect of stress hormones that affect our bodies. Yes, it's true, we can train our brain. It's actually simple; we just have to learn to internalize positive experiences more deeply, while minimizing the harmful effects of dwelling on the negative.

This chapter provides strategies to get those good chemicals flowing and override our brain's negativity bias.

NEUROPLASTICITY

In a nutshell, neuroplasticity is the idea that new neurons can be created. Our brains are vulnerable and can be changed by experiences, for better or worse. Our lifestyle plays a big role in determining what kinds of changes our brains make.

Imagine yourself as the director of your life as a movie. Each scene could be played a thousand different ways. And all of those past events we spend time ruminating about—think of those memories as old movies, each consisting of a different interpretation of those events. Whether you choose to recall the negative or positive ones is up to you.

NEW LEARNING BUILDS NEW NEURAL PATHWAYS

Neural pathways are like superhighways of nerve calls that transmit messages. Every time you learn something new, the neural circuits in your brain are altered. These circuits are composed of neurons, which are simply nerve cells that communicate with one another through special junctions called *synapses*. The synapses' efficiency increases when you learn something new, which facilitates the passages of nerve impulses along a particular circuit.

It used to be the conventional wisdom that after a certain age, the neural circuitry cards we're dealt are the only ones we can utilize long term. Current research now shows that when you learn something new, your brain changes, too. The brain is designed to adapt constantly.

It keeps changing over its entire life span. We have some control over those changes, and by challenging our brains to learn new information, we can change our brain for the better.

The research is clear: we can actually create new pathways in the brain.

Our brains are malleable, and our experiences throughout life continue to shape and inform who we are and what we can do. New learning keeps our brains healthy, and optimal patterns of thought are good for happiness, health, and learning.

With enough time and effort you could, if you so choose, master almost any academic skill. Intelligence is not something that you inherited; you are as smart as you choose to be. The best teachers are always learning new information, new strategies, new ways to present content to their students. Think of the technology that we've had to learn to stay current. Every time there is a new technology tool, I catch myself worrying if I'll figure it out. But, the truth is, I always figure it out. So before you beat yourself up for not knowing how to do something new, take stock of all the new things you've learned in the past six months, and give yourself credit.

Positive experiences are good for the immune system and good for concentration, and positive emotional states help steady the mind for complex reasoning. So in daily life, look for positives and let them sink in. Our thoughts about how we learn are just as important as what we are learning. We learn through our own mental models, and once we are aware of our models, we can challenge them.

CHALLENGE MENTAL MODELS

We do not really see through our eyes or hear through our ears, but through our beliefs.

—LISA DELPIT

Mental models are the mind-sets, values, and beliefs we hold about how the world works. They help us to make sense of the systems we work in, but they are often flawed because the models we have built are simply stories we have created based on our perception. In my role as an instructional coach, I trained myself to listen to the language used by the teachers I worked with so I could help them explore other modes of thinking. For example, teachers often formed assumptions about how they were perceived by the parents of their students, their colleagues, or their administrators. When those models weren't positive, there was often a problematic relationship, which affected the teacher's performance. Often the first step I took was to make those perceptions visible, and help teachers realize that those perceptions weren't always true and that they could reframe the situation. I tried to reframe their mental models and bring awareness to some of their unconscious beliefs by requesting more information or asking open-ended questions, such as "It would help me understand if you'd give me an example of . . ." or "What's another way you might interpret that situation?"

Some of these beliefs have become so ingrained that we aren't even aware of them. Think of the neural pathways in your brain like this. Imagine taking a walk around a lake for the first time. The route you take will be somewhat arbitrary, but the second time you go, if you encounter the tracks that you left the first time, you're likely to follow those tracks. If you continue to take walks around the lake, you're likely to now have a clear path—and you're *very* likely to follow the same pathway, as will others.

Our thoughts create reoccurring pathways that predispose us to perceive things in certain ways.

A TALE OF TWO TEACHERS

Success is peace of mind, which is a direct result of self-satisfaction in knowing you did your best to become the best you are capable of becoming.

—JOHN R. WOODEN

Troubled Tom struggled with technology. Every time he was asked to implement the latest tech tool in his classroom, he balked and complained that he wasn't good at using technology, that he had bad luck with it. He recounted all the times he made the computer freeze. He complained in front of his students and muttered that technology just made things more difficult. He was easily frustrated, called in sick on professional development days devoted to technology, and consequently got further and further behind the technology curve. His "laps around the lake" reinforced that he would always struggle, and often fail, at utilizing the new tech tool.

Positive Pete approached technology as an opportunity to try something new. When asked to try the latest tech tool in his classroom, he was always game. He often asked his students to help him figure it out, modeling that we learn from one another, and he got excited when together they made it work. His "laps around the lake" reinforced that trying new things, asking for support, and persevering paid off.

Both Pete and Tom were reinforcing their assumptions that they had through repetition ingrained into their minds. Before Troubled Tom can change his thought patterns, he has to recognize them for the limiting beliefs that they are.

CHOOSE YOUR STORY

Most of us have built stories about who we are and what we can do. These are just beliefs, not always true, and we can change them. We can be selective about the stories we tell, and we can bring to light the subconscious beliefs that aren't serving us. We always have the opportunity to compose a new story. One way is to inquire into our own belief system.

DON'T BELIEVE EVERYTHING YOU THINK

Perhaps the most important single cause of a person's success or failure educationally has to do with the question of what he believes about himself.

—ARTHUR COMBS

Our thoughts become our words, our words become our story, our story becomes our beliefs, our beliefs become our actions.

Back in 1992, Kagan concluded that "the more one reads studies of teacher beliefs, the more strongly one suspects that this piebald of personal knowledge lies at the very heart of teaching" (85). There are many studies of how beliefs affect outcomes that validate that we are not powerless victims, but instead participants in the life we create. We live our lives based on what we believe. If we think the day ahead will be difficult, it usually is. If we think that our students are going to be a handful during indoor recess, they usually are. If we think our lives are full of stress, they will be.

As the author of your life, you can change your beliefs, which will in effect change your life. Greg Braden (2008) attests that individually and collectively, consciously and unconsciously, we all choose the way we think of ourselves and what we believe to be true of our world. The results of our beliefs are the life we are living.

If you are someone who doesn't like what you see around you, the life you have apparently chosen, that can be a difficult belief to endure. Isn't it worth trying to change this belief? What if you could change your thinking, and the result would change your life circumstances? Isn't it worth trying to subscribe to a healthier mind-set, envisioning what you would like to see in your life? The worst that could happen is that you'd be stuck with your current reality.

I can attest to trying to do this and being successful. When I focused my intention on what I wanted, with clarity, and put forth real effort, I achieved what I set my sights upon. However, it took work, focus, energy, and, most importantly, a belief system that supports this frame of thought.

Most of the beliefs we've inherited and internalized from others originated in what science, history, religion, culture, and family tell us. Think about some of the beliefs you have about your potential in certain areas. For most of us, our first teachers are our parents, followed by the teachers in our school lives. As teachers, we have incredible influence on the students we teach, and if we don't take that seriously, we may unknowingly project some of our beliefs on others, especially impressionable children. Think of the students in Troubled Tom and Positive Pete's classes. In which teacher's classroom would you want your own child? As teachers, we are not just role models, we are downloading long-lasting beliefs into our students' minds.

I remember when I was in fifth-grade chorus and tried out for the solo in the Christmas pageant. I sang "We Three Kings" as loud and as confidently as any nine-year-old ever had. I was full of joy. When the chorus teacher pointed her finger at me and motioned for me to come off the stage, I was positive I had just been chosen for the solo. What she said next stayed with me for the rest of my life. She said, "Lisa, I'm going to let you stay in chorus, but I'm going to move you over to the altos. You can stand with them, but don't ever let any sound come out of your mouth again. You can move your lips, but under no circumstance should you ever sing out loud. You have a voice that wasn't meant to sing."

What happened next is also important. I could have cried. I could have quit, but instead, I looked at the alto section, and it was all boys. I much preferred playing with boys; I found them more fun, drama-free. I smiled and bounded up the steps to join the boys. That's called resilience, and that's something I also learned at an early age.

Something in me didn't let the teacher knock me down, at least not completely. However, can I sing in church now? Nope. In the car? Only if by myself. Do I sing with joy? Not at all; it's a very self-conscious kind of singing. So, her words, her beliefs, did long-term damage. She cared more about how the chorus sounded than the self-esteem of a nine-year-old girl. I don't think she purposefully set out to make me feel bad; she was simply more concerned with the production of a show than the self-esteem of a child. That's an example of a belief I have not been able to change. However, I haven't put forth real effort. If I wanted to change this belief, I would begin with reframing the thought that I still hear: "You have a voice that wasn't meant to sing." I would replace this thought with something like, "My unique voice is a gift and deserves to be heard." Remember, you have to believe what you say. If I had reframed it as "My voice is beautiful," it just wouldn't have worked because I don't believe that. Next, I would have taken some voice lessons, practiced, and with effort I could have changed that belief system by growing new dendrites between nerve cells in the network that held that negative memory. Each time I practiced and applied the new mantra, the link would have become more powerful, just as the connections between the nerve cells would make the network stronger. Just as muscles become stronger when you exercise them, new beliefs must be practiced. Practice makes permanent. If I were enjoying the practice, my brain would release extra dopamine. Positive emotions cause dopamine to travel to more parts of my brain, which would increase my sense of pleasure. We remember more of what we learn if we are in a positive emotional state. Experiencing pride at accomplishing something is also correlated with higher dopamine.

Changing your belief systems begins with questioning your thoughts. This means you have to observe your own thoughts, and when a negative thought intrudes—which will no doubt happen—immediately reframe it into a positive thought. This is the most effective way of dispelling negative thoughts. It takes awareness and practice. When we develop an intentional practice of meditation, we begin to notice our reoccurring thoughts. So often when people first meditate they think that they should be able to stop their thoughts, but this is impossible. Meditation brings awareness to the ever-present cascade of thoughts, many of which simply aren't accurate.

We are often unaware of the damage our thoughts, words, and beliefs do to others, and we are in a profession that needs to be vigilant of the words we use and the impact they can have. My former chorus teacher most likely had no idea of the lasting impact her words had. The effects of what we say and do can be remembered far longer than any content or theory we espouse. I have a poster in my home office of a quote credited to Maya Angelou that reminds me to be vigilant of not only the words I use, but also the intent behind the words: "People will forget what you said, people will forget what you did, but people will never forget how you made them feel."

Take a minute to envision the teacher you want to be and how you want to make your students feel. We are in a position to foster students' self-esteem and to help them reframe any negative mind-sets they may have adopted along the way. But we need to clean up our own thought patterns first.

A WELL-TRAINED MIND: SOCIAL-EMOTIONAL AWARENESS FOR EDUCATORS

Any form of training leads to reconfiguring in the brain, on both the functional and structural levels. As teachers, we've been trained in programs, strategies, behavior modification, and countless other related topics; it's time we had some research-based strategies to develop our own social-emotional awareness.

We normally don't think of well-being as a skill. Neuroscientist and emotion specialist Richie Davidson (2012), founder of the Center for Investigating Healthy Minds at the University of Wisconsin–Madison, does. At a conference hosted by The Mind and Life Institute, Davidson talked about his center's work in the field of contemplative neuroscience. He maintained that you can train your brain to change, that the change is measurable, and that by learning new ways of thinking, you can change it for the better.

The neural circuits that you use most are reinforced and strengthened over time, and those you don't use gradually atrophy. We can take responsibility for our own brains by programming them in ways that are more positive and can lead to the cultivation of well-being. Just as we learn a new language through practice, the same goes for cultivating well-being and happiness. We can begin to think of qualities such as the ability to recognize negative thoughts and fostering positive mind-sets as a skill. A well-trained mind can concentrate on a positive thought amid any negative mind chatter. A well-trained mind can be cultivated.

Curriculum in schools of education has changed in response to changes in society, pedagogy, and technology. As computer technology became an asset in classrooms, schools of education appropriately included that instruction in the curriculum. Many states made similar education program curriculum adaptations in response to multiculturalism, increases in English language learners, and the use of the concrete-connect-abstract progression in math instruction.

Given the neuroscience research implications for teaching, it is time for instruction in the neuroscience of learning to be included as professional development options during in-service days.

An agenda for a well-trained mind might include the following:

- Practicing presence
- Stress-reduction strategies
- Healthy habits for educators
- Optimal wellness
- The myth of multitasking

- Mind-sets, mental models, and beliefs
- Meditation basics
- Emotion regulation
- Cultivating happiness
- Mindful movement
- Engaged educators = engaged students
- Creating lessons that promote student engagement
- Whole-brain strategies for memory and retrieval

The ultimate goal of this type of professional development is to nurture more engaged teachers. Teachers, not programs, make a school great. Great teachers are engaged teachers, who are aware that they are the one variable in the classroom they can control.

Hastings and Agrawal (2015) found that in the United States, K–12 schoolteachers who are "not engaged" or are "actively disengaged" at work miss an estimated 2.3 million more workdays than teachers who are "engaged" in their jobs. The authors define *engaged* teachers as involved with, enthusiastic about, and committed to their work. They know the scope of their jobs and constantly look for new and better ways to achieve outcomes. *Not engaged* teachers may be satisfied with their jobs, but they are not emotionally connected to their workplaces and are unlikely to devote much discretionary effort to their work. *Actively disengaged* teachers are not only unhappy, but also act out their unhappiness in ways that undermine what their coworkers accomplish.

Absenteeism associated with a lack of teacher engagement creates a drain on school productivity. School districts must foot the bill for classroom replacements. And when substitute teachers are relied on to execute a teacher's lesson plans, often with limited advance notice, it can easily create a suboptimal learning environment for students.

Social-emotional awareness is good for us and for our students. The classroom environment is optimal when we are all operating from a calm state that allows us to be happy, relaxed, and curious.

HAPPY, RELAXED, AND CURIOUS

We create a positive emotional state when we are happy, relaxed, and curious.

In the 1960s television show *Laugh-In*, Goldie Hawn was always giggling. It turns out that she had the right idea about laughing. Hawn has employed researchers to develop the Mind Up Curriculum for schools and has done an incredible job of translating the research regarding how the brain works into practical application for teachers to use with students.

Her curriculum is one of many that incorporate neuroscience to help students understand how their brain works, which should be a standard component of all curriculums. We expect our students to learn an incredible amount of knowledge, but we don't always teach them how their brain learns new information. In her book *10 Mindful Minutes*, which is geared toward adults, Hawn (2011) shares that researchers and scientists have provided undeniable proof that that human brain is a living, growing organ. Their findings also support the notion that when we consciously choose how we interact with the world, we can get the best out of life. Hawn contends that researchers have proved yet again that whether we are adults or children, when we are stressed, anxious, bored, or unhappy, we are much less able to cope with problems and take in new information. It's as if our brains are closed tight, like a clenched fist. However, when we are happy, relaxed, and curious, our brains are open and receptive. This not only helps us recall and process information, but also gives us the ability to handle stress.

We spend an inordinate amount of time teaching students content. Do we talk about basic life skills such as how to be happy? Before we can teach students this information, once again, we have to demonstrate it ourselves. Students learn more by observing our actions than listening to our lectures. Let's model how to raise our happiness set point.

HAPPINESS LEAVES CLUES

Ever since researchers have measured happiness and well-being levels, they have noticed an interesting phenomenon: despite the fact that we have more of everything we say we want, we are not any happier. Taylor and Brown (1988) found that lottery winners were not significantly happier than control group participants and that patients with spinal cord injuries "did not appear nearly as unhappy as might be expected." Ever since, many in psychological and social science circles have taken for granted that people return to a relatively stable happiness set point, even after seemingly life-changing events.

According to Lickerman (2012), the set-point theory of happiness suggests that our level of subjective well-being is determined primarily by heredity and by personality traits ingrained in us early in life and, as a result, remains relatively constant throughout our lives.

Fortunately, it's been shown that we can change our happiness set points. When we think, feel, and act in different ways, the brain's plasticity is altered. Davidson (2012) summarizes the findings of one of the world's leading brain scientists: compassion meditation, even in short-term practitioners, induces significant changes in patterns of functional activity in the brain. Davidson believes that, in time, mental exercise will be accepted as something that is as important to general well-being as physical exercise.

On a scale of 1 to 10, how happy are you? Whatever number just came to mind, try to imagine how tomorrow you can raise your number just one digit. So if you are a 7, what could you do to be an 8? First, take the happiness quiz at www.pursuit-of-happiness.org/science-of-happiness/happiness-quiz; your results will be immediately e-mailed to you.

You have a major role in how you feel today; you can alter your happiness set point by diminishing your negativity bias. One of my biggest barriers to happiness was that I worried about things far too much. Now when I am worrying or anxious about doing something, I often visualize what could go right instead of what might go wrong. I'm programming my mind for a positive outcome.

Happiness leaves clues. When I'm in a funk and I don't want to talk to anyone, I tend to retreat and don't want to leave the house. However, I'm aware that the way to get myself out of my own miserable mind is to hurl myself outside and interact with others. Knowing what triggers your own ups and downs can help you navigate to a happier state. Teaching this to students at an early age might help alleviate some of the not-so-good choices they make when they are teens and aren't feeling so good. Rather than self-medicating, if the students were more metacognitive about their feeling states, they could choose a healthier option. Remember my antidepressant prescription in the Preface? Rather than tunneling inside my home, I now choose something on my list of things that make me happy, which alters my feeling state rather quickly.

We are all free to choose happiness over unhappiness. People who grab that present moment and maximize it are living more fulfilling lives than those who don't. It is a choice each of us can make.

Continue to add to the list of the things that make you happy. People with high happiness set points aren't special; they just have different—actually, better—habits. In *The Art of Happiness* (Dalai Lama and Cutler 1988), the Dalai Lama states, "One begins identifying those factors which lead to happiness and those factors which lead to suffering. Having done this, one then sets about gradually eliminating those factors which lead to suffering and cultivating those which lead to happiness" (15).

MIND-SET REVISITED

I wish I had read Carol Dweck's book *Mindset* (2006) prior to raising my children, as well as before teaching for so many years. I would have changed so much of the language I used when praising my children and students for their accomplishments.

When parents and teachers praise their children for being perfect, those children can feel alienated and anxious. By contrast, if they praise children for trying hard and showing effort, they feel motivated. I notice more and more anxious students in our schools, and their mind-set could be a factor contributing to this.

Dweck describes mind-set as the view you have of yourself that affects all the decisions you make about your learning—the effort you put forth, the risks you take, how you deal with failures and criticism, and how much of a challenge you are willing to accept. She defines two different mind-sets, *fixed* and *growth*. People with a *fixed* mind-set believe that talents and personalities are more or less inborn, which fosters the need to prove yourself over and over. Any criticism is seen as an attack on your character. Those with a *growth* mind-set believe that success is a result of effort as much as or more than aptitude. Having a growth mind-set encourages learning and effort. Those who believe they can improve at something will be much more driven to learn and practice. Criticism is seen as valuable feedback and openly embraced. The hallmark of the growth mind-set is the passion for sticking with things, *especially* when they are *not* going well.

My firstborn, Chelsea, reminds me a lot of myself. Nothing came easy for her, but she always persevered and tried her hardest. I used language such as "You are dedicating a lot of time to that project; I can see how hard you are working" when she was doing homework. When she got discouraged, I said things like, "You know you can set your mind to achieve anything you want, just keep at it, you can do it." She grew up believing that her hard work and efforts would pay off, and she was right. She's now a first-grade teacher, and she is making a difference daily in countless students' lives by echoing the words she heard herself for years to her students.

My younger son, Craig, was born with a quick aptitude to learn and memorize new things. I continually praised him, saying things like, "You are so lucky to be born with such a brilliant mind" and "You're so lucky to be smart." However, when middle school hit and learning no longer became easy, he shut down and seemed to just stop trying. I didn't know then that we give up more quickly when we believe our intelligence or ability is innate rather than believing that it's something that can be developed. I had unknowingly programmed a fixed mind-set into my son. The good news is that thanks to my learning about mind-set and neuroplasticity, I changed my approach and the words I used, and his mind-set shifted. He now recognizes that practice, repetition, and hard work make a huge difference in his learning success. He perseveres when things are tough; he is walking proof that neuroplasticity is true—we can rewire our brain.

Dweck's research has found that students of all ages, from early grade school through college, can learn to develop growth mind-sets. It is important to teach our students that their intellectual skills can be cultivated through hard work, reading, education, the confrontation of challenges, and other activities (Dweck 2006).

Understanding that human intelligence is malleable, that it can be changed through exposure to new information or even by looking at what you already know in a different way, means there is no limit to what you can learn, contrary to what some students may think. See page 145 for strategies to cultivate a growth mind-set in students.

Another perspective on mind-set comes from Robert Brooks (2016). He, too, is concerned with the mind-set of the students. His position is that nurturing the social-emotional welfare of students is not an extracurricular that diminishes time for teaching; if anything, it enhances academic instruction. According to Brooks (2015), "Students don't care what you know until they first know you care." Learning at any age is most effective in an environment in which students feel safe, secure, and respected.

At a four-day institute on the topic of the power of mind-sets, Brooks (2016) encourages teachers to recognize that that they have control over a significant dynamic in the classroom—namely, the attitudes and behaviors they choose to adopt and display. I agree, which is why I am also a proponent in investing as much time in teachers' social-emotional wellness as that of students'. I've witnessed a change in the mind-set of a teacher have an immeasurable impact on the students.

Maintaining a positive attitude as an educator these days can be challenging. I am in numerous school districts supervising student teachers and providing workshops for in-service teachers. Everywhere I go, I hear teachers lamenting the time it takes to prepare for and administer the state tests, and the negative impact it has on students. These tests don't provide formative assessment information or allow for data analysis that can help teachers better support their students. The results aren't received until the next year, and rarely are they analyzed in a manner that is used to pinpoint individual student difficulties. Often the scores are used to fuel the public's view that teachers aren't competent.

This is disheartening to teachers and can negatively affect the climate of the school. Not only can individuals have a fixed mind-set, so can entire systems. The stigma attached to being the school or grade level with the lowest test scores is a huge morale problem. Instead of adopting a growth mind-set as a faculty, knowing that their efforts and mind-set can make a difference in student achievement, teachers far too often rationalize why the scores are low—it's the students who live in public housing, it's the unidentified students, it's because we missed so many snow days, and so on. No one is saying all of those things aren't real factors, but they are factors that can't be changed, so we need to instead focus on what can be done.

We need to create schools where the atmosphere is one of hope, optimism, and trust. We need to teach students how their brains work, how to focus their attention, and how to be present. However, we can't do this if we haven't learned how to do it ourselves. How does your own mind-set manifest itself in school, with your colleagues and the students you teach?

As educators, what we say and do in the classroom has a lifelong impact on students. If we accept that we are the "authors of our own lives," we are a step closer to creating classrooms in which positive emotions, meaning, purpose, caring, and learning can thrive. Once again, we have to be able to apply these concepts and then honestly share with students our successes.

It's essential to recall what we learned in Chapter 5 about how we work best. Both adults and children should be pulsing between periods of intense focus and concentration and breaks to allow the brain to synthesize what has been learned. Directing attention skillfully is therefore a fundamental way to shape the brain and one's life over time. Hanson (2009) asserts that mindfulness involves the skillful use of attention to both our inner and outer worlds. Our brains learn mainly from what we attend to, so it makes sense to soak in those good experiences. The longer something is held in awareness and the more emotionally stimulating it is, the more neurons fire and thus wire together, and the stronger the trace in memory (Lewis 2005).

THE DARK SIDE OF NEUROPLASTICITY

When we develop bad habits and we use our brain over and over in a negative way, it's not just that we are thinking the wrong thoughts. We're actually changing the structure of our brains and altering the brain's reward system to some degree. We are creating a new circuitry, which takes on a demon life of its own. That is just one of the examples of the "dark side" of plasticity. We need to be on the lookout for toxic patterns of thought that can impede happiness. Some negative patterns include rumination, catastrophizing or thinking that danger is always looming, or striving to be perfect. These types of stress restrict brain processing. These are the types of mental models we need to challenge. Following are some other examples.

Growth-Focused Evaluation

We can be motivated out of a desire to grow rather than a need to repair our deficiencies. Recognize that you can always grow, improve, and learn more.

Unfortunately, our evaluation systems are currently designed to be deficit oriented rather than growth focused. We start this orientation in our teacher preparation programs. A common scene for a preservice teacher who is student teaching goes like this:

The university preservice teacher and I sat on the steps outside the fourth-grade classroom. She put her face in her hands to hide her tears. "I know I made a total mess of things in there (gesturing toward the classroom). I should have never thought I could be a teacher, what was I thinking?"

Sadly, I wasn't surprised at her outburst; it was more common than not. I began to ask her questions, hoping to shift her judgmental mind.

"What was the best part of the lesson?"

"There was nothing good," she countered.

"Describe when you felt engaged and confident with what was going on."

"Are you kidding, confident? Never! It was a disaster," she said. "There was nothing good."

"Nope, not true," I replied. "Think back through the whole lesson. Was there a student who made you feel as though you were connecting with him or her?"

"Well, Joe did seem to be paying attention," she mumbled.

"What specifically happened during your lesson that showed that your teaching made a difference in students' learning?"

Slowly, she began to recall aspects of the lesson that went right. I pitched another question: "When things are going right when you are teaching, how do you know? What makes it feel successful? What enables you to be at your best?"

She began to describe the students she saw suddenly "get it" in the midst of the lesson.

"What did you learn about your own strengths as a teacher?"

Her body language shifted. She sat up straighter and took her hands away from her face. "Well, just the fact that I kept going even though I knew I had confused a few of them I guess shows I have endurance."

"How can you leverage that learning to invite new possibilities to continue to grow and change?"

And then she began to optimistically describe all the steps she would take to make the next lesson better.

Whatever we focus on, we discover more of. Our current evaluation system focuses on all the ways we don't get it right. No wonder teachers dread observations.

Often teachers' inclination is to reflect on everything that went wrong, what they forgot to say or do, and the ways they should have done better. Honest, candid reflection is certainly important; it helps us refine our craft. However, when I observe pre- or in-service teachers, I begin by asking them to describe everything that worked and that they would do again. If we don't take the time to do this, it's an afterthought, if ever a thought at all. This is a strengths-based perspective.

When people feel judged, they shut down and often don't even hear the actual feedback. Instead, they hear some version of, "I'm not good enough." Physically they hear, but mentally they misinterpret. They may be predisposed to hear something negative when that isn't the intended message. If they use the traditional "three to glow, three to grow" type of feedback (three things that went right, three things to improve on), they are just bracing themselves for the "grow" comments, and not really taking in the "glow."

One of my goals is to lay the groundwork so that as teachers we become self-aware, present, and nonjudgmental. This doesn't mean we don't notice where we can grow—we do, but in a nonjudgmental way. There is a vast difference between observing and stating what could be done differently and judging yourself for messing up. Everyone seems to think if we focus on the positives, no one will reflect on how to improve. In my experience, that just isn't true. When I train instructional coaches, I have them incorporate an appreciative inquiry stance with the teachers they are coaching. I assign coaches to do the following:

- Arrange to visit a teacher's classroom to observe his or her teaching and have a subsequent coaching conversation with that teacher. In a pre-conference, inform the teacher that the focus of the observation will be on discovering strengths and noticing vitality: the things he or she is doing well in the classroom, facilitating student learning and enjoyment.
- During the observation, look for signs of full engagement, both on the part of the teacher and the students. Capture your observations with specific notes so you can share them later with the teacher in the mentoring conversation. Do not attempt to script everything that is said and done.
- Schedule a postconference with the teacher; this can be immediately after the observation or at a later date.
- Prior to the postconference, review your notes and prepare yourself to take an appreciative, strengths-based approach. Remember that you are not going to make suggestions as to what the teacher should be doing differently. For this assignment, you are going to focus on the things that are going well. Notice and set

aside any negative judgments that cross your mind. Remember the mantra: "What we appreciate, appreciates."

Begin the postconference by asking the following appreciative questions of the teacher:

- What was the best experience during the lesson, a time when you felt engaged and happy with what was going on? Describe that moment in detail.
- What do you value most about teaching and yourself as a teacher? How does that come through in your teaching?
- When things go well in your classroom, what helps you to be successful? What enables you to be at your very best?

Offer your own strengths-based classroom observations in ways that confirm and bolster the teacher's answers to the appreciative interview questions. Be sure to note how your observations connect with his or her core values, inherent ambitions, and generative conditions. Affirm the teacher's competence and thank the teacher for the opportunity to collaborate together.

When I first outline this assignment, the coaches in training look at me as if I've lost my mind. They roll their eyes, and comment on how "this won't work in our school." I've learned to say nothing and hold firm that this is the only way I want this observation to be conducted. The majority of the coaches return, incredulous, and comment on how unbelievably insightful and reflective the teachers are, and what a positive experience the entire process is. The teachers themselves share where they'd like to grow and what they could do differently, because for the most part, we all know when we miss the mark and where we could do better. The role of a coach is to create that space where it's safe to acknowledge the specific areas where growth is needed and to let teachers know that they won't be judged, but will be supported.

Social Comparison

Studies show that happier people tend to define their happiness on their own terms and not compare themselves to others or think about how they're always falling short. In this era of social media, I worry more than ever about our youth and the need they have to constantly compare themselves to their peers.

Material Resources Versus Experiences: Gilovich (2015) examined how we devote resources either to material objects and commodities or toward experiences with others. He found time and time again that if we orient the mind toward experience, we fare well in terms of happiness. If we orient toward spending money or pursuing material objects, it costs us in terms of our personal happiness.

Maximizing Versus Satisfying: Barry Schwartz and his colleagues (2002) differentiated two different ways of looking at our experiences. One approach is to maximize pleasure; we try to get as much happiness out of every instant as possible. Another approach is what they call "satisficing"; it's an economic term, which means to find delight in what's given to us. To take pleasure in what we get.

Schwartz and colleagues provide the following example. If you're a maximizer, you would agree with the following statement: "When I am in the car listening to music, I often check other stations to see if something better is playing, even if I am satisfied with what I am already listening to."

Maximizers are always looking for opportunities to maximize more pleasure. And, as you might imagine, Schwartz and colleagues found that the mind-set of always wanting more happiness, trying to maximize our pleasure, costs us in terms of happiness. Maximizers have less satisfaction with life. They tend to be more depressed. When they do well in a circumstance, they actually feel less satisfied. And they're also less optimistic about what the future holds.

I have to admit, I was a constant channel switcher, always on the lookout for the ideal song. However, now that I'm aware of this habit and the research on neuroplasticity, I realize I can reprogram this pattern.

Perfectionism

I've always had a hard time with perfectionists. I feel as though they are just waiting to find fault, and truth be told, often they are. Two perfectionists raised me, and they could easily find fault with just about anything I did. I am about the furthest thing from a perfectionist as anyone could be, and I often felt bad about it. My perspective shifted when I read an essay by Alan Cohen (1996). Cohen describes how a man who considered himself a perfectionist came to the realization that he was an *imperfectionist*. He shared how he lived his life finding flaws and errors that others didn't see. What he realized was that if he were a perfectionist, he would have found perfection everywhere. Instead, he saw only imperfection.

Start to notice how much of your day is consumed by pointing out imperfection, not just in others, but also in yourself. We've all been there. Here's a minute in my mind during a lesson while I was being observed by the assistant superintendent early in my career.

Why in the world did I have them read silently to begin this lesson? I should know better. I know they'll all get done at a million different times. I'm an idiot. How am I going to get their attention? Why didn't I think of one of those cute jingles like the other third-grade teacher uses? It's because I don't do cute jingles, just like I'm not cute. I should have never worn this orange dress. I'm like a giant bulging pumpkin. What adult do you know who wears orange? Oh my god, what is Melvin doing to the back of Amy's hair? I should have moved their desks. Crud, David's done, oh no he's putting his eraser up his nose. I doubt any of them actually like this book. I always pick the wrong book. What's the best question to ask when they're done reading—um, one of those higher-level thinking questions? Oops, I should be walking around the room as they read. OK, here I go. But wait, not too much. I look like a pacing lunatic. What is that assistant superintendent writing? She's been typing nonstop. Oh boy, this isn't going to be good.

Note the chaotic negative stream of consciousness. Our minds are an endless flurry of thoughts, and reining them in is the challenge. Learn to stop midstream, take a deep breath, and fire that negative voice in your head. Ask yourself, would you talk to a friend in this way? If not, then reframe how you talk to yourself.

Personal Practices to Support Mindful Teaching

TAKE CONTROL OF YOUR MIND

Call to mind a past negative experience or a present problem. Recall all the details of the situation, and tune in to how this feels in your body.

Now, try to hold on to that negative experience while tuning in very closely to a sound in the background. It could be the heater kicking on in your room, the clicking of a clock, or the sound of a bird outside. Focus all of your attention on the sound and observe what happens. Most likely the negative experience faded as you tuned into the sounds. With practice, we can learn to redirect our mind.

STOREHOUSE OF POSITIVE MEMORIES

Create in advance a storehouse of positive memories, places, and experiences, things you can envision when you need to shift out of a negative state. To make these quickly accessible, practice by choosing a positive memory. The more this memory is repeated, the stronger the neoplastic neural network is, making this new path your go-to place.

Remember the loving-kindness meditation from Chapter 4? Research shows that not only can the brain rewire neural pathways and change the way it functions, but parts of the brain can grow or shrink depending on their use. Using MRI technology, scientists have been able to show that monks who engage in loving-kindness (compassion-based) meditation have brains that are different from those of people who have just started this practice. These monks' brains are highly charged and developed in areas that deal with compassion and happiness. They prove that we can train our brains to be happier in this way.

ADOPT A GROWTH MIND-SET

Believe that:

- You can train your mind.
- Past performance does not limit your future success.

DOCUMENT THE GOOD

For four weeks, keep a daily log of what you enjoy about your work. At the end of the day, list moments that you enjoyed or that felt good or rewarding—even those that were short and quick.

APPRECIATE THE GOOD

Rick Hanson (2013) describes a method for weaving positive experience into the brain:

1. Look for positive facts, and let them become positive experiences.
2. Savor the positive experience:
   - Sustain the feeling for ten, twenty, thirty seconds.
   - Feel it in your body and emotions.
   - Intensify it.
3. Sense and intend that the positive experience is soaking into your brain and body and registering deeply in emotional memory.

RAISE YOUR HAPPINESS SET POINT

Be intentional about how you spend your free time. It can simply be on the small pleasures of ordinary life. Think of ways you can raise your happiness set point daily.

RELAXATION TECHNIQUES

Rather than simply say you are going to relax, choose one of the following strategies based on what your body or mind needs.

Autogenic Relaxation

This combines both visual imagery and body awareness. In this process, you repeat words or a mantra and imagine a peaceful place as you focus on controlled, relaxing breathing, which gradually slows your heart rate.

Progressive Muscle Relaxation

Yoga nidra uses this type of relaxation technique. You focus on slowly tensing and then relaxing each muscle group. This helps you focus on the difference between muscle tension and relaxation.

Give Your Feet a Break

Our feet literally support us and carry us through our days. Take a moment to tune into your feet. Allow your breath to flow naturally. If you are sitting, move your attention to the soles of your feet on the floor. Feel your heels; notice where your toes touch the inside of your shoes if you have shoes on. Splay your toes. Lift your heels off the floor and release them back down. If you have a frozen water bottle, you can roll your feet on the bottle, noticing the sensations. Possibly invest in a therapeutic massage ball. By rolling your feet on the spiky surface you can release tight muscles and increase blood circulation, and it can help remove toxins.

Remember, when you are present, you are connected with the sensations of life in your body, from the top of your head to the bottom of your feet.

Visualization

Various types of visualizations will help you form mental images. It helps to include sensory detail.

Classroom Connections

If I had influence with the good fairy who is supposed
to preside over the christening of all children, I should
ask that her gift to each child in the world be a sense of
wonder so indestructible that it would last throughout life.

—RACHEL CARSON

Most of the subsequent information is intended to help us in our teaching of students; however, this information can also change how we, as teachers, learn. The same information that benefits student learning benefits us as ongoing learners.

In the past two decades, neuroimaging and brain-mapping research have provided objective support to the student-centered educational model. This brain research demonstrates that superior learning takes place when classroom experiences are relevant to students' lives, interests, and experiences. Lessons can be stimulating and challenging without being intimidating, and the increasing curriculum requirements can be achieved without stress, anxiety, boredom, and alienation as pervasive emotions.

MAKE THE WHY TRANSPARENT

Teach students how their brain works and how *they* best learn. Help them understand the role their brain plays in increasing the capacity to learn, remember, and understand information. For example, when assigning homework, make sure students know *why* they are practicing a skill. Integration of new learning requires repetition. That is the purpose of homework.

At back-to-school night, when explaining my homework policy, I often explain that students need to "use it or lose it." If they don't use or practice what they've learned in the classroom in some way, their brains will delete their new learning to make room for new information that may be more useful to them. In fact, studies suggest that up to 80 percent of what we learn will be forgotten within 24 hours unless some special effort is made to remember it. Homework allows students to store newly learned information into their long-term memory. They do that by making a deliberate effort to remember by using a variety of simple and practical memory techniques. Instead of calling it *homework*, call it *retrieval practice*; it changes their perception when they think of it as a brain-strengthening exercise.

Memory is constructed and stored by patterning, making connections to the brain's prior knowledge before new information is taught. That's why introducing lessons with a memorable anticipatory set, one that hooks the student and grabs their attention, will help students remember and retain new information. They appreciate when we begin a lesson by explaining what they will be learning and why, and then connecting it to what they already know. They remember novel, not "normal," so beginning with an anecdote or an unusual image piques their curiosity.

ENGAGEMENT, MOTIVATION, AND NOVELTY

Do you recall some of your college professors who knew their subject matter but simply lectured for hours without providing breaks? Staying awake became the objective rather than learning and being actively engaged. This is who you don't want to be.

The brain research concludes that optimum learning takes place when classroom experiences are motivating and engaging. Relevant lessons help students feel that they are partners in their education, not passive recipients of knowledge.

WAYS TO PROVIDE NOVELTY

- Change the sound of your voice, volume, pitch, cadence, or infuse a silent pause.
- Change the color of handouts.
- Incorporate movement—have students go to different places in the room to learn new information.
- Use music, rhymes, and rap for transitions.
- Use props and real-world examples.
- Move the desks or rearrange the room.
- Use cooperative learning strategies.
- Have students role-play, pantomime, or use charades to demonstrate understanding.
- Let the students draw or "stop and jot."
- Incorporate games into the lesson.

HELPING STUDENTS TRANSITION FROM FIXED TO GROWTH MIND-SET

- Have students keep a journal and record times that they have persevered and accomplished something that was difficult. This trains them to focus longer on the good events in their life, and it serves as a record of their success.
- Pose questions regarding how much effort students are investing in their own learning. Before taking a test, have them list their study strategies and rate on a 10-point scale how much preparation they invested in studying. Leading them to

the realization that their effort does affect the outcome helps eradicate the mind-set that some students are just smarter.

- Provide frequent focused feedback on work habits. Relate the feedback to the effort. For example: "Craig, I noticed that you created a graphic organizer and that your notes are a combination of illustrations and words. Now try reading them aloud; that will incorporate three modes of learning."
- Ask questions that have multiple ways of answering and increase wait time.
- Encourage divergent thinking. This will encourage "possibility thinking."
- Investigate mind-sets. Explain to students Dweck's (2006) research in kid-friendly terms and foster a growth mind-set by pointing out the opportunities to take on a task or assignment using a growth approach throughout the day. Giving clear examples will make this not just a concept, but a mind-set. Share your own successes with learning new skills.

ADVERTISE UPCOMING LESSON TO PROMOTE NOVELTY AND CURIOSITY

- Put up pieces of a puzzle related to an upcoming unit, and ask students to brainstorm titles of the next unit.
- Create a series of unique photographs that are clues to the next lesson, and ask students to predict the main idea of the next lesson.
- Make a commercial for your topic. Have students make a commercial for the next day's topic.

ASK STUDENTS TO DESCRIBE THEIR BEST LEARNING EXPERIENCE, INCLUDING TWO CHARACTERISTICS THAT MADE IT MEMORABLE

Pay attention to the characteristics they describe; those are clues as to what helps them retain information. For example, one student listed the following activities that helped him solidify information learned in social studies.

Ball-Toss Review: One student names a state and tosses a ball to a partner, who names the appropriate capital.

Snowball Fight: Each student writes a question about the topic or lesson on a piece of paper. The students then stand in two lines, crumple their papers, and throw snowballs at the other team. They then select snowballs to answer.

Four Corners: Mark corners with the letters *A*, *B*, *C*, or *D*. Students can answer multiple-choice questions by moving to the corner that they believe represents the correct answer or go to various corners to discuss.

Based on the learning experiences the student listed, it was apparent that he recalled information best when movement was incorporated into the lesson.

In the last twenty years, the scientific understanding of the brain has literally doubled. Teachers who haven't been trained to understand neuroplasticity are missing out on research-based ways to better engage students. Understanding how students learn can change how we teach.

CHAPTER 7

Can't We Just Get Along?

Collaboration Versus Conflict

2010-2014—The high school cafeteria was filled with over a hundred teachers from grades K–12. Every table was full, and teachers were standing around the perimeter, arms crossed, looking either angry or bored (it was hard to tell). I was the education consultant hired to help them align their resources with the new Common Core Language Arts standards.

Facilitating this task was like herding cats. In the room were teachers from twelve elementary schools, three middle schools, and three high schools, all using a variety of resources and doing their own unique implementation of old and new programs. Teachers from each grade level were complaining that the students came to them not adequately prepared and were blaming the teachers in the grade level prior. There was only one thing they all could agree on: there was a lack of direction, resources, and a clear implementation plan. I was just one more consultant who had been hired to solve all their problems in a day, and so they focused their frustration on me. They were tired of poorly planned professional development and tired of the endless cycle of new innovations that were recycled programs with a different name. I wished I could have provided a solution, but that would have required a long-term professional development plan, not a one-day workshop. I understood that they were frustrated by the lack of leadership and direction, but what I couldn't figure out was why they were so divided among each other. When I tuned into their conversations, most were about each other, and not positive. The room felt charged, but not in a good way. Unfortunately, though not unexpectedly, there wasn't an administrator in sight.

Giant sequoia trees seem as if they should be sturdy enough to weather storms alone. In reality, though, even these magnificent specimens need help. An individual sequoia growing by itself can be blown over in a strong wind. Only by interlocking roots with other trees can a sequoia survive any kind of squall. There's a lesson for all of us here: sequoias fare best when they support each other and so do we as teachers, but we seem to be losing too many good teachers to "strong winds."

—NANCY ROSENOW

The contexts in which teachers work profoundly shape their effectiveness. It is understandable that teachers who work in supportive contexts stay in the classroom longer and improve at faster rates than their peers in less supportive environments. It's common sense that we're happier when we all get along and our students benefit when they're in collaborative, happy environments.

John Dewey, the psychologist and philosopher whose ideas were influential in educational and social reform, is credited with saying, "The deepest urge in human nature is the desire to be important." William James is credited as saying, "The deepest principle in human nature is the craving to be appreciated."

Many teachers don't feel appreciated or important. The profession is under fire, and rather than collaborating, teachers are competing for the scraps of recognition that are attainable. Our egos can make us behave like scavenger dogs. We want to be the teacher whom parents request for their child. We want to be liked, or disliked, popular, or tough, anything, as long as we are *known*. The gains in an educational career aren't monetary; they're more about status and prestige, which require competition. Instead of competing with one another, we need to find ways to cooperate.

Sadly, in schools across the country, I've observed how increased regulatory demands and accountability from the local, state, and federal government have made teachers feel the need to prove their competence by improving scores on standardized tests. This has caused more competition and added to the work stress. We need a new vision, one that is created by those in the trenches, not those glimpsing in from afar.

The next and final chapter of this book is a call for teachers to band together to establish a shared vision. But first, let's have a conversation about creating a collaborative culture within and between classrooms.

As I stood in front of the teachers, the thought crossed my mind that they needed some team building skills. However, if you want to see eyes roll, mention team building to a group of teachers or administrators. I tried to remember what I had learned in my organizational leadership classes. Ironically, though perhaps not surprisingly, managing conflict seemed to have dominated many of the lectures.

TEAM CONFLICT

A good start to managing conflicts is learning how to respond rather than react.

Most schools have teams of teachers who work together. Anyone who has been on a team that doesn't get along well knows how this situation can affect your daily life. Conflict among team members can affect productivity and the emotional well-being of the individuals. It's like living with a dysfunctional family.

Conflicts take up a great deal of our time and dominate our thoughts. It is extremely difficult to stop the negative thought train when you feel you have been victimized in some way. As educators, we have a multitude of potential perpetrators. It can be your principal whom you feel has given you a difficult class, the parents who blame you when their child isn't happy at school, the colleague who talks about you behind your back, or the student who pushes your buttons. The list of potential offenders is endless. Once your mind gets caught up in the negative story, reining it back in is a real challenge.

In my roles as a literacy coach, administrator, and consultant, I have encountered endless conflict among teachers: fractured grade-level teams made up of teachers who wouldn't speak to one another, competing high school athletic departments, judgments about those who taught the lower-level students in the content areas, alienation of the special education specialists, and so on.

In one elementary school, I encountered two teachers who refused to talk to the other three teachers in their grade level because of a rift that had taken place years ago over a fifth-grade field trip. I know middle school teams that refused to collaborate and coordinate their resources because they were competing to produce students with the highest test scores. It's no wonder; their evaluations depended on the students' scores. In another district, the addition of a new high school meant that selected teachers from the two existing high schools had to be merged to create a new high school, none of whom wanted to leave their "home school." A decade later, they still only associate with those who came from their original home school.

These scenes are replicated in schools with different players and scenarios all across the country. Districts build new schools, and redistricting occurs. Teachers are transferred, grade-level changes are made, new teachers are hired, and others retire or change careers. Personnel changes are common in schools. Among all these changes, new teachers come with new ideas, experiences, and expectations. We need to welcome them and foster their growth and success.

On my daughter's first day as a first-grade teacher, she walked into her classroom to find the other first-grade teachers had made her a welcome card, which said, "We share our crayons here." Sounds sappy, but from that moment on, she was made to feel part of the team. She loves her job. Not only does she enjoy the students, her colleagues are her friends, and she *wants to go* to work because she is surrounded by people who know and care about her. Her colleagues and principal continue to be tremendously supportive and because of this supportive kindness, she will no doubt support the next new hire.

So, how does a new teacher develop strong networks?

BANISH GOSSIP

Be known as the teacher who doesn't talk about others.

Some teams can feel exclusive, with some individuals feeling alienated. This often happens when teachers chat about others. Think about how much happier and more productive we could all be if we abolished gossip. Sadly, it's often what brings people together. The chance to talk about someone else can make you feel included and connected to your co-gossiper. We can't change other people, but we can influence them by not engaging in gossip or joining the negativity parade.

So what do you do when you are the focus of gossip?

My first year as teacher on assignment (another name for instructional coach) was full of opportunities to ponder this question. The role was new and many incorrect assumptions were made, usually behind closed doors. I adopted the mantra, "What you think of me is none of my business."

Keep in mind that our perception of events is often distorted. Many of our thoughts involve reactions to others, but how often do we take into consideration their reactions to us? Perception is a mirror, not a fact. What we often perceive is our own state of mind, reflected outward. Often what we see is determined by what we want to see. Our world reflects our mind. We see schools that are not peaceful collaborative environments, in part because our own minds are not at peace. Usually when we're triggered, we make the other person into the enemy and forget that we are also responsible.

No one can make you feel bad about yourself or unworthy in any way. How you react to difficult people is always your choice; you can choose to take it personally or ignore the situation. I know that I am 100 percent responsible for myself, and myself only. The more we are focused on pleasing others, the more complicated our lives become. The more we live our own authentic life, the more manageable our life will become, and the gossip and drama will, on their own, simply fall away, or we won't even notice it!

WORK AND RELATIONSHIPS
When you point your finger at another person, look at where the other fingers point.
—JAMAICAN PROVERB

Mihaly Csikszentmihalyi (1990) found that more than anything else, the quality of life depends on two factors:

1. How we experience work, and
2. Our relations with other people.

The Organization for Economic Cooperation and Development is one of many international bodies concluding that new realities demand that people bring a different set of competencies to the workforce than they used to. In the 1970s, writing, computation, and reading made the top of the list of skills most sought after by employers. Today teamwork, problem solving, and interpersonal skills trump the list. Teachers who are able to work with one another, manage stress, and be resilient are going to be happier, and thus remain in the workforce longer. Futurists have made it clear that knowledge is no longer power, because it's accessible to so many. Teachers who can connect with their students and garner their attention are needed.

Once we have their attention, we need to model strong interpersonal communication. We may need to model some healthy modes of communicating, and we may need to infuse more emotional intelligence concepts into our classes.

When I facilitated strategic planning, we projected what the workforce would look like and value in thirteen years, when our kindergartners would graduate. What skills did we need to model to support these students in becoming productive members of society? We found that the skills most needed would be emotional intelligence and innovation. Essentially, we need innovative relationship workers who have empathy, can collaborate, listen to others' viewpoints, and be creative and open to new experiences. We need teachers who are willing to fail. If you do enough new things, you are going to fail. And that's OK. Thinking outside the box won't be enough; we need to create new boxes. Connecting the dots will be replaced with making new dots.

Collaboration is key. And the good news is that collaboration and innovation can be learned, but our students need mentors to demonstrate them.

GROUP PROCESSES

Teachers know instituting classroom norms and procedures helps the classroom run smoothly. The same principle applies to getting teams of teachers to work together. Spending time with a group up front to discuss how they can best work together will help them to do so. Over time, this may mean beginning a meeting by asking teachers to characterize an effective group and for leading members to agree on some norms. This process can include soliciting and attending to individuals' preferred work habits and learning styles. I've done this with groups in my role as a coach, and I can't tell you how grateful they are for the attention to process. At first, everyone groans when they see they have to follow a process, but once they experience how much time a process can save, they are sold. The Personal Practices to Support Mindful Teaching section (page 160) has a few different group process tools that can be easily referenced. However, all the processes in the world won't change the fact that we will encounter difficult personalities.

DEALING WITH DIFFICULT PERSONALITIES
Problems are our friends.

—MICHAEL FULLAN

Conflict presents us with opportunities, not just problems. Possibly those people we perceive as problematic aren't really as difficult as we think. When we begin to practice self-care and self-compassion, we can shift how we perceive others and how we relate to the world. We begin to pause more, we move through the day with more intentionality, we see instead of just look, and we slow down and start to really notice others around us. In seeing more deeply, we can notice the goodness in others that, although buried deep, is still there.

A mantra I repeat often when triggered by difficult people comes from the book *A Course in Miracles*: "I could see peace instead of this" (Schucman 1976, 51). This is one of the lines I've memorized and used more times than I can recall.

Everyone we meet helps us in some way. Some help by being kind, and others by challenging us to be kind when they are not so kind. Although your inclination may be to avoid difficult people at all costs, those same people can be your greatest teachers. Consider the challenge as an opportunity. When faced with a challenging personality, consider how this difficult person has helped you grow. Has he or she taught you to think before you react? Possibly this person has enabled you to speak your truth and say what can be difficult. Has he or she provided opportunities for saying no or asking for what you want? There are countless benefits you might have gained, or still might gain, from someone who triggers you. Imagine that they are part of your life curriculum, just another lesson plan that you have to implement, but the lesson is really for you in how to handle the situation.

If we could walk in others' shoes, we would most likely change our perceptions of them and thus our judgment of their actions. None of us have any idea of what others have been through or are dealing with. When people act in a hurtful way, stop and recognize that you don't know the whole story.

Tara Brach, a renowned mindfulness teacher, uses a metaphor that has often helped me reframe situations when people are acting unkind. Imagine a little dog is barking and barring its teeth, lunging at you. Your first reaction may be fear or anger. But then you pause, look closer, and you notice that the little dog has its back leg caught in a trap; it's raw and bleeding. Wouldn't you want to help the dog first get out of the trap, and then comfort it? Many people we encounter are like that little dog, literally in pain, either emotionally or physically. If you can pause and create the space so that you don't react, often a conflict can be avoided. By practicing presence and compassion, it's much easier to see when someone has her or his leg in a trap. It doesn't mean that you don't set boundaries—you do—but there is understanding, not judgment in your heart.

By pausing before responding, we deepen presence. This world has so much disease. We need to cultivate the capacity to see the goodness in others. One of the greatest gifts we can give others is to see them as they really are, their essence, their true self.

Let's look at some of the common characters that can be found in schools:

The chaotic colleague: She or he is underprepared, leaves things to the last minute, and is always rushing.

The dramatizer: He or she thrives on and continually creates drama in relationships with other teachers, administrators, and parents.

The controller: He or she tries to control all aspects of an agenda and feels a need to be right. When controllers are right, they feel in control, but when questioned, they become defensive.

The perfectionist: She or he can't handle when someone else is in charge and insists on doing everything her or his way, rarely accepting help. Perfectionists may act like martyrs, seeming to want to make others feel guilty because of all the work they are doing.

The pleaser: This person feels that she or he must make everything right and keep the peace on grade-level or departmental teams. Pleasers feel responsible for keeping everyone happy.

The chatterer: This person talks just to hear him or herself talk, and rarely listens.

The isolationist: This individual prefers to work alone, doesn't want to share, and doesn't want to be part of any type of collaboration.

HOW TO DEAL WITH THE CAST OF CHARACTERS

Accept them all. If you want to live in a peaceful work environment, extend your compassion to your colleagues, students, and the parents of your students. The characteristics listed are their iniquities, not their strengths. Look for the good; everyone has it. Change your perspective and reframe how you see your coworkers, and either they start to behave differently or you notice that you are less inclined to be triggered by their behavior. Challenge your perceptions and remember everyone has the same desire to belong, be accepted, and be happy. Bring compassion to the situation. You may be thinking, "That is the last thing I want to do," but if what you're doing now isn't working, isn't this worth a try?

REPLACE JUDGMENT WITH COMPASSION

When another person makes you suffer, it's because he suffers deeply within himself, and his suffering is spilling over. He does not need punishment, he needs help. That's the message he is sending.

—THICH NHAT HANH

There is nothing compassionate about judgment. When you become aware of all the judgments you make, all day long, you realize that much of your life is spent categorizing, labeling, and deciding who or what is right or wrong. To accurately judge another person, you would have to be aware of an inconceivably wide range of information about his or her past and present. You would also have to be certain there is no distortion in your perception. Who is in a position to do this? Not I.

Most teachers I know are extremely compassionate toward their students. The more problematic the student, the more they attempt to bring compassion to the situation. Extending this stance of compassion to adults seems to be much more difficult.

A teacher I worked with for years had good relationships with everyone in the school. One day I witnessed another teacher accelerate past her and take the last parking space in the main parking lot in front of the school. It was that kind of action that was clearly wrong, but this teacher didn't react. As we walked into school, after she had to carry multiple bags from about a half mile away, I asked her about it. How was it she didn't get angry at that kind of behavior? She said, "I have a good memory." I said, "You mean you'll get even later?" "Oh my gosh no," she replied, "I have a good memory because I only remember the good."

Now that's the kind of memory I'd like to have. I thought about the colleague who had humiliated my daughter in elementary school. She summoned my nine-year-old to stand in front of all the fourth-and fifth-grade students in the cafeteria during lunch and publically demonstrate the "short shorts test" where you hold your arms straight down along your sides and if the hem of your shorts does not fall below your fingertips, your shorts are considered too short, which means you are dressed "inappropriately." My daughter was wearing a new outfit her grandparents had gotten her from Disney World. Her shorts were deemed too short in front of all of her peers, and she was sent to the nurse to change. That day when she got off the bus she cried like I'd never seen her cry, sobbing for hours. I drove to the school to request a meeting with this teacher, but unbelievably she was in a reception receiving the "teacher of the year" award from our local union. I drove home in tears. It took me a long time to let go of that anger. Clearly I needed more practice remembering only the good. Trust me, I know that forgiveness isn't easy, but if you can forgive, you will see things differently.

PROJECTION IS PERCEPTION

Consider that the greatest teachers are those who rub us the wrong way. They may be shining a light on our triggers and repressed feelings. Those triggers are clues; pay attention, they have something to teach us. Awareness of those triggers can be a gift. Acknowledge that everyone is different, but at the same time, we are all alike. If you look closely, you will realize that you can usually see yourself in others, the good, bad, and ugly.

What if those who annoy you most are possibly mirroring some of your own characteristics right back at you? I know this seems inconceivable; I denied this for a long time myself. Start paying attention. That person who infuriates you mirrors, consciously or unconsciously, something you sense that is similar in yourself that you don't like. That person is a reflection of qualities you try to suppress. Her or his behavior strikes a chord in you, which you identify with at some level. Or, she or he may have qualities that you, at some level, wish you had.

However, perception is a mirror, not a fact, and what I look on is my own state of mind. Projection makes perception. Rather than attempting to change people, change your mind about them. For example, I've been known to hurry, and anyone who stands in the way of me completing my to-do list is perceived as a huge inconvenience. I used to look at those people with frustration. I now look at them with respect; they are helping me to slow down. Something about their methodical manner represents how I wish I could be. Their pace illuminates how ridiculous my frenetic pace is.

RECOGNIZE YOUR TRIGGERS

A. A. Milne's classic character Eeyore, a friend of Winnie the Pooh, was a threadbare, gray donkey who was always moping around talking to himself and awaiting his inevitable misfortune. People like that often triggered me. I couldn't believe they would utter all of their misfortunes aloud. Then I realized I did the same thing, just internally. Their negative "poor me" chatter sounded familiar because I had the same type of internal dialogue going on inside.

Here's a quick check to take stock of what similarities you may have with those who trigger you. Notice someone at work who is difficult for you to deal with. List the qualities about this person that trigger a negative reaction inside you. Circle any qualities that you also have.

Accept that at their core, everyone is simply trying to fulfill their basic need for love and acceptance. We need to begin by accepting ourselves. Next, accept your colleagues for who they are, instead of who you want them to be. On some level, even if you say nothing, others know when you are judging them. They can feel your condemnation and it affects your relationship. Most people are strongly influenced by the feelings, thoughts, and energy of others. Subconsciously, we all know pretty darn well how others feel about us without anyone saying a word. Have you ever walked into a room and felt the negative charge, even though those in the room weren't saying anything? That charge is always there; it can be positive, negative, or neutral. You are always giving off energy, and if you tune in, you can read the energy of others. There is a ripple effect to that energy that extends to the students in your classroom, which could then extend to their family and even your own family. We all know what it's like to bring our negative work sagas home. We are susceptible to other people's energy, good or bad. Our connection to one another is profound, and taking responsibility for our own energy is the first place to start.

Although it can be useful to recognize that you can learn from those who trigger you, it doesn't mean you have to constantly surround yourself with those who drain you. Take an inventory of those who sap your good energy, and limit the amount of time you spend in their presence.

When I was an administrator, I had the opportunity to observe teachers in ten different elementary schools in the school district. I often felt as if I was entering Epcot at Disney World. Each school had its own distinct culture. I could feel what I called the "happiness gauge" of a school the second I walked in the door.

Each school has a feel, a vibe. It begins in the front office where you sign in; that initial feeling is usually a good indication of the culture of the school. The custodian, support staff, and cafeteria workers are all part of the school culture and have a tremendous role. Everyone has a role. I think one of the mistakes that we make is waiting for the principal in a school to improve the culture; teachers have the real internal influence and power, and every teacher has the capacity to lead.

In the Personal Practices to Support Mindful Teaching section are some ideas that might help create a more collaborative culture.

Personal Practices to Support Mindful Teaching

This segment is organized a bit differently than in other chapters. Listed here are some strategies to create a culture of collaboration that could be choices for faculty development. Each topic could be a segment at a faculty meeting or a menu of opportunities for an in-service day.

AN AGENDA FOR CREATING A COLLABORATIVE CULTURE

- Circle of Support
- Mindful Mondays: No Complaining Challenge
- Mindful Listening
- Silence
- Complaint-Free Zone Staff Lounge
- Team Building
- Enneagram
- Task Versus Maintenance Behaviors
- Written Reflection
- Gossip-Free Faculty Room
- Monthly Birthday Breakfast Book Club
- Appreciative Interviews

CIRCLE OF SUPPORT

According to Christakis and Fowler (2008), every friend or positive person you have in your life increases your own happiness by 9 percent! Collecting positive people in our lives is a multiplier; the more you have, the more you get, spreading like a virus. Staying present and focused in the moment means our brains don't drift into autopilot and we more thoroughly appreciate who and what is around us.

One way to take stock of the relationships in your life is to visually draw a circle of support. List the names of the four people you spend the most time with (see Figure 7.1). Complete one for personal and one for professional relationships.

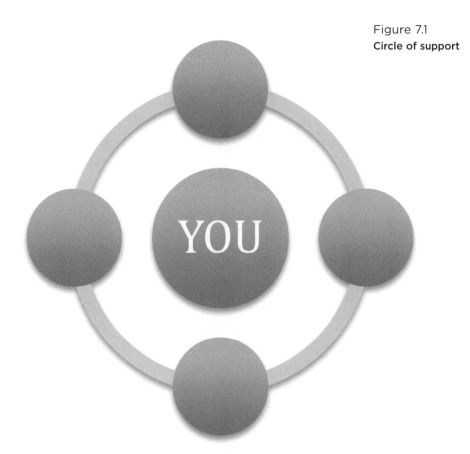

Figure 7.1
Circle of support

Draw lines connecting each name to yours.

Draw a straight bold line (_____) if that source of that support is strong and reliable.

Draw a broken line (_ _ _ _ _) if the source of support is unpredictable.

Draw a zigzag line (/\/\/\/\/\/\) if that person creates tension and stress.

Research on culture has shown that people "catch" feelings from others. Looking at your circle of support, consider the energy that surrounds you. Energy is an actual force, which takes many forms. Trees, plants, flowers, and rocks have energy. The food we eat, the clothes we wear—everything about you has energy. Your thoughts and feelings have energy and can be negatively or positively charged. Energy moves in pulses like waves. We can feel each other's energy. Every word has a vibratory energy, and depending on the negativity or the positivity of the words, it can have an effect.

Next, reflect back to the previous section on dealing with difficult personalities. Determine whether you need to work to improve the relationship or limit the time you spend in their presence.

MINDFUL MONDAYS: NO COMPLAINING CHALLENGE

Great minds discuss ideas; average minds discuss events; small minds discuss people.

—ELEANOR ROOSEVELT

If you listen carefully to the conversations swirling around you, begin to notice the language people use. You may find that complaining is often a staple in many conversations.

Complaints are often used as conversation starters. For example, someone asks, "How are you doing?" If I respond, "Great, life is good," it's a conversation stopper. They assume I'm slacking on my work or being sarcastic. If, however, I respond by sharing how exhausted I am, or how lousy I feel, I not only get a response but may make a connection and also get some empathy. We complain about our busyness almost as a badge of honor. We bond together over how overworked and exhausted we are. I noticed often we would attempt to outcomplain one another in a competition of "ain't it awful."

All the complaints in the world don't change anything, except possibly by generating more negative energy. Complaining is simply non-acceptance of what is, and it is rarely solution oriented. The complaining words we use can have a negative charge that affects our internal state of mind and the way that we feel. So what can we possibly do to minimize the amount of complaining we encounter?

We begin with ourselves. We have the opportunity to choose the words we want to use. Affirming words can be inspiring. Negative words can be devastating. Funny words can make us laugh, and sad words can bring us to tears. Encouraging and supportive words can boost morale and self-esteem, and judging and condemning words can destroy our confidence.

Begin the day by looking for the positives, appreciating the small things that go well. Recall what we discovered in the previous chapters about taking in the good rather than complaining about the bad.

In my search to reduce my own complaining, I stumbled on a book by Jon Gordon (2008), *The No Complaining Rule*. Gordon uses a narrative to describe how a company created and implemented a no complaining policy. After reading this text, I initiated the no complaining rule in one of my teacher preparation classes at the university. The purpose was to heighten awareness of the words we used and how often we used complaining language. I explained the concept and then challenged my students to see how long they could endure without uttering a single complaint. None of them made it through the first day. Neither did I. I shared my experience with one of my colleagues, the director of a preschool where I had provided a workshop on gratitude for her staff. She was intrigued, borrowed the book, and decided to introduce the concept to her staff. At a staff meeting, she summarized the concept of the book, and interested teachers completed a self-assessment to see how much of a "complainer" they were. The school then had a three-day no complaining challenge. Participation was optional. Those who participated gathered together on day three to discuss their experiences. Their reactions ranged from feeling more at peace to feeling lost without anything to talk about. Overall, the complaints decreased enough to make it worth the effort.

As teachers, we choose our words and, in the process, construct the classroom culture for our students and ourselves. Complaining does not work as a strategy. We all have finite time and energy. Any time we spend complaining detracts from achieving our goals. And complaining won't make us happier in the long run. Next are ten strategies to help reduce complaining.

STRATEGIES FOR CREATING A COMPLAINT-FREE WORK ENVIRONMENT

Keep your thoughts positive because your thoughts become your words. Keep your words positive because your words become your behavior. Keep your behavior positive because your behavior becomes your habits. Keep your habits positive because your habits become your values. Keep your values positive because your values become your destiny.

—MAHATMA GANDHI

1. Take a long, deep breath before you speak.
2. Monitor the words you use.
3. Notice your thoughts and change the negative thoughts you think.
4. Monitor your self-talk and your internal meanderings.
5. Notice the words others use. Become aware of the language you hear.
6. Judge less, accept more. Look for the good in others and their actions rather than mistakes.
7. Envision those who are annoying you as small children in a sandbox waiting for their turn for the shovel.
8. Practice gratitude. Take in the good and record it if possible.
9. Decide whether you want to be right or be happy.
10. Decide what's worth complaining about. If you have to complain, intentional complaining is better than mindless complaining.

I've continued the no complaining challenge with teachers and pre-service teachers. Each semester I pair university students with hosting cooperating teachers. The challenge is simple: Monday will be deemed a day of no complaining. We introduce this challenge with a potluck breakfast where we review the ten strategies for a complaint-free work environment, administer the complaining self-assessment, and outline the challenge. Any practicum student-cooperating teacher pair that can refrain from complaining on Mondays will earn a token, and twice a year a drawing is held and the recipient receives a gift card and a mindful Monday certificate. I've organized the no complaining challenge at various schools, and many report a change in climate.

The ultimate goal is to heighten awareness of the words we use, which will ultimately have an impact on the children we teach. Who couldn't benefit from more gratitude and less negativity in our lives? What we do and say in front of children when we think they aren't paying attention matters. We have an opportunity to model gratitude, kindness, forgiveness, and compassion. Imagine a world where children embraced these concepts instead of the frenetic pace and stressful living that they are accustomed to seeing all around them. I think every teacher would agree that it's a lesson worth modeling.

MINDFUL LISTENING

Remember not only to say the right thing in the right place, but far more difficult still, to leave unsaid the wrong thing at the tempting moment.

—BEN FRANKLIN

Far too often we aren't truly present when someone is talking to us. We may listen only partially; often our attention is divided. I notice that in my home often we are shouting from room to room in the morning as we all struggle to get out the door in time, and simply hearing is an issue. I've made a house rule that if someone wants a response from me, that person needs to be in the same room as I am. We're still working on it!

As teachers, our attention is often divided, and multiple voices can beg for attention at once. When working in a school environment, conversations can feel rushed. Usually teachers have minimal preparation time when they aren't with students, and they tend to be taking care of what's urgent rather than engaging in meaningful conversations.

Listening is a skill that, if practiced, can be sharpened. The following activity is a way to practice and get in the habit of giving your full, undivided attention when listening. I should warn you, most teachers report that this exercise feels uncomfortable. However, it has helps bring awareness to our communication patterns.

1. Choose a partner.
2. One person is the speaker, the other the listener.
3. The speaker has one minute to describe a stressful event.
4. The listener may not contribute to the conversation and should simply listen. Direct all of your attention as the listener to the speaker. Notice his or her body posture, facial expression, the rhythm of speech, and the pitch of his or her voice.
5. Pay attention to your own need to relate the speaker's story to yourself. Instead, use only nonverbal communication.
6. At the end of the minute, both the speaker and listener should tune in and notice how they feel and whether they can pinpoint anywhere in their body that they are holding on to stress.
7. Conclude with three deep, cleansing breaths, switch partners, and repeat the exercise.

SILENCE
Speak only if it improves upon the silence.

—MAHATMA GANDHI

Start to notice how uncomfortable silence can be for some people. Cultivating silence sounds so simple, but the truth is, it takes practice. One of the many things I noticed during a retreat I attended was how much chatter there is, when in fact, silence would be optimal. Consider having five minutes of silence at the start or the end of the day. It will give everyone a well-needed reprieve.

TEAM BUILDING
Conflict can destroy a team which hasn't spent time learning to deal with it.

—THOMAS ISGAR

One way to help school-based teams work effectively together is to take the time to build relationships, making the time and space to help foster a shared vision. However, I've participated in enough team-building seminars that have been poorly timed and facilitated. To develop a culture of collaboration, I would choose carefully when and what the teams did. I would begin by providing some autonomy.

At the end of a school year, most teachers' minds are on the much-needed reprieve from school. Often schools end the year with a professional development day, and having facilitated many of these days, I know the bodies may be present, but the minds are elsewhere. Instead of having a traditional professional development session, consider a range of options for individual exploration. Adult learning theory indicates that adults appreciate choice and independence. Options could be provided for teachers to learn remotely, on their own time. When the school reconvenes, time would be set aside for follow-up discussion and reflection. Listed here are three options that teachers could explore on their own.

1. Enneagram: A Tool for Self-Discovery
I've tried various tools: True Colors, Myers-Briggs, and Strength Finder, just to name a few. All have excellent qualities, but the one tool that has helped me understand myself and others the most has been the Enneagram.

Riso and Hudson (1999) introduced the Enneagram (pronounced "ANY-a-gram") as a geometric figure that maps out the nine fundamental personality types of human nature and their complex interrelationships. The Enneagram is a diagnostic tool to determine one's emotional outlook on life. The practice of self-observation and an understanding of what one's experiences mean are components of presence. The Enneagram system can enable us to have more insight into others and ourselves. It helps discern our masks and filters more clearly and provides effective ways of dealing with them. It is a useful guide to begin to understand how we all perceive the world differently. It portrays the strengths and limitations of our inner habits of attention and response.

2. Task Versus Maintenance Behavior

Cooperative learning is a method that many teachers use to help groups of students work together productively. This same method can be used with teachers. Each teacher completes a Task Versus Maintenance Behavior Instrument. The results help the group collectively better understand each individual's work habits and collaborate more productively to complete projects.

Those who are task oriented tend to focus on getting the job done. Those who are more maintenance oriented prefer to keep an open ear, resolving team problems and supporting the team decision. Having a mix of both tendencies among team members help the team work productively and contentedly.

Once you have taken this self-assessment, you will never again *not* notice how individuals contribute to a group. This awareness will help you relate to those who are different than you with more appreciation and understanding.

3. Written Reflection

Whether you're keeping a journal or writing as a meditation, it's the same thing. What's important is you're having a relationship with your mind.

—NATALIE GOLDBERG

We need to take the time to ask teachers how they could best contribute their talents. This written reflection is an opportunity to discover strengths and hidden talents that many teachers may not have ever shared before. Teachers ask the following questions:

1. In what distinctive way can you contribute to make our school even better?
2. What are your unique talents and skills, and who would benefit from them?
3. What are the qualities you look for in a quality work environment?

GOSSIP-FREE FACULTY ROOM

Ten percent of conflicts are due to difference in opinion.
Ninety percent are due to wrong tone of voice.

—UNKNOWN

This concept is similar to the no complaining challenge, but instead focuses on cultivating a gossip-free school environment, beginning with the faculty room. Every time teachers refrain from gossiping, they toss a token with their initials into a jar. Once a month, a name is drawn to win an award. I have to admit, we had multiple months when the jar was empty. At least we were honest gossipers.

APPRECIATIVE INTERVIEWS

Appreciative inquiry is an approach to organizational change that focuses on what's working rather than trying to fix what is not. In a world of educational reform, where standards, assessment, and accountability are buzzwords, we can balance those words with relationships, inquiry, and moral purpose. Deep down, we all want to be seen, to be recognized, and to have someone take the time to know us. Having dialogues about strengths, successes, values, hopes, and dreams are in themselves transformational. An inquiry-based activity is described next and provides a process to build relationships, focusing on individual potential. It encourages seeing and supporting the best of others to create a more collaborative community.

In one school district, we used this process for strategic planning. We also used this process to launch a new year with new inductees. New teachers were paired with a mentor and invited to "walk and talk." What a wonderful way to begin the school year. Following are some sample interview questions.

As you think back to your first teaching experience, recall some of the emotions you felt: nervous, excited, anxious, alone, and so on. Think about your mentoring experiences and the people who were there to guide you, support you, and strengthen you.

1. Was there someone you encountered that made a difference in your life and helped you grow and develop? (If there was no one, describe what you wished someone could have provided and proceed to question 3.)
2. At what point did this person come into your life?
3. Without being humble, describe a time when you empowered and supported someone.

4. How did that make you feel?

5. What is one small step we could take to support new teachers entering the field of education?

Classroom Connections

Colleague collaboration is for adults what social-emotional learning is for students. Several studies show that academic learning increases with an investment of time, money, and energy into social-emotional learning. Teaching skills such as empathy and altruism helps students be successful not only in school but also later in life. In the classroom, teachers foster the conditions where students feel connected with others and have the opportunity to practice social and emotional skills with others.

There are a multitude of resources for teachers to learn more about creating social-emotional classrooms. I used the texts and resources from the Responsive Classroom (www.responsiveclassroom.org). Responsive Classroom is a research-based approach to K–8 teaching that focuses on the strong link between academic success and social-emotional learning. The text *The Power of Our Words* (Denton 2014) influenced the no complaining challenge, *The First Six Weeks of School* (Northeast Foundation for Children Inc. 2000) helped me establish my routines, and the *Morning Meeting Book* (Kriete and Davis 2014) provided ways to build a positive classroom community.

COLLABORATION WITH COLLEAGUES

Through collaboration, a good idea can grow and evolve into something wonderful. Teams that function well together collaborate, and the students benefit from wonderful experiences. Good collaboration is diversity of thought and ideas. Collective genius can occur when the right teams work well together.

Diane, one of my first-grade teacher teammates, always shared her great ideas. She had great project ideas, and she didn't keep them to herself. She included the team, and as a result, more students got to experience these great activities.

One idea she shared was a book jacket fashion show, which is an opportunity for a younger student to pair with an older student to put on a fashion show based on a book they had read together. The two students choose a book, read it together, and then create a book jacket that the younger student "models" while the older student narrates. Together they create invitations that are sent to parents, and both classes create a "fashion show" presentation, including a red carpet stroll and photo ops that parents absolutely love.

The multiage project benefits both classrooms and helps foster a school community. My former students who are now adults always mention how much they enjoyed this event. Students remember what is novel; it's a nice break from the routine and it brings teachers together to collaborate.

CHAPTER 8

Envisioning Endless Possibilities for Education

Envision and Establish Mind-Set

2014–2016—My mentee from the university and I sat across from each other, each of us working on our own writing projects, typing away on our laptops. I noted how distracted I was. I was writing a grant proposal to fund a summer workshop on healthy habits for educators. I minimized my grant document and checked my e-mail for the eighteenth time that day. This was the day I had a feeling the editor from Stenhouse would be "pitching" my book proposal to the review board.

My mentee and I met biweekly to catch up at a local restaurant, and then simply write. Both of us were in the midst of writing a book, several articles, and grants. Our routine was pretty standard: eat, converse and catch up, then write. Our meeting norms were pretty simple as well: Don't interrupt once we finish eating and catching up. I broke our norm. "I can't stand it. I keep checking e-mail to see if Stenhouse has contacted me. This waiting is making me nuts. Listen to the last e-mail they sent." I read aloud the e-mail. "What do you think—is it a hopeful tone?"

As I read aloud the last communication I had received, the editor's name, William Varner, flashed on my screen—I had just received an e-mail from him. "Oh my god, he just e-mailed me."

I scanned the e-mail:

> *Hi Lisa,*
> *Well, I met with everyone this morning. Your voice, vulnerability, and the advice you've learned the hard (and real) way appealed to everyone. So, we'd like to offer you a contract for the book!*

Tears poured down my face. The best way I could describe the excitement was a feeling of relief, extraordinary happiness, and mostly gratitude that my ideas might help others.

This achievement was interesting in that it happened the way most good things in my life occurred. It began with a dream, in which I had envisioned what I wanted. Next the work began: middle-of-the-night writing, endless editing. Throughout the process, I had a deep knowing that I would publish this book.

ENVISION

The future is not some place we're going, but one we are creating. The paths are not to be found, but made. And the activity of making them changes both the maker and their destination.

—JOHN SCHAAR

This final chapter is about envisioning possibilities and maybe remembering why we went into education. Being an educator is a calling, not a job. I believe there are infinite possibilities ahead for the future of education. As teachers, we can't risk standing still. We have to make a choice: do we want to live out of circumstance or live from a vision? This book has provided strategies to become aware of our habitual thinking. We control our thoughts. When we begin to think differently, new feelings emerge and we feel differently, which then allows us to act differently. Different actions create different results.

In the words of the poet Mary Oliver (1990), "Tell me, what is it you plan to do with your one wild and precious life?" (60).

To begin with, let's envision what a fully present teacher would look like. Keep in mind, we are all a work in progress, but this is what we're moving toward, and it is a real possibility.

PORTRAIT OF A PRESENT TEACHER

Teachers who are present love their jobs and just about everything about their lives. They rarely complain, grumble, or moan. There is an acceptance of what is. They accept their teaching assignment, their colleagues, and their students. They look for the good in every situation, and they enjoy the present moment.

These teachers are eternal learners. Every moment represents an opportunity for knowing more. They learn from their students. They are doers and helpers.

They don't worry, so they are free from anxiety. They don't dwell on the past, so they aren't wishing for things to be different than they are. They don't spend present moments ruminating about the past, or worrying about the future. They are independent of the good or bad opinion others may have of them; there is an absence of approval seeking. They are internally directed and content. They smile and laugh often. To them, each day is an adventure. They are honest and hardworking and have the discipline to complete tasks without drama. They are not problem free, but they recover quickly from setbacks and they pursue solutions.

They have the same teacher manuals that everyone else has, but they use them as guides because they know that the present moment offers opportunities that the manual can't anticipate. They don't teach in the same way each year, because each year is different, just as each student is different. When they don't do things right, they try again. They are not afraid of failure. They are creative, and they have high energy. They are never bored because they are always curious. They enjoy teaching and care deeply about their students. Although they are steeped in the present moment, they like to imagine, dream, and envision.

So, let's begin to envision. And let's not dwell on how much needs to be changed, let's focus on the parts that are within our reach. How we show up each day is within our reach. Simply take one present moment at a time.

BRAVE CHANGE AGENTS

Life shrinks or expands in proportion to one's courage.

—ANAIS NIN

We are living in a time of significant change. Citizens are banding together, rising up against current establishments. All over the world, people are working tirelessly to bring about the positive aspects of change. Change is accelerating at a pace that has left few institutions untouched. Let's use this to our advantage. Our educational system could certainly benefit from some thoughtful, brave change agents. As educators, we can play an important role in a pivotal time in education. We have a chance to recommit, to make our schools places where students and teachers look forward to attending and places that foster a new generation of dreamers.

What kind of legacy are you leaving to the next generation? How do you inspire children to be more confident and more involved in creating a better world? Are you actively working to improve the world in a way that will preserve it for the youth? Do you interact with young people in a way that inspires them to follow their dreams and discover their true passions? As educators, one of the greatest gifts we can give is to use words that help ignite dreams. Our language should elicit "possibility thinking" so that challenges are seen as opportunities to grow. Don't ever underestimate the impact you can have; it's farther reaching than you'll ever realize.

BE PRESENT

Are you living each moment for everything it's worth? Do you have the intention, attention, and attitude to show up each day fully present?

One of the worst ways to spend your days is to live only for the time when you are "off" or "retired." What a waste of precious moments. Those who live for the weekends and days off are bypassing about 75 percent of their life. How can you reframe this perspective? Start using the minutes you have more intentionally. There are 1,440 minutes in each day—that's 1,440 opportunities to be fully alive and present.

I am always dismayed to hear seasoned teachers counting down the years until they can retire. They aren't truly present for all the possible moments of each day because they are future focused, as if all the joy in life is boxed up, sent ahead to that magic day when they don't have to roll out of bed and drive to work. Life doesn't work that way. In fact, remember when I mentioned that *after* a stressful event is when we get sick. I've known too many people who retire, and then really retire—meaning they pass and leave this life.

I had a weeklong consulting contract for a summer workshop on integrating writing using the Collins Writing Program. My point of contact was a lovely gentleman who had been in the district for thirty-eight years. Every time I talked with him, he shared how many days he had until he could retire. He had been counting down the days for the last two years of his employment. He shared that my first day of the workshop would be his first day of retirement, but assured me his replacement would greet me and have all the logistics prepared for the workshop. His replacement did greet me and was extremely organized. All of the details—the handouts, food, beverages—were in place, and we began the workshop without a hitch. A few hours later, midmorning, she reappeared, looking distraught. She informed the group that her predecessor had gotten up that morning, went out to start the car to begin his first day of retirement, and had suffered a massive heart attack. He died—on his first day of retirement. Wow. The lesson in this is obvious: live for now, not the idyllic future.

A NEW VISION

When you are inspired . . . dormant forces, faculties, and talents become alive, and you discover yourself to be a greater person by far than you ever dreamed yourself to be.

—PATANJALI

I can't begin to recount all of the innovative ideas I've heard from teachers about creating new visions for the future; my intent here is to spark innovation and invoke possibility thinking. Most new ideas that have resulted in change in our society were at one time scorned. People doubted Einstein and the Wright Brothers and ridiculed the suffragettes and abolitionists. Stop waiting for change; be the change.

EARLY CHILDHOOD AND ELDERLY CARE CENTERS

I have always been an early childhood advocate. The research is clear that the formative years are the most important in a child's development. That early childhood teachers are paid half of what teachers in a K–12 system earn makes absolutely no sense. Another system that is broken is our elderly care. Having firsthand experience of parents and grandparents in nursing homes, I am frustrated at the lack of compensation earned by those working with our older people. I could focus about the inequities and injustices of both of those systems, or I could envision something better.

Imagine if we could have early childhood and retirement centers adjacent so that both could benefit from singing, dancing, drawing, storytelling, and simply enjoying each other's company. I've started to see this happen. I have a video clip that I show to my students at the university of preschool students visiting a nursing home. There is not a dry eye in the class when the video is over and many students vow to start their own early childhood-elderly care centers.

Where there are problems, start dreaming and do what I call *possibility thinking*.

FRIDAY FIELD TRIPS

Another recurrent complaint I hear from teachers is that there is no time to plan creative lessons. Imagine changing the workweek so that every Friday was a day for students to attend field trips, complete special projects, or perform community service work under the guidance of the administrators and specialists in the district. University pre-service students could also participate. Classroom teachers would be given time to plan and collaborate to create engaging, meaningful, creative lessons for the following week and work on curriculum. Administrators need to stay connected to the realities of teaching, and most I know would welcome the change to spend one day a week with students. When I was an administrator, I missed being with the students and would have loved more interaction with them. When we're with students, we remember that they are *all* our students and that we share responsibility for their learning. Rather than shake your head no and think "never in my school," instead think "how in my school?"

LABORATORY SCHOOLS

At the university, our pre-service teachers need to complete field hours, which means they are placed in schools with students to gain various classroom experiences. It is an enormous task to find these placements. I have often wondered why *all* universities with education students don't have infant-through-grade 12 laboratory schools. They could be staffed with preservice students and faculty from the colleges of education, social work, and counselor education. They would be sites for research and hands-on learning. Faculty members could enroll their children, and the children from the local community could also attend. These schools would be focused on innovative techniques and project-based learning. This is already happening in various sites across the county; these are good models that could be replicated and expanded.

THE VILLAGE: UNIVERSITY-COMMUNITY PARTNERSHIP

In the middle of our small town, within walking distance from the university, a beautiful building stood vacant. Every time I walked by, I envisioned all the possibilities that could be housed to benefit the community in that building. I imagined the college students who were majoring in social work holding parent workshops while education majors tutored the parents' children. One room could hold adult and child exercise classes taught by the kinesiology students. A healthy juice and smoothie bar would be a place where the nutrition majors offered classes on healthy eating and food preparation. Meditation classes could be offered for adults and children by the students majoring in contemplative studies. The possibilities are endless.

CONTEMPLATIVE CENTER

When I first arrived at the university, I learned that it housed a stress reduction center. I searched for the building and found only a professor in her office. She and a handful of other professors *were* the center—no building, no funding, just some mindful people with a vision. She has since moved on to facilitate workshops for teachers using a program she developed, Learning to Breathe (learning2breathe.org). With another colleague, I conducted a research study using this program with preservice teachers. We found that the mindfulness training helped these future teachers control impulsive behavior and respond more flexibly to stressful emotions (Kerr et al. 2017; Lucas and Kerr 2016). The results provided evidence for the usefulness of mindfulness training to enhance emotional well-being in preservice teachers. I have no doubt that society needs future educators to be not only academically competent but also emotionally balanced to educate the next generation.

A decade ago, mindfulness in education was perceived as odd; today, mindfulness in education is mainstream and there are a number of available resources, many of which I've provided in the Resources section. Now at the university, we have a Contemplative Center on campus. This is an actual facility where students and teachers can meditate and participate in a variety of contemplative activities such as yoga and t'ai chi ch'uan. This dream began years ago when I met that professor in her office, and it has slowly evolved. Imagine if *all* schools could have a contemplative room on site, a place for teachers to read, meditate, and find stillness.

PATHWAYS TO PRESENCE: IGNITING MORE VISIONS

We must not, in trying to think about how we can make a big difference, ignore the small daily differences we can make which, over time, add up to big differences that we often cannot foresee.

—MARIAN WRIGHT EDELMAN

Deep down, I always felt I was called to do something, but I was never quite sure *what* that something was. I think we all feel that way, but so often we let others dim our light.

This book began as a vision: that it will encourage educators to be present, so that they can contribute to a culture of kindness and compassion, beginning with themselves. Having a teaching force of happier, emotionally balanced teachers is not only good for society, schools, and students, it's good for us as individuals. Students don't remember the administration or the name of the superintendent, but they remember the teacher who encouraged them to express their opinions and who cared about them. They felt "seen" because that teacher was present. I intentionally focused this book on teachers rather than students. System change begins with personal change. For us to improve the current system, we have to operate from a place of presence.

Let's approach each day from a place of positivity, so that we are in a better position to optimistically influence our students. We have to not only practice what we preach, but model what we believe. Our ability to foster sustainable growth and development of our students rests on our own inner state. That's why intentional words and actions are so important.

You can be the architect of the new systems we create. This book has given you a process. First, get clear and center yourself. Next, use what you've learned to foster in others the desire to become more balanced. You won't have to say a word; they will notice your calm demeanor and will wonder what changed. A calm, confident inner knowing precedes a compelling vision. Our work as teachers provides us with a unique opportunity to model living authentically, from a place of presence. This isn't a book on being present only for yourself; the purpose is for you to be a light in the world to ignite sparks everywhere. We receive what we give, and then, somehow, we receive more and the cycle continues.

Personal Practices to Support Mindful Teaching

If you want to teach people a new way of thinking, don't bother trying to lecture or instruct them. Instead, give them a tool, the use of which will lead to new ways of thinking.

—BUCKMINSTER FULLER

This text has been intentionally filled with tools that will lead to a new way of thinking, which can result in a new way of being. We get further by doing something small every day, and before you know it, all those small acts end by changing our lives in ways we could have never managed.

Remember, reading this entire book won't change a thing, until you take action. As teachers, we've been conditioned to assume that we can read a book and comprehend the main idea. That may be true, but superficial comprehension isn't the goal here, real knowing is, and that has to be felt, not with just our brains, but with our whole self. You have to actually try the strategies outlined in this book if you want to really know them. Some will work for you, others you might discard, but none of them will work if you don't actually try them on for size.

ENVISION AND ESTABLISH MIND-SET

We need time to dream, time to remember and time to reach the infinite. Time to be.

—GLADYS TABER

To envision something different, something better, or something more interesting is to push the existing world into a state of change. Some of the greatest revolutionary acts of our time came to be because someone had the courage to imagine something new. Nothing has ever been created that wasn't first imagined. So if our imagination creates our reality, then we can see ourselves as alchemists, able to transform society and the culture at large with our thoughts, words, and ideas. We can begin the process of change by documenting our ideas. Let's envision something radically better, for ourselves and our students.

BEGIN WITH A LIST

Make a list of all the things you would like to do as an educator, but believe you cannot. Question and look fearlessly and honestly at the limitations you've imposed upon yourself. Adopt possibility thinking. Our lives are meant to be adventures where we dream, envision, and expand. Now more than ever we need to be brave; we're investing in the most precious commodity in the world, our children.

What would you like to change, create, or modify about our educational system? This is a brainstorming exercise meant to elicit possibility thinking. Think about what would best serve our students.

The process below may help expand your vision.

Envisioning Process

No more than twenty minutes are required for this exercise.

This is a short and powerful process to brainstorm ideas. It can be used with departments, grade-level teams, anywhere people want to brainstorm possibilities.

Roles to be played:

- Teacher/envisioner
- Process facilitator
- Timekeeper
- Recorder (notetaker)
- Brainstorm team

It begins with a teacher who has a vision. Gather together three to five trusted colleagues. Assign a timekeeper and a notetaker. All participants are part of the brainstorm team.

As a warm-up activity, have the team brainstorm anything for one minute (types of cereals, movies, books, favorite beverages). This is needed to get everyone in the brainstorm mode.

Steps

Step One

(4 minutes) The teacher has four uninterrupted minutes to *describe the vision*. The process facilitator makes sure no one interrupts. The recorder takes notes. Everyone else stays silent until the four minutes pass. This is key! The teacher gets four *uninterrupted* minutes.

(2 minutes) The brainstorm team can ask a clarifying question if needed related to the goal or desired outcome.

Step Two

(4 minutes) This is a brainstorm. Everyone chimes in with ideas about creative options regarding what they just heard. It is *not* a time to clarify the details or to ask questions. It is not a time to give speeches, lectures, or advice. The notetaker keeps record and numbers the ideas. The process facilitator must make sure this is a brainstorm. Everyone gets a chance to contribute his or her brilliant ideas. No one must be allowed to dominate. The teacher listens without interrupting. He or she must not talk or respond.

Step Three

(5 minutes) Now the group has a dialogue led by the facilitator; the goal is to have the teacher select a direction. *Focus on the positive points only* and not on what can't be done.

Step Four

(5 minutes) The process facilitator asks the teacher to determine steps that are doable using the Action Plan Template. The recorder records these notes on the Action Plan Template.

ACTION PLAN TEMPLATE

Use this Action Plan Template to identify specific steps you need to take to achieve the vision. Tip: Make each action step as simple and specific as possible, breaking down complex actions into single steps.

OVERARCHING VISION

VISION	RESPONSIBLE PERSON	TIME LINE	NECESSARY RESOURCES	POTENTIAL CHALLENGES	POSSIBILITIES
What needs to be done?	Who could take action to complete this step?	When could this step be completed?	What do you need to complete this step?	Are there any potential challenges that may impede completion? How will you overcome them?	Any new possibilities identified in the process?

INDECISION: FLIP A COIN—NOT THE WAY YOU THINK!

The longer we are able to hold a positive thought, the stronger that energy around us becomes.

—MADISYN TAYLOR

Sometimes you are torn about where to invest your energy. You may be torn between two choices. I have a process that works every time. First, find a coin. Before flipping, designate heads one option, tails the other. Imagine that you will commit to whichever the coin lands on. Flip the coin and notice your intuitive reaction to the result. If you feel delighted, that is your decision; if you are disappointed, go with the other alternative. This helps hone your inner compass.

BANISH DOUBTS

Finish each day and be done with it. You have done what you could. Some blunders and absurdities have crept in; forget them as soon as you can. Tomorrow is a new day. You shall begin it serenely and with too high a spirit to be encumbered with your old nonsense.

—RALPH WALDO EMERSON

Interrupting a pattern of negativity takes a great deal more work than simply beginning the day with a clear intention and a purposeful, planned practice. Pay attention to your energy before it hijacks you into negative thinking. *Act as if* what you want to feel is already happening.

Be careful who you share your vision with—naysayers can cause you to doubt yourself. Sadly, not everyone wants to see your dreams come true. You know who your real supporters are; only share with them. Often our dreams take us away from the status quo, and for close friends and family, that may not always be comfortable. I used to say, "Don't go to the gas station for milk," but now our gas stations actually do sell milk. You know what I mean. Don't assume everyone who loves you will be behind your dreams. If you do start to doubt yourself, be aware, and put the brakes on.

If you still feel less than optimistic, you may try to reach for a better-feeling emotion. Aim for an emotion that is just a tad better than where you are. You are trying to find thoughts that give you relief from the current emotion you are feeling. It's a way of deliberately setting an intention that induces an emotion that moves you up the vibrational scale to a better feeling. An improved feeling means releasing resistance, and releasing resistance means a greater state of allowing what you really want.

One of the ways to reach that better-feeling emotion is to cycle back to what I shared about gratitude. We can always find something to be grateful for. If you've truly incorporated that practice into your daily life, you might be ready for a variation on the practice. I've added another gratitude practices to my morning in an effort not to get complacent with my usual routine.

Envision one person in your life and think of five things you are grateful to that person for. Or, choose someone at work you are having a difficult time with and keep focusing on your co-worker's positive attributes. It really doesn't matter what process you use; the goal is to shift the energy to have more optimal, inspired thoughts.

Trying to achieve that better-feeling emotion is where my beliefs differ from traditional mindfulness and the books on mindfulness in education. Traditional mindfulness focuses on being OK with what is, accepting, and not resisting the emotions you are feeling. Although I agree with not resisting the emotions you are feeling, I suggest reaching for a better emotion that can move you forward.

MASTERMIND CABINET

"One can't believe impossible things," Alice said. "I daresay you haven't had much practice," said the Queen. "When I was your age, I always did it for half an hour a day. Why, sometimes I've believed as many as six impossible things before breakfast."

—LEWIS CARROLL

Admittedly, this process is a little out there, but it's better than ruminating and feeling stuck about a conflict or problem. Often right before I fall asleep, I call a meeting of those I respect most in the world. I call them my "cabinet." They consist of the world's greatest thinkers, and I pose my possibility thinking to them and then let it go. My cabinet consists of those living and nonliving. Right now I have an author and coach whose work I respect, a nun who was my mentor when I started teaching, and my Dad, the former newspaper editor, in my cabinet. My cabinet changes according to the topic. The number of times I've woken up with greater clarity has convinced me it's a process worth keeping.

JUST IMAGINE

The future belongs to those who believe in the beauty of their dreams.

—ELEANOR ROOSEVELT

We know now that the research is clear: What you think about truly affects your mind-set. The problem is that you can't fake your way out of what you really think, because your body feels the difference. So, when you need a perspective change, take the time first thing in the morning, before you go out and encounter the stresses of the world, to imagine the way you'd like things to be. Envision as clearly as you can the outcome. What you are actually doing is reprogramming your mind to focus on what you want, rather than what you don't want. You will notice that you start to see more of what you want in your everyday life. Whatever you pay attention to grows; attention is focused awareness. Paying attention allows you to fully engage in the moment. Focused intention is the source of most creative, successful endeavors.

Keep in mind that you don't need to know how exactly you're going to achieve what you want, but you do need to be clear on the desired outcome.

CLARIFY YOUR VISION OF SCHOOLS AS LEARNING ORGANIZATIONS
Thoughts are energy and you can make your world or
break your world by your thinking.

—SUSAN TAYLOR

The building blocks of a better educational system are its teachers. *We* can significantly affect a child's development and the future of our society. Investing the time to clarify what is important to us so that we operate from a place of intentional purpose and vision has to happen or we'll remain stagnant and aimless. The very place to begin the change process is within us.

One of the things I realized about myself when I first started envisioning was how very little detail I was able to provide about what I wanted. Clarity was clearly missing. My thoughts were scattered in a variety of directions.

This actually made sense. I am a "big picture" type of thinker; I'm great at creative brainstorming, but that old adage that the devil is in the details is my downfall. So to get clear about what I wanted, I had to really focus. If my attention was murky, my outcomes were murky. I had to invest the time to get clear. With clarity came focus, and I began to relax and not try so hard. Once you achieve clarity, the right people, books, opportunities, and information flow toward you. When we are ready to transform, we realize that we already had everything we needed, inside. When I applied my mind to a specific vision, one that I was passionate about, my thoughts gathered together and became undistracted. I could then simply respond to the opportunities that naturally came my way. However, to get to this place, I had to get quiet.

SOLITUDE
The ability to be alone, with your own thoughts and no distractions, can take some practice. It's called *solitude*, and our best thoughts often come when we're quiet. The process that follows is incredibly simple, but can yield profound insights. Try repeating a mantra from the book *A Course in Miracles* (Schucman 1976):

> *Where would you have me go?*
> *What would you have me do?*
> *What would you have me say, and to whom?*

Then, try to really listen to inner guidance. This is the hardest part. To listen when your head is full of different thoughts is a real challenge. Learning to silence the thoughts and tune in to the wise, still voice takes practice. I developed a two-minute micro-meditation to help get you there.

ONE PERSON'S WEED IS ANOTHER'S WILDFLOWER

People are like stained glass windows: They sparkle and shine when the sun is out, but when the darkness sets in their true beauty is revealed only if there is a light within.

—ELISABETH KÜBLER-ROSS

As a child, I often sat in the front yard, blowing those white balls of dandelion seeds that I called wishes. I would close my eyes, and they would scatter. One day my Mom saw me, and she reprimanded me, explaining that I was making more weeds and that I was ruining the yard. I wondered why she thought the "wishes" were weeds; to me, they were thousands of opportunities for my wishes to come true. On the day of her funeral, as I came down Pepperdine Hill, I glanced to the left, and the entire sky—and I mean the entire sky—was filled with wishes. It was like being in a cloud of happiness. I have never seen anything like it. In that moment, I had a flash of recollection.

I recalled how unbeknownst to my mom, when I was little I had continued blowing wishes, but had done my wishing from high up in a tree. A memory flashed in my head of pretending to be a superhero, picking all the wishes, stuffing them in my navy blue sweatshirt pocket, and climbing up as far as I could in the tree in our front yard to make wishes for everything I thought would make the world a better place.

I could hear my mom telling me, "Lisa, you are a bright light, and others want nothing more than to snuff out that light. Don't you dare let them."

Don't let anyone dim your light; your vision may be someone else's weed, but that doesn't matter. Follow your dreams. Try and recall what you wanted to do when you were young and life hadn't yet got a hold of you. Take stock and remember why you really want to be a teacher. There is no nobler occupation. If you want to experience greater joy and fulfillment in your role as a teacher, be the teacher you always dreamed of being.

IGNITE A VISION IN OTHERS

Change the story and you change perception; change perception and you change the world.

—JEAN HOUSTON

As educators, we need to be the activists who bring peace, presence, and clarity to the educational systems that are failing our youngest, our brightest, and our poorest. There is no time like the present; in fact, it's all we have.

How do you inspire other people? Do you help people laugh or ponder a question that perhaps they have never thought of before? Can you help others reframe problems as possibilities? Do you add value to the lives of people you may only interact with once, but know they will somehow look at things differently after meeting you? Do you help your colleagues see the potential in a struggling student? Can you inspire others to follow their visions? When we live inspired lives, we have more energy, enthusiasm, and passion. We enjoy the present moment.

Hopefully you've adopted some new habits as a result of this book. If you haven't, all I can hope is that I've planted a seed. I'm well aware that often we don't see the effects of our efforts and that things can lie dormant before taking form.

Whatever you think you can do, or believe you can do, begin it, because action has magic, grace, and power in it. The moment one definitely commits oneself, then Providence moves too. All sorts of things occur to help one that would have never otherwise occurred . . . unforeseen incidents, meetings, and material assistance which no man could have dreamed would have come his way.

JOHAN WOLFGANG VON GOETHE AND W. H. MURRAY (THE SCOTTISH HIMALAYAN EXPEDITION)

Resources

Chapter 1

Practicing Presence: This is my own website for information on coaching, educational consulting, and workshops: www.practicingpresence.life.

***Everybody Present: Mindfulness in Education* by Nikolja Flor Rotne and Didde Flor Rotne**: *Everybody Present* is a wonderful primer for those who want to explore more about the transformative effects of mindfulness on educators, students, and their classrooms.

***Peace in the Present Moment* by Eckhart Tolle and Byron Katie**: This small book combines beautiful photography with quotes from two popular spiritual writers.

***Gratitude: A Journal* by Catherine Price**: Keep a daily record with this gratitude journal filled with a year worth of insightful prompts, inspiring quotes, and ample room for reflecting on all the things that you are thankful for.

***Living in the Moment* by Anna Black**: This book contains short and simple meditations that can be done anywhere.

***The Precious Present* by Spencer Johnson**: This simple parable about finding presence in a fast-paced world will give you something to muse about. Although it can be easily read in less than 30 minutes, I recommend reading it slowly—it's meant to be thought-provoking.

Chapter 2

"Positive Emotions Broaden and Build" by Barbara Fredrickson: The work of Fredrickson and her colleagues has made an impact on the study of happiness. They advocate that we should all strive for "happiness habits" of the positive emotions (specifically the "big ten" most common positive emotions: joy, gratitude, serenity, interest, hope, pride, amusement, inspiration, awe, and love).

The Greater Good magazine: Published by the Greater Good Science Center at the University of California, Berkeley, this magazine has an abundance of resources that support these "happiness habits." (greatergood.berkeley.edu/about)

Sleep Phones: When I wake in the middle of the night, instead of beginning the vicious cycle of rumination, I have a plan. I purchased something called sleep phones. They are developed by a family doctor to provide a safe, all-natural way to provide restful, audio-assisted relaxation without bulky headphones or uncomfortable earbuds. (www.sleepphones.com/)

Yale Center for Emotional Intelligence: The *Emotion Revolution for Educators* is a joint initiative between the Yale Center for Emotional Intelligence and the nonprofit organization New Teacher Center. Their mission is to build awareness around the critical role of emotions in teaching, learning, and educator wellness and effectiveness. (ei.yale.edu/what-we-do/emotion-revolution-educator/)

"7 Little-Known Benefits of Sunlight" by Dr. Michael Murray: This is a quick read on the benefits and cautions of sun exposure. (www.care2.com/greenliving/7-little-known-benefits-of-sunlight.html#ixzz3rgvqf2G6)

HeartMath Institute: HeartMath provides research regarding psychophysiology, heart-brain interactions, and coherence. (www.heartmath.org/research/research-library/)

The Penn Program for Mindfulness: Operated within a variety of centers in and around Philadelphia and New Jersey, this program adapts traditional meditation-based techniques to make them practical, easy to learn, and relevant to modern life. (www.pennmedicine.org/mindfulness/)

Responsive Classroom: This evidence-based approach to elementary and middle school teaching focuses on the strong link between academic success and social-emotional learning. (www.responsiveclassroom.org/about/research/)

"Reminder to Pause" Bracelet: I wear this bracelet that often reminds me to reframe my thoughts. (www.mcssl.com/store/meaningtopause/)

Mindfulness Apps:
- Calm (itunes.apple.com/us/app/calm-meditate-sleep-relax/id571800810)
- ConZentrate (itunes.apple.com/us/app/conzentrate/id493897333)
- Get Some Headspace (getsomeheadspace.com/shop/headspace-meditation-app. aspx)
- Insight Timer (insighttimer.com)
- Mind (itunes.apple.com/us/app/id419702358)
- The Mindfulness App (www.mindapps.se/)
- Mindfulness Daily (mindfulnessdailyapp.com)
- Mindfulness Meditation (www.mentalworkout.com/store/programs/mindfulness-meditation/)
- Simply Being: Guided Meditation for Relaxation and Presence (itunes.apple.com/us/app/simply-being-guided-mediation/id347418999)

Chapter 3

"Why Your DNA Isn't Your Destiny" by John Cloud: This article in Time magazine describes how the field of epigenetics is showing the way your environment and your choices can influence your genetic code and that of your children. (www.time.com/time/magazine/article/0,9171,1952313,00.html#ixzz1uYwktiRt)

The Biology of Belief **by Bruce Lipton:** In its simplest form, epigenetics proves that our perceptions of life shape our biology. The old belief that biology is destiny is no longer true. That's why Bruce Lipton, a cell biologist, authored a groundbreaking book that exposed how a cell's life is controlled by the physical and energetic environment and not solely by its genes. Lipton explains that the genes you are born with are basically fixed but do not control how you will live. The choices you make can contribute to whether these genes turn on or off. Just like a single cell, the character of our lives is determined not by our genes but by our response to the environment.

Super Genes: Unlock the Astonishing Power of Your DNA for Optimum Health and Well-Being **by Deepak Chopra and Rudolph Tanzi:** Chopra and Tanzi concur with Lipton's theory and assert that our genes are fluid, dynamic, and responsive to everything we think and do. The basis for their book is that gene activity is largely under our control.

Who Gets Sick? **by Blair Justice**: In his book, Justice estimates that genes account for about 35 percent of longevity, and lifestyles, diet, and other environmental factors, including support systems, are the major reasons people live longer. Our consciousness—our beliefs, prayers, thoughts, intentions, and faith—often correlate much more strongly with our health, longevity, and happiness than our genes do. After reading the research, I was struck by the importance of support systems, and I realized my lack of support was a tremendous issue.

The Extraordinary Healing Power of Ordinary Things **and** *One Mind* **by Larry Dossey:** The executive editor of *Explore*: *The Journal of Science and Healing* offers another important perspective. In his latest books, Dossey reports on several studies that indicate that what one *thinks* about one's health is the most accurate prediction of longevity.

Affirmations: Wanting to think more positively, I committed to memory a handful of positive affirmations. Affirmations are simply short, powerful statements that you intentionally think. Various sources have estimated that, on average, we have between 45,000 and 60,000 thoughts a day and for most people 80 percent of those thoughts are negative. Left to my own devices I could fall into habitual thinking which wasn't always positive but taking this research into consideration, I intentionally developed a more vigilant thought system. I crafted a list of positive affirmations and every day chose an affirmation that felt appropriate. I also sent those that participated in my Healthy Habits Workshops an affirmation on "Mindful Monday."

Having repeated these so often now, they are thought systems in my problem-solving repertoire that are at my disposal. The following list includes some of my favorite affirmations for general well-being and having too much to do, but consider developing your own.

- My day begins and ends with gratitude and joy.
- Opportunities are everywhere. I have a multitude of choices.
- I see the best in everyone.
- I get the help I need, when I need it, from various sources.
- My support system is strong and loving.
- Everyone I meet today has my best interest at heart.

- I view all experiences as opportunities for me to learn and grow.
- I am willing to slow down and take the time to nourish myself.
- Everything will get done; there is enough time in this day for everything I need to complete.
- I am clear, focused, and productive.
- I see what needs to be done with precision and clarity.
- I will remember to be present, and do one thing at a time.

Chapter 4

The Harvard Medical School Guide to a Good Night's Sleep **by Lawrence Epstein with Steven Mardon**: Epstein details his six-step plan for overcoming sleep problems.

Bella Grace **Magazine**: This 160-page publication features beautifully penned stories and striking photographs that capture life's beautiful journey. (stampington.com/bella-grace)

The Art of Extreme Self-Care **by Cheryl Richardson**: In this book, Richardson guides you through a year of strategies to transform your life one month at a time.

Kripalu Center for Yoga and Health: This beautiful retreat center in Lenox, Massachusetts offers hundreds of transformative programs and trainings designed to inspire, educate, and empower. (www.kripalu.org)

Omega Institute: Located in Rhinebeck, New York, Omega offers diverse and innovative educational experiences that inspire an integrated approach to personal and social change. (www.eomega.org)

Mindful Awareness Research Center: MARC is located at the University of California, Los Angeles, and also offers free guided meditations on their website. (http://marc.ucla.edu/body.cfm?id=22)

Franklin Covey Planners: These planners help keep me organized. (franklinplanner.fcorgp.com/store/)

Chapter 5

Collins Writing Program: This phenomenal program provides teachers, schools, and districts with a unified, research-based writing program that can be used successfully in all classrooms and all subjects. Although it's designed for K—12, I continue to use the principles of Collins Writing in my university classroom. This program is the best writing program I've ever encountered. (collinsed.com/)

Responsive Classroom Zenergy Chime: A great audio signal to get students' attention. A great gift for student teachers! (www.responsiveclassroom.org/product/zenergy-chime/)

Mind Yeti: Mindfulness for Kids: Guided mindfulness sessions to help calm children, focus their attention, and prepare for whatever's next. (www.mindyeti.com/)

GoNoodle: GoNoodle provides movement and mindful exercises. (www.gonoodle.com/)

"Are You Breathing? Do You Have E-mail Apnea?" by Linda Stone: This article suggests that not only are many of us suffering from too much screen time, we're also experiencing "screen apnea," temporary cessation of breath or shallow breathing while working in front of screens. (lindastone.net/2014/11/24/are-you-breathing-do-you-have-email-apnea/)

"Creative People Say No" by Kevin Ashton: This is an excerpt from *How to Fly a Horse: The Secret History of Creation, Invention and Discovery* by Kevin Ashton. Reading this helps diminish any guilt you may feel when you respond no. (medium. com/@kevin_ashton/creative-people-say-no-bad7c34842a2)

Sound Sleeping: This online sound generator is great for creating background white noise to help with sleep. (www.soundsleeping.com)

Holosync: I've used this form of neuro-audio technology to relax before going to sleep. It's an audio technology designed to support meditation. (www.centerpointe.com)

"All It Takes Is 10 Mindful Minutes" by Andy Puddicombe: In this TED Talk, mindfulness expert Puddicombe describes how 10 minutes of "doing nothing" can be life-changing. (www.ted.com/talks/andy_puddicombe_all_it_takes_is_10_mindful_minutes)

CARE for Teachers: Developed by the Garrison Institute, this professional development program uses mindfulness to help teachers cope with stress and burnout. When I attended this conference, I formed wonderful connections with many mindful educators and left with lots of print resources. (www.care4teachers.com/)

Mindmapping: Mindmaps can be a great tool for thinking/brainstorming and visually organizing information. (www.tonybuzan.com/about/mind-mapping/)

Mindful **Magazine**: This magazine features stories, advice, and practices to live a more mindful life. (www.mindful.org/magazine/)

Chapter 6

Neuroscience for Kids: This website provides lots of brain information and interactive activities for students and features clear illustrations of a brain. (www.Neuroscienceforkids.com/)

Happiness Quiz: This quiz is based on numerous scientific studies that focus on lifestyles and habits that relate to long-term psychological well-being. (www.pursuit-of-happiness.org/science-of-happiness/happiness-quiz/)

RADteach: This blog by Judy Willis contains an abundance of information on neuroplasticity. (www.radteach.com)

Richie Davidson: The founder of the Center for Investigating Healthy Minds at the University of Wisconsin-Madison has a website detailing his research. (richardjdavidson.com/research/)

Animoto: Use this website to create a video online to summarize information from class or readings. (www.animoto.com)

Make Beliefs Comix: Students love making their own comics. This site includes summarizing, storytelling, and plot description activities. (www.makebeliefscomix.com/)

Tagxedo: Here, students make word clouds to illustrate "big ideas" in text. (www.tagxedo.com/)

Mindful Intentions **by Louie Schwartzberg and Miraval**: This book is full of breathtaking photographs that are paired with quotations and intentions. Miraval is a resort with a reputation as the destination for the practice of mindfulness and creating life balance.

"The Happiness Revolution": This great YouTube video details how to truly obtain happiness. (www.youtube.com/watch?v=17FaSaEZOZI)

Chapter 7

Appreciative Inquiry (AI) Commons: AI is about the search for the best in people and their organizations, creating a fundamental shift in the overall perspective toward seeing a system's strengths, possibilities, and potential throughout the process of organizational change. (appreciativeinquiry.champlain.edu/learn/appreciative-inquiry-introduction/)

The No Complaining Rule **by Jon Gordon**: This book helps to create a positive culture. (jongordon.com/books/no-complaining-rule/)

Exchange **Magazine**: This magazine supports early childhood education professionals worldwide in their efforts to craft thriving environments for children and adults. (www.childcareexchange.com/home/)

Just Listen **by Mark Goulston**: Goulston's book gives you tools to get along with absolutely anyone.

The Center for Courage and Renewal: This website has an abundance of resources related to four compelling themes: the shape of an integral life, the meaning of community, teaching and learning for transformation, and nonviolent social change. It features the work of Parker Palmer. (www.couragerenewal.org/resources/books)

The Cooperative Classroom: Empowering Learning by **Lynda Baloche:** This text is a phenomenal resource that guides teachers learning the skills needed to empower their students and themselves in classrooms where cooperation is a way of being. Lynda shared her resources and helped me better understand how to create a cooperative learning environment.

Real Happiness At Work: Meditations for Accomplishment, Achievement, and Peace by **Sharon Salsberg:** We used this book for our book club in our Teaching, Learning, and Assessment Center at the university.

Chapter 8

Imagine: What America Could Be in the 21st Century **edited by Marianne Williamson:** This multiauthor text is a collective response to the realm of highest possibilities for America.

Inspiration 365 Days a Year by **Zig Ziglar**: This is a book full of inspiring quotes and photographs.

TED: This is the place to go to find out what the world's greatest thinkers are pondering. For those of you who are inspired to do your own TED talk, the book *TED Talks* by Chis Anderson is a must read. It's the official TED guide to public speaking. (www.ted.com)

Wisdom 2.0 Conference: These are regular gatherings for those passionate about living with greater mindfulness, meaning, and wisdom in our modern age. (www.wisdom2summit.com/)

Inward Bound Mindfulness Education: This nonprofit is doing some amazing work around mindfulness with teens and parents. (ibme.info/)

"Dos and Don'ts When Teaching Mindfulness" by Deborah Schoeberlein David: This *Huffington Post* article provides some advice about whether or not to bring mindfulness to your classroom. (www.huffingtonpost.com/deborah-schoeberlein/mindfulness-practice_b_2629114.html)

The Greater Good: The Science of a Meaningful Life: This site provides science-based insights for a meaningful life. Every year the Greater Good holds a summer institute for educators at the University of California, Berkeley, where they provide the latest research and articles on mindfulness. It was a phenomenal professional development experience and the website has an abundance of valuable resources. (greatergood.berkeley.edu/)

Passageworks Institute: The website for the Institute is full of resources to support engaged teaching activities. I use the text *The 5 Dimensions of Engaged Teaching* in my Engaging Learners course at the university. (http://passageworks.org/)

The Center for Contemplative Mind in Society: The Center supports the use of contemplative practices and perspectives to create active learning and a research environment in service of a more just and compassionate society. (www.contemplativemind.org)

Center for Courage and Renewal: This center provides online resources and retreats and programs using the Circle of Trust approach. (www.couragerenewal.org)

Center for Mindfulness at University of Massachusetts Medical School: This center at UMASS offers the traditional MBSR program. (www.umassmed.edu/cfm/index.aspx)

Collaborative for Academic, Social, and Emotional Learning (CASEL): The mission of CASEL is to help make evidence-based social and emotional learning an integral part of schools. (www.casel.org)

Garrison Institute: The signature program, CARE for Teachers, is a unique professional development program that introduces contemplative techniques to educators to enhance their well-being and help them create school environments that support children emotionally, socially, and academically. This conference provided me with practical resources and the retreat center was so peaceful I never wanted to leave. (www.garrisoninstitute.org)

Learning to BREATHE (L2B): This sequenced mindfulness program can be used to introduce adolescents to the practice of mindfulness. L2B is appropriate for many settings (e.g. schools, universities, clinical settings, after-school programs, residential facilities, etc.). CASEL includes L2B as one out of only four programs in the mindfulness category that meet their standards for evidence-based programs. I used this program with my student teachers at the university. I highly recommend this program. (www.learning2breathe.org)

Mindfulness in Education Network (MIEN): MIEN sees mindfulness as an anecdote to conflict and confusion in educational settings. I've attended their annual conference for many years and always leave rejuvenated and optimistic about the future of our schools. (www.mindfuled.org)

Mindful Schools: This organization supports and trains educators to bring mindfulness into schools. (www.mindfulschools.org/)

Mindfulness in Schools Project: .b (pronounced "dot be") is the UK's leading mindfulness curriculum for 11- to 18-year-olds in schools. .b stands for "stop and be," a simple practice at the heart of this ten-lesson course. (mindfulnessinschools.org/what-is-b/b-curriculum/)

MindUP: This program, a product of the Hawn Foundation, was created with educators, for educators to help students improve focus and engagement in learning. (mindup.org/)

The American Mindfulness Research Association (AMRA): The mission of AMRA is to support empirical and conceptual efforts to establish an evidence base for the process, practice, and construct of mindfulness; promote best evidence-based standards for the use of mindfulness research and its applications; and facilitate discovery and professional development through grant giving. (goamra.org/)

References

AI Commons. "Introduction to Appreciative Inquiry." https://appreciativeinquiry.case.edu/intro/whatisai.cfm.

American Psychological Association. 2013. *Stress in America: Missing the Health Care Connection*. American Psychological Association. https://www.apa.org/news/press/releases/stress/2012/full-report.pdf.

Beck, M. 2001. *Finding Your Own North Star*. New York: Three Rivers Press.

Bowers, T. 2004. "Stress, Teaching and Teacher Health." *Education* 13 (32): 73–80.

Boyle, G. 2011. *Tattoos on the Heart: The Power of Boundless Compassion*. Tampa, FL: Free Press.

Braden, G. 2008. *The Spontaneous Healing of Belief: Shattering the Paradigm of False Limits*. Carlsbad, CA: Hay House.

Breaux, A. L., and H. K. Wong. 2003. *New Teacher Induction: How to Train, Support, and Retain New Teachers*. Mountain View, CA: Harry K. Wong P.

Breines, J. 2015. *Four Great Gratitude Strategies*. https://greatergood.berkeley.edu/article/item/four_great_gratitude_strategies

Broderick, P. C. 2013. *Learning to Breathe: A Mindfulness Curriculum for Adolescents to Cultivate Emotion Regulation, Attention, and Performance*. Oakland, CA: New Harbinger.

Brooks, R. 2016. "The Power of Mindsets: Promoting Positive School Climates and Motivation in Students." Summer institute, the Learning and the Brain, Boston, MA.

———. 2015. *Positive Emotions and Purpose in the Classroom*. http://www.drrobertbrooks.com/positive-emotions-and-purpose-in-the-classroom/

Brooks, R., S. Brooks, and S. Goldstein. 2012. "The Power of Mindset: Nurturing Engagement, Motivation, and Resilience in Students." In *Handbook of Research on Student Engagement*, ed. S. Christenson, A. Reschly, and C. Wylie. New York: Springer.

Burns, D. 1989. *The Feeling Good Handbook*. New York: William Morrow.

Cameron, J. 2002. *The Artist's Way: A Spiritual Path to Higher Creativity*. New York: Penguin Putnam.

Carter, C. 2016. *Tuesday Tip: Focus On One Thing At A Time*. https://www.mindful.org/achieve-more-by-doing-less/

———. 2015. *The Sweet Spot: How to Find Your Groove at Home and Work*. New York: Ballantine Books.

———. 2015. "Achieve More By Doing Less." *Mindful*. https://www.mindful.org/achieve-more-by-doing-less/

Carter, T., and T. Gilovich. 2012. "I Am What I Do, Not What I Have: The Differential Centrality of Experiential Material Purchases to the Self." *Journal of Personality and Social Psychology* 102 (6): 1304–1307.

Chang, M. 2009. "An Appraisal Perspective of Teacher Burnout: Examining the Emotional Work of Teachers." *Educational Psychology Review* 21: 193–218.

Chiesa, A., R. Calati, and A. Serretti. 2011. "Does Mindfulness Training Improve Cognitive Abilities? A Systematic Review of Neuropsychological Findings." *Clinical Psychology Review* 31: 449–464.

Chopra, D. 2013. "The Conscious Lifestyle: Awareness Skills—Holding Focus." LinkedIn. https://www.linkedin.com/pulse/20130511004156-75054000-the-conscious-lifestyle-awareness-skills-holding-focus

Chopra, D., and R. Tanzim. 2015. *Super Genes: Unlock the Astonishing Power of Your DNA for Optimum Health and Well-Being*. New York: Harmony Books.

Christakis, N., and J. Fowler. 2008. *Dynamic Spread of Happiness in a Large Social Network: Longitudinal Analysis over 20 Years in the Framingham Heart Study*. British Medical Journal. http://www.bmj.com/content/337/bmj.a2338.full

Church, D. 2008. *The Genie in Your Genes: Epigenetic Medicine and the New Biology of Intention*. Santa Rosa, CA: Energy Psychology.

Cloud, J. 2010. "Why Your DNA Isn't Your Destiny." *Time*. http://content.time.com/time/magazine/article/0,9171,1952313,00.html#ixzz1uYwktiRt

Cohen, A. 1996. *A Deep Breath of Life: Daily Inspiration for Heart-Centered Living*. Carlsbad, CA: Hay House.

Collins Education Associates. 2016. "Is Oral Reading Still the Best Way to Check Your Work?" *Collins Writing Program Blog*. http://collinsed.com/2016/10/15/is-oral-reading-still-the-best-way-to-check-your-work/.

Csikszentmihalyi, M. 1990. *Flow: The Psychology of Optimal Experience*. New York: Harper Collins.

Dalai Lama, and C. Cutler. 1988. *The Art of Happiness: A Handbook for Living*. New York: Riverhead Books.

Davidson, R. 2012. *The Emotional Life of your Brain. How Its Unique Patterns Affect the Way You Think, Feel and Live—and How You Can Change Them*. With S. Begley. New York: Hudson Street.

DeFreitas, S., and M. Garrison. 2015. *Choice*. 13 (2),10-11.

Denton, P. 2014. *The Power of Our Words: Teacher Language That Helps Children Learn*. 2nd ed. Turners Falls, MA: Northeast Foundation for Children.

Dweck, C. 2006. *Mindset: The New Psychology of Success*. New York: Random House.

Dickenson, E. 2016. "The Cult of Busy." *Johns Hopkins Health Review* 3 (1). http://www.johnshopkinshealthreview.com/issues/spring-summer-2016/articles/the-cult-of-busy.

Dispenza, J. 2014. *You Are the Placebo: Making Your Mind Matter*. Carlsbad, CA: Hay House.

———. 2012. *Breaking the Habit of Being Yourself*. Carlsbad, CA: Hay House.

Dodd, M. L. 2016. "All Together Now." *Yoga Journal* 282, 71-75.

Dongen, H., G. Maislin, J. Mullington, and D. Dinges. 2003. "The Cumulative Cost of Additional Wakefulness: Dose-Response Effects on Neurobehavioral Functions and Sleep Physiology from Chronic Sleep Restriction and Total Sleep Deprivation." *SLEEP* 26 (2) https://www.ncbi.nlm.nih.gov/pubmed/12683469.

Dossey, L. 2013. *One Mind*. Carlsbad, CA: Hay House.

———. 2006. *The Extraordinary Healing Power of Ordinary Things* New York: Three River.

DuBose Heyward, E. 1955. *The Country Bunny and the Little Gold Shoes*. New York: Houghton Mifflin.

Duckworth, A., P. Quinn, and M. Seligman. 2009. "Positive Predictors of Teacher

Effectiveness." *The Journal of Positive Psychology* 4 (6): 540–547.

Duhigg, C. 2012. *The Power of Habit: Why We Do What We Do in Life and Business*. New York: Random House.

Dunham, J., and V. Varma, eds. 1998. *Stress in Teachers: Past, Present, and Future*. London: Whurr.

Dweck, C. 2006. *Mindset: The New Psychology of Success*. New York: Random House.

Eccles, J. S., and R. Roeser. 1999. "School and Community Influences on Human Development." In *Developmental Psychology: An Advanced Textbook*, 4th ed., ed. M. H. Bornstein and M. E. Lamb. Mahwah, NJ: Lawrence Erlbaum.

Emmons, R. A., and M. E. McCullough, eds. 2004. *The Psychology of Gratitude*. New York: Oxford Press.

Emmons, R. A. 2013. *Gratitude Works*. San Francisco, CA: Jossey Bass.

Emoto, M. 2005. *The Hidden Messages in Water*. New York: Atria Books.

The Enneagram Institute. 2017. https://www.enneagraminstitute.com/.

Epstein, L., and S. Mardon. 2007. *The Harvard Medical School Guide to a Good Night's Sleep*. New York: McGraw Hill.

Ericson, J. 2013. "75% of Americans May Suffer from Chronic Dehydration, According to Doctors." *Medical Daily*. http://www.medicaldaily.com/75-americans-may-suffer-chronic-dehydration-according-doctors-247393.

Fredrickson, B. L. 2013. "Positive Emotions Broaden and Build." In *Advances in Experimental Social Psychology*, Vol. 47, ed. P. Devine and A. Plant, 1–54. San Diego, CA: Academic Press.

Fullan, M. 1993. *Change Forces: Proving the Depths of Educational Reform*. London: The Falmer Press.

Gard, T., J. Noggle, C. Park, D. Vago, and A. Wilson. 2014. "Potential Self-regulatory Mechanisms of Yoga for Psychological Health." *Frontiers in Human Neuroscience (8)*: 770. http://journal.frontiersin.org/article/10.3389/fnhum.2014.00770.

Gilovich, T. 2015. *The Wisest One in the Room: How You Can Benefit from Social Psychology's Most Powerful Insights*. New York: Free.

Goleman, D. 2013. *Focus: The Hidden Driver of Excellence*. Sydney, Australia: Harper Collins.

Gordon, J. 2008. *The No Complaining Rule*. Hoboken, NJ: Wiley.

Gottman, J., and J. Silver. 1999. *The Seven Principles for Making Marriage Work: A Practical Guide from the Country's Foremost Relationship Expert*. New York: Three Rivers.

Hallowell, E. M. 2006. *Crazy Busy: Overstretched, Overbooked, and About to Snap!* New York: Ballantine Books.

———. 2015. *Driven to Distraction at Work: How to Focus and Be More Productive*. Boston, MA: Harvard Business Review.

Hallowell, E. M., and J. J. Ratey. 2006. *Delivered from Distraction: Getting the Most Out of Life with Attention deficit Disorder*. New York: Ballantine Books.

Hanson, R. 2013. *Hardwiring Happiness: The New Brain Science of Contentment, Calm and Confidence*. New York: Harmony Books.

———. 2007. "Pay Attention." *Just One Thing*. https://www.rickhanson.net.

Hanson, R. (with R. Mendius). 2009. *Buddha's Brain: The Practical Neuroscience of*

Happiness, Love, and Wisdom. Oakland, CA: New Harbinger.

Hartman, T. 2006. *Walking Your Blues Away: How to Heal the Mind and Create Emotional Well-Being.* Rochester, Vermont. Park Street.

Hastings, M., and S. Agrawal. "Lack of Teacher Engagement Linked to 2.3 Million Missed Workdays." Gallop. http://www.gallup.com/poll/180455/lack-teacher-engagement-linked- million-missed-workdays.aspx.

Hawkins, D. 2012. *Letting Go: The Pathway of Surrender.* West Sedona, AZ: Veritas.

The Hawn Foundation. 2011. *The mindUP Curriculum: Grades Pre-K Through 8 Brain-Focused Strategies for Living—and Learning.* New York: Scholastic.

Hawn, G. (with W. Holden). 2011. *10 Mindful Minutes: Giving Our Children-and Ourselves—The Social and Emotional Skills to Reduce Stress and Anxiety for Healthier, Happy Lives.* New York: TarcherPerigee.

Holden, R. 2005. *Success Intelligence.* Great Britain: Hodder and Stoughton.

Holt-Lunstad, J., T. B. Smith, and J. B. Layton. 2010. "Social Relationships and Mortality Risk: A Meta-analytic Review." *PLoS Med* 7(7): e1000316. https://doi.org/10.1371/journal.pmed.1000316.

Horowitz, S. 2010. "Health Benefits of Meditation." *Alternative and Complementary Therapies* 16 (4): 223–228. doi:10.1089/act.2010.16402.

Howard, S., and B. Johnson. 2004. "Resilient Teachers: Resisting Stress and Burnout." *Social Psychology of Education* 7: 399–420.

Idler, E., and S. Kasl. 1991. "Health Perceptions and Survival: Do Global Evaluations of Health Really Predict Mortality?" *Journal of Gerontology* 46 (2): 55.

Institute for Economics and Peace. 2015. *Global Peace Index: Measuring Peace, Its Causes and Its Economic Value.* Institute of Peace Report No. 34. http://economicsandpeace.org/wp-content/uploads/2015/06/Global-Peace-Index-Report-2015_0.pdf

Jennings, P. A., and M. T. Greenberg. 2009. "The Prosocial Classroom: Teacher Social and Emotional Competence in Relation to Student and Classroom Outcomes." *Review of Educational Research* 79 (1): 491–525. doi:10.3102/0034654308325693.

Johnston, P. 2004. *Choice Words: How Our Language Affects Children.* Portland, ME: Stenhouse.

Justice, B. 2000. *Who Gets Sick?* Houston, TX: Peak Press.

Kabat-Zinn, J. 2013. *Full Catastrophe Living.* 2nd ed. New York: Bantam Books.

———. 2009. *Letting Everything Become Your Teacher: 100 Lessons in Mindfulness.* New York: Random House.

Kagan, D. M. 1992. Implications of Research on Teacher Belief. *Educational Psychologist* 27: 65–90.

Keller, G., and J. Papasan. 2013. *The ONE Thing: The surprisingly Simple Truth Behind Extraordinary Results.* Austin, TX: Bard.

Keng, S., M. J. Smoski, and C. J. Robins. 2011. "Effects of Mindfulness on Psychological Health: A Review of Empirical Studies." *Clinical Psychology Review* 31: 1031–1056.

Kerr, S. L., L. J. Lucas, G. E. DiDomenico, V., Mishra, B. J. Stanton, G. Shivde, A. N. Pero, M. E. Runyen, and G. M. Terry. 2017. *Is Mindfulness Training Useful for Pre-service Teachers? An Exploratory Investigation.* Teaching Education. DOI: 10.1080/10476210.2017.1296831.

Killingsworth, M. 2011. *Matt Killingsworth: Want to Be Happier? Stay in the Moment.* TED. http://www.ted.com/talks/matt_killingsworth_want_to_be_happier_stay_in_the_moment

Klusmann, U., M. Kunter, U. Trautwein, O. Ludtke, and J. Baumert. 2008. "Teachers' Occupational Well-Being and Quality of Instruction: The Important Role of Self-Regulatory Patterns." *Journal of Educational Psychology* 100 (3): 702–715.

Konnikova, M. 2016. "How People Learn to Become Resilient." *The New Yorker.* http://www.newyorker.com/science/maria-konnikova/the-secret-formula-for-resilience.

Kriete, R., and C. Davis. 2014. *The First Six Weeks of School.* Turners Fall, MA: Northeast Foundation for Children Inc.

Kyriacou, C. 2001. "Teacher Stress: Directions for Future Research." *Educational Review* 53: 27–35.

Lambert, R., and C. McCarthy, eds. 2006. *Understanding Teacher Stress in an Age of Accountability.* Greenwich, CT: Information Age Publishing.

LeDoux, J. E. 2003. *Synaptic Self: How Our Brains Become Who We Are.* New York: Penguin.

Levitin, D. 2015. *The Organized Mind: Thinking Straight in the Age of Information Overload.* New York: Dutton.

Levy, D. 2016. *Mindful Tech: How to Bring Balance to Our Digital Lives.* New Haven, CT: Yale University Press.

Lewis, M. D. 2005. "Self-Organizing Individual Differences in Brain Development." *Development Review* 25: 252–277.

Lickerman, A. 2012. *The Undefeated Mind: On the Science of Creating an Indestructible Self.* Deerfield Beach, FL: Health Communications.

Lipton, B. 2008. *The Biology of Belief: Unleashing the Power of Consciousness, Matter, and Miracles.* Carlsbad, CA: Mountain of Love Productions.

Lucas, L. 2017. "Words Create Words." *Exchange Magazine* 39 (2): 41—43.

Lucas, L. J., and S. Kerr. 2016. "Remembering to Breathe: The Challenges and Rewards of Teaching Mindfulness Practices to Pre-Service Teachers." *Journal of Educational Thought.* University of Calgary: Routledge.

Lykken, D. 1982. "Research with Twins: The Concept of Emergenesis." *Psychophysiology* 19 (4): 361–372.

Lyubomirsky, S., K. Sheldon, and D. Schkade, 2005. "Pursuing Happiness: The Architecture of Sustainable Change." *Review of General Psychology* 9 (2): 111–131.

Marzano, R. J., J. S. Marzano, and D. J. Pickering. 2003. *Classroom Management That Works.* Alexandria, VA: Association for Supervision and Curriculum Development.

Matos, K., and E. Galinsky. 2014. "National Study of Employers." Families and Work Institute. http://familiesandwork.org/site/research/reports/NSE_2012.pdf

MetLife. 2013. *The MetLife survey of the American Teacher: Challenges for School Leadership.* https://www.metlife.com/assets/cao/foundation/MetLife-Teacher-Survey-2012.pdf

Mindfulness in Schools Project. https://mindfulnessinschools.org/wp-content/uploads/2014/10/Evidence-for-Mindfulness-Impact-on-school-staff.pdf.

Murray, M. 2013. "7 Little-Known Benefits from Sunlight." Care2. http://www.care2.com/greenliving/7-little-known-benefits-of-sunlight.html#ixzz3rgvqf2G6.

Nagendra, R., N. Maruthai, and B. Kutty. 2012. "Meditation and Its Regulatory Role on Sleep." *Frontiers in Neurology*. http:// journal.frontiersin.org/ article/10.3389/fneur.2012.00054/full

National Union of Teachers. 2013. *Tackling Teacher Stress*. https://www.teachers.org. uk/help-and-advice/health-and-safety/t/ tackling-teacher-stress.

Northeast Foundation for Children Inc. 2000. *The First Six Weeks of School*. Turner Falls, MA.

Northrup, C. 2015. *Goddesses Never Age: The Secret Prescription for Radiance, Vitality and Well-Being*. Carlsbad, CA: Hay House.

Oliver, M. 1990. *The House of Light*. Boston: Beacon Press.

Organization for Economic Cooperation and Development. 2016. "About the OECD." http://www.oecd.org/about/.

Pick, M. 2011. *Are You Tired And Wired? Your Proven 30 Day Program for Overcoming Adrenal fatigue and Feeling Fantastic*. 2nd ed. New York: Hay House.

RAND Corporation. 2012. "Teachers Matter: Understanding Teachers' Impact on Student Achievement." http://www.rand.org/pubs/ corporate_pubs/CP693z1-2012-09.html.

Rately, J. 2008. *Spark: The Revolutionary New Science of Exercise and the Brain*. New York: Little Brown.

Rath, T. 2004. *How Full Is Your Bucket?* New York: Gallup.

Responsive Classroom. 2017. What Is Responsive Classroom? https://www. responsiveclassroom.org/.

Richardson, C. 1999. *Take Time for Your Life*. New York: Broadway Books.

Riso, D., and R. Hudson. 1999. *The Wisdom of the Enneagram*: *The Complete Guide to Psychological and Spiritual Growth for the Nine Personality Types*. New York: Bantam Books.

Rowe, M. B. 1987. "Wait Time: Slowing Down May Be a Way of Speeding Up." *American Educator* 11: 38–43, 47.

———. 1972. *Wait Time and Rewards as Instructional Variables: Their influence on Language, Logic, and Fate Control in Resources in Education, Education Resources Information Center*, Presented at the National Association for Research in Science Teaching. Chicago, Illinois: http://eric. ed.gov/?id=ED061103.

Sapolsky, R. 1994. *Why Zebras Don't Get Ulcers: A Guide to Stress, Stress Related Diseases and Coping*. New York: Holt.

Schoen, M. 2001. *When Relaxation Is Hazardous to Your Health*. Calabasas, CA: Mind Body Health Books.

Schucman, H. 1976. *A Course in Miracles*. Mill Valley, CA: Foundation for Inner Peace

Schulte, B. 2015. *Overwhelmed: How to Work, Love, and Play When No One Has Time*. New York: Picador.

Schultz, W. 2006. "Behavioral Theories and the Neurophysiology of Reward." *Annual Review of Psychology* 57: 87–115.

Schwartz, A. 1997. *Guided Imagery for Groups: Fifty Visualizations That Promote Relaxation, Problem-Solving, Creativity, and Well-Being*. Duluth, MN: Whole Person Associates.

Schwartz, B., A. Ward, J. Monterosso, S. Lyubomirsky, K. White, and D. Lehman. 2002. "Maximizing Versus Satisficing: Happiness is a Matter of Choice." *Journal of Personality and Social Psychology* 83 (5): 1178–1197.

Schwartz, T., and C. McCarthy. 2007. *Manage Your Energy, Not Your Time.* Boston, MA: Harvard Business Review.

Seligman, M. 2011. *Flourish: A Visionary New Understanding of Happiness and Well-Being.* New York: Free Press.

Seligman, M. P., T. A. Steen, N. Park, and C. Peterson. 2005. "Positive Psychology Progress." *American Psychologist 60* (5): 410–421. doi:10.1037/0003-066X.60.5.410.

Senge, P. 2004. *Presence: An Exploration of Profound Change in People, Organizations, and Society.* New York: Random House.

Shimoff, M. 2008. *Happy for No Reason: 7 Steps to Being Happy from the Inside Out.* New York: Free Press.

Stahl, B., and E. Goldstein. 2010. *A Mindfulness-Based Stress Reduction Workbook.* Oakland, CA: New Harbinger.

Taylor, S. E., and J. D. Brown. 1988. "Illusion and Well-Being: A Social Psychological Perspective on Mental Health." *Psychological Bulletin* 103 (2): 193.

University of Maryland Medical Center. 2017. Ginkgo biloba. http://umm.edu/health/medical/altmed/herb/ginkgo-biloba.

Ury, W. 2007. *The Power of a Positive No: Save the Deal, Save the Relationship—and Still Say No.* New York: Bantam Books.

Weaver, L., and M. Wilding. 2013. *The 5 Dimensions of Engaged Teaching: A Practical Guide for Educators.* Bloomington, IN: Solution Tree.

Wooten, Virgil. "How to Fall Asleep." How Stuff Works. http://health.howstuffworks.com/mental-health/sleep/basics/how-to-fall-asleep2.htm

Index

abstinence activity, gratitude and, 52

acceptance, self, 159

acknowledge the weary activity, 55

action plan template, 181

ADD, 121

aerobics, focus and, 103-104

Aesop, 41

Agrawal, S., 132

amygdalae, stress and, 47

Apache blessing, 45

appreciation, 143

Are You Tired and Wired? (Pick), 75

Artist's Way, The (Cameron), 86

Art of Happiness, The (Lama and Cutler), 134

attention, 15, 102-103

attention, practice and, 73

attention fatigue, 103

attitude, learning and, 127-128

autogenic relaxation, 144

behaviors, self-regulatory, 12

beliefs

  changing, 130

  inherited, 129

  systems and, 129

  thoughts and, 128-129

bells, 120

bilateral activities, 89

blessings, counting, 53

body scans, 50

Bowers,?, 62

Brach, T., 155

Braden, G., *Spontaneous Healing of Belief, The*, 128

Breaking the Habit of Being Yourself (Dispenza), 54

breathing, 49, 118

Breaux, A.L., 12

Breines, J., 43

Brilliant, A., 88

Brooks, R., *Power of Mind-sets, The*, 136

Brown, J.D., 133

buckets: fuels, drains and, 27-28

Buddha, 77

Buddha's Brain (Hanson), 124

Burns, D., 65

Calati, R., 24

Cameron, J., *Artist's Way, The*, 86

career changers, teaching profession and, 17

Carnegie, D., 103

Carroll, L., 183

Carson, R., 145

Carter, C., *Sweet Spot, The*, 28, 95

catastrophizing, 37

Chang, M., *Educational Psychology Review*, 62

change agents, 173-174

Chiesa, A., 24

choices, making, 18

Chopra, D., 60, 76, 101

Christakis, N., 160

Church, D., 67

circle of support, 160-162

Cirillo, F., 111

clarity, vision of schools and, 184

classroom connections, 145-148

  acknowledge the weary, 55

  advertising upcoming lessons, 147

  collaboration, colleagues and, 169-170

  daydreaming students, 121

  engagement, motivation, novelty, 146

  ever-present bell, 120

fixed to growth mind-set, 146-147

four corners, 148

four-corners observation, 33

gratitude journals, 55

just listen, 32

make the why transparent, 145-146

mind map for students, 120

mini-Pomodoros for students, 121

modeling presence, 120

morning exercises, 55

music, 122

novelty, 146

play, 93

present lesson planning, 33-34

rest and, 92

seeing with fresh eyes, 33

snowball fight, 148

student learning experiences, 147-148

tally your thoughts, 92

thirty-second laugh, 92

"write 'em up box," 55

zoom in, 32

zoom out, 32

zoom out/zoom in, 31-32

Clean Sweep tool, 27

Clear Focus app, 112

Cloud, J., "Why DNA Isn't Your Destiny," 58

cognitive distortions, 36

Cohen, A., *Deep Breath of Life, A*, 141

collaboration

  banishing gossip and, 152-153

  conflict versus, 151-152

  difficult personalities and, 154-156

  group processes and, 154

  work, relationships and, 153-154

collaborative culture, agenda for, 160

Collins, J., 98

Combs, A., 128

compassion, judgment versus, 157-158

compassion fatigue, 57

complaint-free work environment, 163-164

complaints, 162-163

conflict

  collaboration versus, 151-152

  opportunities and, 155

  pausing and, 155

  responding, reacting versus, 155

  team, 151-152

contemplative centers, 177

context switching, 95-96

control fallacies, 37

cooperation

  benefits of, 150

  See also collaboration

Course in Miracles, A (Schucman), 155, 184

Covey, S., 23, 107

Crazy Busy (Hallowell), 80, 96

Crenshaw, D., 104

Csikszentmihalyi, M., 25-26, 153

  Flow, 100

"Cult of Busy, The" (Dickinson), 104

Davidson, R., 131, 133-134

decisions, 21

Deep Breath of Life, A (Cohen), 141

DeFreitas, S., 112

delegating techniques, 118-119

delegation, productivity and, 107

Delivered from Distraction (Hallowell and Ratey), 96, 96-102

Delpit, L., 126

Denton, P., 39

  Responsive Classroom, The, 39

Denton, P., *Power of Our Words, The*, 169

Dewey, J., 150

Dickinson, E., "Cult of Busy, The," 104

difficult personalities, 154-156

  common, 156

  solution for dealing with, 156

digital distraction, 99

Dillard, A., 85

Dispenza, J.

Breaking the Habit of Being Yourself, 54

Your Are the Placebo, 59

distorted thinking, 37-38

distractibility deterrents, 97-100

background music, 98-99

being observant, 98

scheduling e-mail times, 99

standing, reading aloud, 98

unplugging, 97

distractibility deterrents. *See* productivity tips

documenting the good, 143

Dodd, M., *Yoga Journal*, 82

Dongen, H., 46

dopamine, 130

Dossey, L., 58

doubts, banishing, 181-182

drains, 27-28

Driven to Distraction at Work (Hallowell), 96, 120

Duckworth, A., 12

Duhigg, C., 20

Power of Habit, The, 29, 74

Dunham, J., 66

Dweck, C., 65, 134-135, 136

Dyer, W., 88

early childhood, elderly care centers, 175

Eccles, J.S., 12

Edelman, M.W., 177

education, epigenetics and, 59

Educational Psychology Review (Chang), 62

Einstein, A., 118

Eisenhower, D., 28

e-mail, scheduling time for, 99

"e-mail apnea," 30

Emerson, R.W., 181

Emmons, R.A., 42-43

emotional reasoning, 38

Emoto, Dr. Masaru, 43

enneagram, self-discovery and, 167

envisioning, 172-173

outcomes, 183

process, 179-180

steps, 180

epigenetics, 57-59

body response to stress and, 61-62

defined, 58

education and, 59

manageable stress and, 64

mind-set and, 65-66

present, joyful lives and, 67

stress, responding to and, 59-60

stress statistics and, 60-61

workplace stress and, 62-64

Epstein, L. and S. Mardon, *Harvard Medical School Guide to a Good Night's Sleep*, 74-75

Families and Work Institute, The, 16

fatigue, 74-75

recognizing, 103-104, 113

sleep, nutrition and, 74

fatigue, recognizing, 103-104

feet, relaxation and, 144

First Six Weeks of School, The (Northeast Foundation for Children Inc.), 169

5 Dimensions of Engaged Teaching, The (Weaver and Wilding), 68-69

fixed mind-sets, 135

flow, defined, 100-101

focus, aerobics, 103-104

Focus (Goleman), 116

four-corners observations, 33

Fowler, J., 160

Franklin, B., 165

Franklin Covey Planner, planning tools and, 71

Fredrickson, B., 39

Friday field trips, 176

Frontiers in Human Neuroscience, 82

Fuels and Drains survey, 110

Fullan, M., 154

Full Catastrophe Living (Kabat-Zinn), 24

Fuller, B., 178

Gandhi, M., 163, 166

Garrison, M., 112

Gilovich, T., 141

global labeling, 37

Godon, J., *No Complaining Rule, The*, 162-163

Goethe, J.W., 97, 186

Goldberg, N., 167

Goleman, D., 121

  Focus, 116

gossip, banishing, 152-153

gossip-free faculty room, 168

Gottman, J., 124

gratitude, 41-43

  commitment and, 42

  files, 53

  fourteen habits of, 51-53

  identifying, 22-23

  journals, 55

  practices, 182

  practicing, decision and, 43

  state of distraction versus, 42

  thoughts and, 41

  writing and, 53

Greater Good Institute, The, 43

Greenberg, M.T., 11

group processes, 154

growth mind-sets, 135

Guided Imagery for Groups (Schwartz), 116

guided meditation, 116

habits, 20

  changing, 21-22

Hallowell, E., 108

  background music and, 98-99

  Crazy Busy, 80, 96, 113

Driven to Distraction at Work, 96, 120

Hallowell, E. and J.J. Ratey, *Delivered From Distraction*, 96-102

Hanh, T.N., 157

Hanson, R., 102, 125, 137, 143

  Buddha's Brain, 124

happiness, 40-41, 133-134

  material resources, experiences and, 141

  maximizing versus satisfying and, 141

  quiz, 134

  set point, 40, 133, 144

  social comparisons and, 140-141

happy files, gratitude and, 53

Happy for No Reason (Shimoff), 40

Hartman, T., *Walking Your Blues Away*, 89

Harvard Medical School Guide to a Good Night's Sleep (Epstein and Mardon), 74-75

Hastings, M., 132

Hawkins, D., 17

Hawn, G., 132-133

  10 Mindful Minutes, 133

health-care alternatives, 90

heart coherence technique, 50-51

Heartmath, institute of, 50

Hebb's rule, 54

Hippocrates, 89

Holden, R., *Success Intelligence*, 108

Horowitz, S., 48

Howard, S., 62

How Full is Your Bucket? (Rath), 27

hugs, gratitude and, 53

humor, 79-80

identification, behavior change and, 11

Idler, E., 59

imagine if, 52

information overload, 117-118

  productivity and, 106

inner vision, 121

instructional coaches, 139-140

intention, focus on, 77

intentional transitions, 83-84

interviews, appreciative, 168

   questions and, 169

Isgar, T., 166

James, W., 65, 101, 150

Jennings, P.A., 11

Johnson, B., 62

Johnston, P., 39

Journal of Managerial Psychology, 62

journals

   gratitude, 53

   perseverance and, 146

Justice, B., *Who Gets Sick?*, 58

Kabat-Zinn, Dr. R., 2

   Full Catastrophe Living, 24

Kagan, D.M., 128

Kasl, S., 59

Keng, S., 24

Kerr, S.L., 177

Killingsworth, M., 100

kindness, noticing, 53

Kleiser, G., 84

Klusmann, U., 12

Kriete, R. and C. Davis, *Morning Meeting Book*,
   169

Kübler-Ross, E., 185

Kutty, B., 47

Kyriacou, C., 59

laboratory schools, 176

Lama, D., and C. Cutler, *Art of Happiness, The*,
   134

Lambert, R., 59

laughter, 79

LeDoux, J.E., 124

Leonard, T., 27

Leshan, E., 79

lesson planning, present, 33-34

"let down effect," 62

Levitin, D., *Organized Mind, The*, 106

Levy, D., *Mindful Tech*, 99, 106

Lickerman, A., 133

lifestyle choices, importance of, 67

Lindbergh, A., 18

Lipton, B., 58

listening, just listen and, 32

lists, beginning with, 179

Lucas, L., 177

   "Words Create Words," 164

Lykken, D., 40

Lyubomirsky, S., 40

McCarthy, C., 59, 97

McCullough, M.E., 42, 43

mantras, gratitude and, 53

Maruthai, N., 47

Marzano, J.S., 12, 77

Marzano, R.J., 12, 77

meditation, 23-25, 47, 48-49, 114-116

   changing belief systems and, 130

   guided, 116

   loving-kindness, 90-91

   practice, 24

   sitting, 115

memory, patterning and, 145-146

memory loss, stress and, 63

mental models, 126-127

MetLife Survey of the American Teacher, The, 77

micromoments, 117

Milne, A.A., 158

Mindful Based Stress Reduction (MBSR) clinic,
   24

mindful listening, 165

mindful meditation, 114-116

mindful Monday challenge, 164

mindful Mondays, no complaining, 162-163

mindfulness, 15, 182

Mindfulness in Schools project, 62

mindful teaching, 50-54, 68-69

  body scan and, 50

  gratitude habits and, 51-53

  heart coherence technique and, 50-51

  personal practices and, 84-85

  purposeful planning, ending day and, 54

  rent a strategy and, 68-69

  should to could and, 68

mindful teaching practices, 142-144

  adopt growth mind-set, 143

  appreciate the good, 143

  appreciative interviews, 168

  appreciative interviews, sample questions, 169

  circle of support, 160-162

  collaborative culture, agenda for, 160

  complaint-free environment, strategies for, 163-164

  control your mind and, 142

  document the good, 143

  gossip-free faculty room, 168

  mindful listening, 165

  mindful Mondays, no complaining challenge, 162-163

  raising happiness set point, 144

  relaxation techniques for, 144

  silence, 166

  storehouse positive memories, 143

  team building, 166-168

mindful teaching productivity tips

  breathing, 118

  delegating techniques, 118-119

  deterring distractibility, 110-111

  fatigue and, 113

  focused energy, 111

  information overload, 117-118

  meditation, 114-116

  mind map, identifying distractions, 109-110

  power of no, 119

  present moment living, 116-117

  reframing responses, 114

  time management, 111-113

Mindful Tech (Levy), 99, 106

mindlessness, 2

  blur, 44

  recognizing, 44-45

mind mapping, distractions and, 109-110

mind reading, 37

mind-set, 134-137

  envisioning, establishing, 179

  growth, 143

  stress and, 65-66

  types of, 135

Mind Up Curriculum, 132-133

mini-retreats, 85-87

  health care and, 90

  injuries, illnesses and, 88

  meditation and, 90-91

  rhythms of the year and, 87-88

  special occasions and, 87

  suggestions and, 86-87

  un-plugging and, 88-89

  walking and, 89-90

mirror neurons, 79

modeling, strong interpersonal communication and, 154

morning exercises, 55

Morning Meeting Book (Kriete and Davis), 169

multitasking, 95-96, 109-110

  myth of, 104

  technology and, 110

Murray, Dr. M., 48

music, 122

Nagendra, R., 47

National Commission on Teaching and America's Future, 3

National Union of Teachers, 62

negativity

  bias, 124-125

focus, 37
stopping, 38
nervous system, the, 72-73
neural pathways, new learning and, 125-126
neurobiological response, 79
neurons, 125
neuroplasticity, 115, 125
growth-focused evaluation and, 137-140
negativity effects and, 137
Nin, A., 173
No Complaining Rule, The (Gordon), 162-163
Northeast Foundation for Children Inc., *First Six Weeks of School, The*, 169
Northrup, C., 79

observations, four-corners, 33
OECD (Organization for Economic Cooperation and
Development), 153
Oliver, M., 173
Organized Mind, The (Levitin), 106
overcommitment, 107-108
overgeneralization, 37
Overwhelmed, (Schulte), 16
Oz, M., 57

partnerships, university-community, 176
past-future-present, 117
Patanjali, 175
pauses, presence, 29-30
perception, 153
perfectionism, 141-142
personalization, 37
personal practices, mindful teaching and, 26-31, 84-85
action plan template, 181
buckets: fuels, drains and, 27-28
doubts, banishing, 181-182
envisioning, establishing mind-set and, 179
envisioning process, 179-188

health care and, 90
imagine, just, 183
injuries, illnesses and, 88
lists, 179
loving-kindness meditation, 90-91
mastermind cabinet, 183
mini-retreats and, 85-87
personal visions and, 185
presence pause and, 29-30
PRES strategy and, 30-31
prioritizing tools and, 27
purposeful planning, beginning day and, 28-29
solitude and, 184
steps, 180
unplugging and, 88-89
vision of schools, 184
visions, igniting others, 185-186
walking, 89-90
Personal Practices to Support Mindful Teaching, tool, 19
Pick, M., 47
Are You Tired and Wired?, 75
Pickering, D.J., 12, 77
planning tools, Franklin Covey Planner and, 71
pleasing others, 153
polarized thinking, 37
Pomodoros, mini, 121
Pomodoro Technique, 111-113
positive emotional states, 132-133
positive feelings, 125
positive memories storehouse, 143
possibility thinking, 175
Power of Habit, The, (Duhigg), 29, 74
Power of Mind-sets, The (Brooks), 136
power of "no," 119
Power of Our Words, The (Denton), 169
presence
benefits to students of, 12
cues, 111
defined, 1-2, 10

how to become present and, 15

listening and, 10

mindfulness, versus, 3

pathway to, 2

pause, 29-30

PRES strategy, 30-31, 49

when to be present and, 12-14

where to be present and, 14

who needs to be present and, 11

why, 14-15

presence pause, 29-30

Presence (Senge), 73-74

presense

being present and, 174-175

present moment practice, 73-74

present momment living, 116-117

present teachers, portrait of, 173

PRES strategy, 30-31, 49

prioritizing, 18-19

making choices and, 18

tools, 19, 27

productivity tips, 95-108

crazy busy persona and, 104-105

distractibilty deterrance, 97-100

do it or delegate, 107

fatigue, recognizing, 103-104

focused energy, 100-101

information overload and, 106

multitasking and, 95-96

paying attention, 101-103

power of "no," 107-109

slow down, 105-106

tests and, 101-102

See also distractabilty deterrants

progessive muscle relaxation, 144

projection, perception and, 158

Proust, M., 67

purposeful planning, 19-21, 28-29

ending day and, 54

routinizing and, 20

Quinn, P., 12

Rately, J., *Spark*, 103

Rath, T., *How Full is Your Bucket?*, 27

reacting, internal state and, 15

reframing, 38-39

situations, 110-111

relaxation techniques, 144

autogenic relaxation, 144

feet and, 144

progresive muscle relaxation, 144

visualization, 144

Rent a strategy, 68-69

responding, reacting versus, 3, 151-152, 155

Responsive Classroom, The, (Denton), 39

rest, renewal, 45-48

eating and, 47

meditation and, 47

sound-generated white noise machine and, 47

sunshine and, 47-48

television and, 46-47

retreats. *See* mini-retreats

Richardson, C., 27

Riso, D. and R. Hudson, *Wisdom of the Enneagram, The*, 167

rituals, incorporating, 22-23

Robins, C.J., 24

Roeser, R., 12

Roosevelt, E., 162, 183

routines, 20

realistic, 23

Rowe, M.B., 105

Sapolsky, R., 65

say "thank you," gratitude and, 52-53

Schaar, J., 172

Schkade, D., 40

Schoen, M., *When Relaxation Is Hazardous to Your Health*, 62

Schucman, H., *Course in Miracles, A*, 155, 184

Schulte, B., *Overwhelmed*, 16

Schwartz, A., *Guided Imagery for Groups*, 116

Schwartz, B., 141

Schwartz, T., 97

seeing, fresh eyes and, 33

self-assessment, work stress and, 71-72

self-awarness, self-sabotaging versus, 75-77

self-blame, 37

self-care, 12-13, 70-72, 75-77

   conscious choices and, 76

   finding time for, 72

self-compassion, 77-78

   exercise, 78

self stories, view of self and, 128

Seligman, M., 12, 43

Senge, P., *Presence*, 73-74

Serretti, A., 24

Sheldon, K., 40

Shimoff, M., 52

   Happy for No Reason, 40

Shirky, C., 106

Siddhartha, 2

silence, 166

silence, practice, 117

Silver, J., 124

singing bowls, 121

sleep, 113

   benefits of, 75

   debt, 46

slowing down, productivity and, 105-106

Smoski, M.J., 24

social-emotional awareness, 131-132

solitude, 184

Spark (Rately), 103

Spontaneous Healing of Belief, The (Braden), 128

Steindle-Rast, Brother David, 52

stillness, 23-25

stress

   distorted thinking and, 37-38

"let-down effect" and, 62

lifestyle choices and, 59-60

manageable, 64

memory loss and, 63

mind-set and, 65-66

physical reaction to, 61-62

statistics, 60-61

teachers and, 62-63

workplace, 62-64

stressors, top ten, 64

Success Intelligence (Holden), 108

sunshine, rest and renewal and, 47-48

suppression, repression, 17

Sweet Spot, The (Carter), 28

synapses, 125

Taber, G., 179

Tanzi, R., 76

task, maintenance behavior versus, 167

Taylor, M., 181

Taylor, S., 184

Taylor, S.E., 133

Taylor, T.L., 51

teachers

   attrition rates of, 3

   engaged, 132

   preparation for, 3

   presence and, 3-4

   ruminations and, 124

   self-criticism and, 124

   sense of being flattened and, 16-17

teaching, stress and, 62-63

team building, 166-168

   enneagram, 167

   task, maintenance behavior versus, 167

   tools, 166

   written reflection and, 167-168

technology, multitasking and, 110

television, 44-45

   sleep and, 46-47

10 Mindful Minutes (Hawn), 133
theme for the day, gratitude and, 52
thirty-second body scan, 115-116
thoughts
  beliefs and, 128
  emotions and, 11
  reframing, 2
time, 25-26
Tolle, E., 100
transitions
  intentional, 83-84
  techninques for, 49
triggers
  insights and, 158
  recognizing, 158-159
Tzu, L., 107

Ury, W., 19

Varma, V., 66
visions, igniting, 185-186
visualization, 144

walking, 89-90
Walking Your Blues Away (Hartman), 89
Weaver, L. and M. Wilding, *5 Dimensions of Engaged Teaching, The*, 68-69
well-trained mind, agenda for, 131-132
When Relaxation Is Hazardous to Your Health (Schoen), 62
white noise machines, 47
Who Gets Sick? (Justice), 58
"Why DNA Isn't Your Destiny," (Cloud), 58
willpower, 74
Wisdom of the Enneagram, The (Riso and Hudson),
  29, 167
Wong, H.K., 12
Wooden, J.R., 127
"Words Create Words" (Lucas), 164

workplace stress, 62-64
work stress self-assessment, 71-72
"write 'em up box," 55
written reflection, 167-168

yoga, 80-83
Yoga Journal (Dodd), 82
You Are the Placebo (Dispenza), 59

zoom in, 32
zoom out, 32
zoom out/zoom in, 31-32